KU-661-196

OFFICE ORGANIZATION AND MANAGEMENT

INCLUDING SECRETARIAL WORK

PUBLISHED BY PITMAN

OFFICE ORGANIZATION AND MANAGEMENT

INCLUDING SECRETARIAL WORK

BY

THE LATE

LAWRENCE R. DICKSEE

AND

SIR HERBERT E. BLAIN

C.B.E.

THIRTEENTH EDITION

BY

STANLEY W. ROWLAND, LL.B., F.C.A.

LECTURER IN ACCOUNTING, LONDON SCHOOL OF ECONOMICS AND POLITICAL SCIENCE, UNIVERSITY OF LONDON

LONDON

SIR ISAAC PITMAN & SONS, LTD.

SIR ISAAC PITMAN & SONS, LTD.
PITMAN HOUSE, PARKER STREET, KINGSWAY, LONDON, W.C.2
THE PITMAN PRESS, BATH
PITMAN HOUSE, LITTLE COLLINS STREET, MELBOURNE
UNITEERS BUILDING, RIVER VALLEY ROAD, SINGAPORE
27 BECKETTS BUILDINGS, PRESIDENT STREET, JOHANNESBURG

ASSOCIATED COMPANIES
PITMAN PUBLISHING CORPORATION
2 WEST 45TH STREET, NEW YORK
205 WEST MONROE STREET, CHICAGO

SIR ISAAC PITMAN & SONS (CANADA), LTD.
(INCORPORATING THE COMMERCIAL TEXT BOOK COMPANY)
PITMAN HOUSE, 381–383 CHURCH STREET, TORONTO

THE PAPER AND BINDING OF
THIS BOOK CONFORM TO THE
AUTHORIZED ECONOMY STANDARDS

MADE IN GREAT BRITAIN AT THE PITMAN PRESS, BATH
D5—(B.1545)

PREFACE

The object of this volume is to provide business men with a practical handbook of reasonable proportions, to which they may refer from time to time for information upon matters ordinarily arising in the management and general conduct of the office work in connection with business transactions both large and small. No attempt has been made to exceed these limits by needlessly specializing either in the direction of accountancy or of law, or in connection with the more technical details of the practical conduct of different classes of business undertakings. Such an extension of the scope of the work would, it is thought, have been in the highest degree undesirable; for, apart from the difficulty of dealing with these larger subjects effectively within anything approaching the compass of the present volume, it is at least open to serious doubt whether a knowledge of them can be imparted effectively by means of a book of any description.

Chapters XXI and XXII deal with the various legal matters concerning which all business men should possess some knowledge. Obviously, however, they do not profess to be exhaustive, or to avoid the necessity of legal assistance in all cases where serious complications or disputes arise. Their aim is rather to point out to the reader the desirability of employing such assistance in circumstances in which it should be invoked than to attempt the impossible task of indicating how the average layman, with no special training or experience, can hope to succeed in carrying on an important business for any appreciable period of time without incurring some expenditure by way of law costs. Attempts at economy in this direction are in general as futile as in connection with the professional audit of accounts, and it is certainly not claimed that the most attentive reader of the present volume will be able with safety to dispense with the services of either his solicitor or his professional accountant.

NOTE TO TWELFTH EDITION

In revising for the Press the present twelfth edition I have been indebted to numerous reviewers and correspondents for helpful suggestions. In view of the evident popularity of the book amongst students of commerce, I have taken special pains to bring every chapter under close scrutiny and to be mindful of the rapidity of the changes which characterize modern conditions. Consequent on this attitude of mind many passages, and one whole chapter, have been entirely rewritten. One of the most prominent points calling for fresh attention has been the fact that in modern counting houses mechanical aids are now the rule rather than the exception. Within the obvious limits laid down by the restricted scope of the work special attention has therefore been devoted to mechanical methods, although, in relation to accounting proper, care has been taken not to lose sight of the fundamental principles of double entry which must necessarily underlie all the apparent complications of modern methods.

S. W. R.

NOTE TO THIRTEENTH EDITION

The note to the twelfth edition applies with equal force to this, the thirteenth. I am indebted to several correspondents and friends for their helpful interest.

S. W. R.

CONTENTS

OFFICE ORGANIZATION AND MANAGEMENT

CHAPTER I

Introductory, dealing generally with the importance of organization in business matters, and the qualifications necessary for those who undertake it

No one who is in touch with commercial offices can have failed to notice the vast changes in methods of organization which have characterized the last few decades. The period of economic stress through which the whole world has been passing has increased the competition in business of every description, and the great efforts which have been made by other nations to tap the trade of the world have quickened the activities and added an additional spur to the ambition of the English-speaking race, who realize that new methods are necessary if the headway gained by their forefathers is to be maintained. There has also been a noticeable commercial invasion of Great Britain by our American cousins, and there is a never-ceasing stream of representatives of foreign nations whose success in establishing profitable business connections in this country is apparent. With new men come always new methods and often new manners, and it has been found necessary by all who desire to keep abreast of the times that these new methods should be studied, and—where telling for increased efficiency or economy—adopted. There is no branch of manufacture of which the cost has not been materially reduced by labour-saving machinery, and the modernizing influences have spread gradually but surely from the manufactory and the works into the office itself, until now there are but few offices which do not bear unmistakable signs of the revolution which has taken place in commercial ideas since the last generation.

The day has gone past never to return when great commercial undertakings could afford to have their offices conducted on the slow, if steady and reliable, lines of old, and it is now realized that the office is to a business what the main spring is to a watch. The office of a successful business organization must be the brains of the whole concern : it must be the nerve centre of the entire mechanism, and so responsive in its organism that it shall instantly feel any weakness or failure in any outlying branch. The aim of the present book is to show the directions in which new methods may be found of advantage, and to suggest a systematic organization of every detail of office work.

Let it be assumed that a new business is being established, say, of a manufacturing character, with its own drawing office and works, its own travellers and agents, its own branches, and, of course, its own managing and clerical staff. This will enable us to take a "bird's-eye view" of the various departments of the business, to map out the scope and working of each, to consider the relationships which will combine all into a smoothly working whole—each having separate responsibility, but always acting in harmony with the one general plan, and co-operating with the others to secure a successful issue.

Successful organization implies a capable organizer, and it may be well at the outset to consider the qualifications necessary for the Manager of any large business undertaking. Notwithstanding the numerous examples there are of self-made men, they would probably be the first to admit that their efforts had been much hampered by want of education, and it is quite certain that they have risen not *because* of their want of education, but rather *in spite of* it. A good sound commercial education is a most remunerative investment, and is now within the reach of anyone of reasonable industry and average ability. It is not the function of this book to go into details as to what should comprise a good commercial education, the desire being to compile information and make suggestions which may be found useful to those who are either about to organize an office, or wish to improve their existing scheme of management.

A sound commercial education having been acquired, it is necessary for this education to be trained. Management should not be undertaken without training and the implied experience in office organization, otherwise it is probable that the experience will be dearly bought by the business whose Manager so acquires it. The young business man, ambitious ultimately to hold managerial reins, should lose no opportunity of acquiring an insight into every branch of work, be it correspondence, book-keeping, travelling, costing, store-keeping, advertising, manufacturing, or even legal. There is no knowledge which equals the knowledge possessed by one who has actually *done* work similar to that to be organized, who knows its difficulties, who has tested its possibilities of economy, and who has not been content merely to execute it but has endeavoured, as he has gained aptitude and experience, to improve upon its details and to facilitate rapidity of completion.

For the more marked success, organizing ability of the highest order is, of course, necessary. But, after all, what is organizing ability, and is it not possible to acquire it, at all events to a fair extent? It is true that many men have that gift of intuition which enables their minds to grasp almost with lightning rapidity the bearings of a case, that logical faculty which marshals up without difficulty the *pros* and *cons* of a knotty point which must be settled, that ability of foretelling results or events which is almost uncanny in its far-sightedness, that grasp of method and of detail which makes their brain like an orderly cabinet from which may be obtained at a second's notice whatever information may be required, and that capacity for rapid and accurate decision which almost amounts to genius. But, on the other hand, much of each of these qualities may be attained by that "infinite capacity for taking pains," which, we are told, is akin to genius, and is asserted by some to be genius itself. The cultivation of a habit of business accuracy, the thoughtful study of varying idiosyncrasies and types of character, the careful tracing of cause and effect, research into sources of commercial information, the compilation of useful notes, a tactfully exercised curiosity acted upon by a *soupçon* of that "gospel of discontent," which is so powerful an incentive to those who desire to mount life's ladder, will go far to foster powers of organization, and there are many ways in private and social life in which useful experience may be obtained. Honorary secretaryships of some of the numerous organizations which play so large a part in modern life offer most useful opportunities of acquiring valuable experience, and are of unmistakable benefit from the training point of view when the duties connected with them are undertaken with intelligence, enterprise, and industry.

Will power is no mean equipment. It is not merely necessary for the successful Manager to be able to "make up his mind," as the saying goes; having made it up, it is equally important that he should be mentally strong enough to adhere to, and to carry out, his decision. The adage, "the man who hesitates is lost," is more true in business life than in almost any other sphere. Decision and firmness should be twin qualities, and, in management, a decision should not be arrived at without due consideration of all the factors of the situation. When a decision has been given, it should be altered only when proved to be wrong by actual experience. It is better thus to buy experience once than to shake the confidence of the staff by constant changes of decision, reversals of policy, and the incessant alteration of arrangements before there has been a fair opportunity of testing what results will be brought forth.

Adaptability is a useful power in business life—not merely adaptability in dealing with one's fellows, but adaptability in connection with business methods. How often do we see men turn out business failures for no other reason than that they will not, or cannot, adapt themselves to those with whom they are brought into business relationships, or will not change their methods to suit alterations made necessary by competition or other influences? Many fortunes have been made by men who have set out upon certain lines, and have adapted themselves or their businesses to some changed condition which they have been quick to notice and to fall in with.

Originality and imagination are important factors in business management and success. The trend of commercial life is all in the direction of improvement, and it is the man with originality of ideas, who has trained his imagination to come into play in business life, who outstrips his fellows. It is not well to run after novelties for the sake of novelty, but it is often the presentation of an old idea in some new form which brings business, and which, in course of time, marks out a man as one who does not run in a groove but has brains to think out new ways. Cultivate the imagination—it is a powerful aid against business mediocrity, and (more important still) a preventer of monotony.

The successful Manager must cultivate self-control. Coolness, quietness of demeanour and utterance, firmness of manner, and uniform command of temper are certain to ensure obedience and respect. Shouting, blustering, and bullying may appear to have a temporary effect, but continued indulgence will soon be recognized as a sign of weakness, and induce contempt and perhaps even hatred in the minds of subordinates. For a like reason sarcasm is generally to be avoided. Even if regarded only from the selfish point of view, it is better to be surrounded by cheerful, willing assistants, whose pleasure it is to earn commendation, when they know appreciation is always expressed, rather than by cowed, discontented, and disloyal workers. Cultivate a spirit of fellowship in the staff, take an interest in their doings, and let them feel that they are regarded not as machines but as brains whose active and sympathetic co-operation in the progress of the undertaking will be welcome, whose interest is invited and whose welfare will be safeguarded. Self-control is to some extent a matter of health. The bilious, " livery " man will at times find it difficult to maintain his evenness of temper, and it is therefore important, from the business point of view, that bodily health should be as good as possible. Modern science has taught much in connection with the " healthy body," and much help in this direction will be derived from the regular use of some of the physical exercises now so widely recommended. By their means all exercise really necessary for health's sake can be obtained, so to speak, " in tabloid form," and this without interfering in any way with the exigencies of business.

CHAPTER II

Personnel of Staff—General points to be considered in connection with the engagement of Clerks, Travellers, Agents, Foremen, etc.—Qualifications required in each case—Female Labour—Apprentices—Remuneration—Terms of Hire—Termination of Hire

One of the most important factors in commercial success is the power to read character, and the selection of a staff is one of the matters which should always secure the personal attention of the capable Manager, as upon its wisdom depends to an even greater extent than is generally recognized the success of the whole undertaking. No trouble should be regarded as too great to be taken in the endeavour to find just the right man for each appointment. It is hardly necessary to say that no appointment should be made until the applicant has been personally interviewed. Written references should not be relied upon. It is a matter of common knowledge that some firms, not specially noted for commercial morality, try to get rid of their indifferent employees by giving them a strong recommendation in support of applications for other appointments, while, on the other hand, some houses make it a rule never to give written references. A personal interview with the Manager of the firm giving the recommendation is always advisable if it can be obtained, whilst an indirect inquiry amongst the colleagues of the applicant will sometimes throw an unexpected light upon his character and capabilities.

The Manager's Principal Assistant or Chief Clerk should possess, as far as possible, the qualifications of the Manager himself, as the latter must have someone upon whom he can rely to take charge in his absence. Some Managers prefer to appoint to this position one having a good knowledge of some parts of the work with which they themselves are least familiar, and, in cases where the Manager has not a good all-round knowledge, probably this is advisable.

Very special care must be exercised in the selection of travellers and agents, as their duties are necessarily performed outside the immediate supervision of the Manager. Although there is a widespread belief that a smart and experienced traveller can effect sales of *anything*, it is of undoubted importance for him to have a good knowledge of the various manufactures of the firm he represents; and one who is already personally known to buyers in the particular line of business will have access to many a private office which would be closed to a new man. Readiness of wit and a good address are essentials to these appointments.

In regard to agents, it is very necessary that, prior to appointment, their commercial status should be inquired about through one of the commercial inquiry offices. It is useless to expect an extension of business in a given neighbourhood unless the agent is a man of good standing locally, and the careful Manager should not content himself until he has made personal inquiries in the district which it is desired to open up.

In selecting book-keepers and clerks, there is a good deal to be said in favour of requiring certificates in such subjects as book-keeping and shorthand, although it should not be imagined that the possession of these certificates indicates that their holders are trained men of business. Employers are often inclined to complain of our system of commercial education, and that there is room for improvement may be readily admitted. It is, however, useless to expect that any conceivable system of scholastic training can take the place of actual experience, and the danger is that, if the opposite be assumed to be true, the first duty of a new entrant to an office will be to unlearn a good deal of what has been inculcated outside. What is wanted is a good foundation of general knowledge—supplemented by an acquaintance with common commercial terms and general routine—and a receptive mind. There is no good reason why a youth of 16 or 17 who has any intention of filling a place in the huge business machine should not have acquired some idea of the difference between, say, a Letter of Credit and a Credit Note, as well as the ability to cast, correctly and quickly, a column of figures, to write a good hand, and to use, rather than abuse, his mother tongue. It is satisfactory to find that such subjects as shorthand, book-keeping, commercial law, business routine, commercial geography, etc., are now receiving some of the attention they deserve, and are being given a proper place in the educational curriculum. Certificates in these and other subjects are now awarded by several trustworthy examining bodies, notably the Endorsed Certificate in Commerce awarded by the Board of Education to successful examination candidates who have taken an approved three-year course of study. Such certificates possess a secondary value which should not be overlooked; they not only indicate a certain acquaintance with the subjects specified, but they also serve as an indirect testimony to the industry and ambition of the applicants who possess them, and, from this point of view, they are a valuable endorsement of the personal references furnished by a previous employer. In may be added that several of the newer Universities, not only the University of London, now grant Degrees in Commerce. The curriculum preparatory to graduation in this faculty is naturally somewhat severe, but the value of the qualification, when obtained, is correspondingly high.

A would-be book-keeper should have a good grounding in the *principles* of book-keeping, as well as the knowledge and mental agility necessary to enable him to apply those principles to particular requirements. In addition, he should possess certain mental and moral qualifications without which his technical knowledge will be worse than useless. In the first place, he should, of course, be accurate and reliable and absolutely above suspicion, especially if filling one of the higher positions in his department. These are all-important considerations, while neatness and quickness are also essential to the best results.

Correspondence clerks should be really expert typists definitely trained to get the best out of their machines. Additionally they should either have a good knowledge of shorthand (both as to writing and reading) or should be trained to use the dictating machines to be mentioned in Chapter III. The Manager of a busy office cannot afford to waste time dictating letters to clerks who are unable to "take down" at the desired rate or who cannot type those letters in a creditable manner. A good knowledge of English is another desideratum, as it will save the clerk from many a pitfall, and it will be to the employer's interest to look for this qualification in his correspondence clerks. Nothing but discredit is reflected on an office sending out badly typed, badly spelt, or badly punctuated letters; and, although it may be sometimes necessary as a corrective to careless work to insist on a letter being re-typed, this is an expensive and vexatious remedy which it should not be necessary to apply as a regular practice.

There is some difference of opinion as to the desirability of the apprentice system in offices. It has grown to be very unpopular in some districts, owing largely to its abuse by employers who run their offices with young apprentices, who are promptly discharged when their periods of apprenticeship have expired. The apprentice system of olden days furnished opportunities for a youth to be thoroughly grounded in every branch of the business to which he was bound, and left him, at the end of his time, a valuable assistant well worthy of a permanent place in the establishment, and, if this method is followed to a legitimate extent, it will be found useful.

The question of remuneration is one which it is difficult to discuss in detail, owing to the infinite variety of circumstances existing in businesses of various kinds and magnitudes. There are, however, some general considerations which it will be well to bear in mind. Cheap labour from the point of view of the salaries list does not necessarily imply economy when the final balance of profit or loss is considered, and a really good clerk is always worth good pay. The results obtained will be a faithful reflex of the ability of the individual members of the staff, and it is well to remember, particularly in businesses where competition is keenly felt, that a good clerk lost may be an important gain to a competitor. The Manager should have a clear idea of the qualifications necessary for the various appointments to be filled, and a proper acquaintance with what is regarded as the market value attached to such positions. Given this knowledge, it follows that a payment higher than the ordinary market value for the leading positions will secure a variety of choice and a standard of applicant which will assist materially in the quest of the best assistants. It will not be found more expensive to obtain men and girls of fair education, appearance, and address than those of a more common grade, and due attention should be paid to these points, particularly in connection with positions the holders of which necessarily come into contact with customers or the general public. If the Manager is not favourably impressed with an applicant for one of these posts, he should not forget that, while appearances are often deceptive, the impression made on others may be not unlike his own, and the success of the business may be prejudiced by the very defects which lead him to look unfavourably on the applicant.

As regards the actual engagement of employees, the law is that in the case of a partnership every partner has implied authority to engage and to dismiss a servant unless it is otherwise provided in the articles of partnership. An employee cannot, however, be compelled by one partner to leave the premises if the other partner or partners authorize him to remain.

For all except the most subordinate positions, written agreements should, of course, be the rule. Not that an agreement by word of mouth is unenforceable if supported by proper evidence; but the mere existence of a written contract has a marked effect in *preventing* disputes, as well as in assisting materially in their settlement should they arise. In the case of an engagement which, by its nature, cannot be performed within a year, the Statute of Frauds, 1677, enacts that no action can be brought (in England) unless some note or memorandum of it is in writing and signed. The essential points of an agreement are—

(1) It must contain the names or other sufficient description of the parties thereto;
(2) It must contain the terms of engagement. (These cannot be varied by any outside evidence);
(3) It must be shown that the agreement is mutual;
(4) It must be signed—by both parties for preference, though it is sufficient if each party has the signature of the other.
(5) It must be stamped (see below).

If an agreement is unenforceable because these requirements have not been complied with, the master cannot effectively object if the servant leaves before the expiration of the time specified; and the servant, if dismissed before that time, has no right of action on that account, though he is entitled to be paid a reasonable sum for such work as he may have actually performed. At or before the time of signing, the document may be stamped with an adhesive 6d. stamp, otherwise it must be impressed at an Inland Revenue Stamp Office within fourteen days from the date of the first signature. The effect of not properly stamping an agreement is that, if either party wishes to enforce the agreement, he will not be able to use the written document as evidence of it, except under a penalty of £10 in addition to the duty originally payable. An agreement for the hire of an "artificer" or "labourer" is specially exempted from stamp duty.

The period for which a servant is engaged depends upon the terms of the contract. Where the contract is indefinite, it is presumed to be for a year, and if it is continued after the year it is presumed to be for another year, and so on. The mere fact that wages are paid quarterly, monthly, or weekly does not *necessarily* alter the presumption that it is a yearly hiring. Both the period of service and the time at which wages will become due should be definitely stated, but where nothing is said as to the time of payment, wages will be payable at the end of the period or periods for which the servant is engaged—whether weekly, monthly, quarterly, or yearly. But where payments have in fact been made quarterly or at other periodical dates, that fact would, notwithstanding that the hiring is yearly, be sufficient to warrant a jury in inferring that there was an agreement that the wages should be so paid. In certain employments the time is fixed by custom.

Where a servant is *not* engaged for any definite period, he is to be paid by the hour, day, etc., his wages becoming due at the end of each complete hour's or day's work, although as a matter of fact they may be paid only at the end of a week or other period. Where payment is by the job, the workman is not, in the absence of special agreement or custom, entitled to payment until the completion of the work; and, if the work is not completed, the employer might, in certain circumstances, be justified in not paying any wages at all. For extra work, an employee is not entitled to special remuneration unless the work was distinctly outside the scope of the employment for which he was engaged.

The Truck Acts provide that the wages of a workman, i.e. a person engaged in manual labour, must be paid in coin (or other legal tender money), except by his consent, and the deductions which may be made therefrom are strictly defined by statute. Deductions for bad or negligent work, for instance, are lawful only if specified in the contract, and fines can be deducted only if so specified, or if the particulars are set out in a notice kept in some place in or about the workshop where it may be easily seen, read, and copied. Every employer should make himself acquainted with the provisions of these Acts, which are of a more comprehensive nature than is frequently supposed. Some of the provisions are special to certain trades and circumstances, and it is impossible to indicate them fully here.

It has been held that a servant is bound to obey his master's orders, no matter how inconvenient and unreasonable, provided they are lawful and within the scope of the servant's employment.

He is not, however, bound to risk his life in his master's service. He must also exercise reasonable care and skill. The acceptance of employment implies the possession of a certain amount of competence to perform the work undertaken. The amount of skill to be expected must, of course, depend to some extent on the nature of the work, the remuneration to be paid, and other circumstances. The employer, too, must bear his share of the responsibility, for, if he knowingly engages a man to do something which the man has never done before, he cannot complain of incompetence. It should be borne in mind also that an employer can generally be compelled to indemnify his servant against all responsibilities incurred by him in the course of his employment, when acting in pursuance of the employer's orders, expressed or implied.

The length of notice required to terminate an engagement should be stated in the agreement in all cases, unless it is to be governed by custom. In the absence of express stipulation, it has been held that a clerk or commercial traveller is entitled to three months' notice. But, in the case of clerks or other servants engaged by the week or the month at a weekly or a monthly wage, a week's or a month's notice (as the case may be) only is necessary. As a general rule where the engagement is determinable upon a "reasonable" notice, such notice may be given at any time; but an engagement for one whole year, and so from year to year as long as the parties may please, can be determined only by a reasonable notice ending with such year. Although an employer may give wages in lieu of notice, it is not open to an employee to do the same thing.

Where an engagement is for a definite period, no notice is required to terminate it at the expiration of that period. A master may dismiss a servant without notice for, *inter alia*, the following reasons: disobedience to orders properly given, immorality, drunkenness, dishonesty, gross negligence, absolute incompetency, claiming to be a partner, conduct incompatible with his duties, permanent disablement through illness (mental or physical), or fraudulent concealment of some material fact at the time of his engagement. The receipt of an illicit commission by a Company Manager has also been held to be a justifiable reason for dismissal. An employer need not state why he dismisses a servant, but, if the servant brings an action for wrongful dismissal, the employer will have to justify what he has done. In certain circumstances, an employer dismissing a servant for misconduct may do so in the presence of a third party, as a witness to what is said, without rendering himself liable to an action for slander. A servant rightfully dismissed without notice will not be entitled to any wages in respect of the broken period subsequent to the last date at which they became due and payable.

A contract of service may be put an end to at any time by mutual agreement, and, in the absence of any stipulation to the contrary (express or implied), it is determined by the death of either party. In the latter case, wages are due up to the date of death. An engagement, even if for a specified period, will be terminated by the death of any partner unless from the actual terms of the agreement the contrary intention is implied. Voluntary dissolution will constitute wrongful dismissal or breach of contract, but, if a re-constituted firm offers to employ a servant on the same terms as before and he refuses to remain, he will be entitled to nominal damages only.

An employer is not legally bound to furnish a character, but, if he gives one, it must be true. Such a statement, whether in writing or by word of mouth, is privileged if made only to the parties interested. If made by telegram or by post card, however, the statement ceases to be privileged. In certain cases, it is allowable for a master to communicate to other employees (for his own and their protection) his reasons for dismissing a servant. Good faith is, of course, necessary to the maintenance of the privilege in any circumstances. Not only is a malicious statement of a derogatory nature actionable, but a master who, by giving a laudatory character which he knows to be false, induces another person to employ a servant, will be liable for any injury which the new master may suffer in consequence. Contracts with managers, travellers, and others frequently provide that the employee shall not engage in the same business within a limited area after the termination of the contract. These restraints must be such as are reasonably necessary for the master's protection. If the restraint is too wide it will be void, being deemed by the law to be against public policy.

In a business of any pretensions to size, a systematic record should be kept of each employee, including references received, references given, notes as to conduct, duties performed, cause of leaving, etc. The card system is very suitable for such records.

CHAPTER III

Office Accommodation—Importance of suitable situation and arrangement—Effect on efficiency of organization—General equipment of Office, drawing special attention to modern labour-saving devices, card and loose-leaf systems, Typewriters, Dictating Machines, Calculating Machines, etc.

Of primary importance in connection with office organization and management is the question of office accommodation, and, in many quarters, the extent to which efficiency of organization is hindered by the inappropriateness or insufficiency of physical accommodation is not adequately appreciated. In the establishment of a new business, very careful consideration should be given to the selection of a suitable position for the office. It is quite customary to find that banks and insurance companies, as well as some other large concerns, select very central positions upon which to erect imposing and convenient offices. Recent years have shown the increasing importance of this factor in establishing, in a purely material sense, the stability of these undertakings. But it is not only businesses of this description which find it useful to pay due regard to the question of the site upon which to conduct their work, though necessarily different factors must be considered in connection with different businesses. In these busy times, thought must be given to accessibility to customers. The channel through which inquiries (which may lead to purchases) are directed may be governed by nearness to purchasers' own premises, or to such places as may be convenient to their buyers or principals in their daily visits to their exchanges, etc. It is undoubtedly this consideration which has led to special centres being largely patronized by firms doing a particular class of business, especially where inspection and comparison of samples as well as prices are necessary. For internal time-saving, too, it is important to consider the proximity of banks, post offices, the trade exchange—in fact, of all places to which it may be necessary to pay daily, and even more frequent, visits. It is false economy to endeavour to save a few pounds per annum by placing the office in some cheap but out-of-the-way locality which will necessitate loss of valuable time every day on the part of principals and clerks in journeying to and from the centres of business activity. This consideration has a distinct bearing also on the number of office assistants required.

If the business is so large as to make advisable the building of its own offices, then the Manager must of necessity devote personal attention to the consideration of plans in consultation with the architect who is employed, and he must not allow the purely operative departments to be the only ones to be considered. The fact that the architect will receive a commission on the gross cost of erection has to be borne in mind, and every care must be taken to see that no unnecessarily lavish expenditure is incurred. Provision must be made not merely for the business of to-day, but for the probable extensions required in the future. There are few more costly things than to find that buildings specially planned for the accommodation of a particular business are outgrown, entailing a forced disposal and the provision of a larger building. No one should contemplate building unless the business is of an assured character, and, in this case, accommodation for extension should always be reserved and the selection of a site should be governed by this wise prevision.

In most cases, however, it will not be the building but the renting of office accommodation which will be the subject of consideration, and here to some extent the Manager may find his hands tied by questions of locality quite as much as of suitability, though it will generally be found that landlords are willing to make any reasonable alterations to their premises required by good tenants. If the business is of even moderate magnitude, numerous small rooms are not desirable and are distinctly bad from points of view of supervision, lighting, heating, and ventilation. Separate rooms may be necessary for the Manager and for some of the chiefs of departments, particularly those whose work necessitates interviews with callers, etc., but, where possible, the general office staff should be placed in one large room where oversight can easily be given. Needless to say, the arrangements should be such that no chance caller can see confidential documents. Where privacy for interviews is necessary for the Chief Clerk, it may be found useful to have his office raised above the level of the general office, from which it should be partitioned off with glass, this giving the desired confidential character to interviews whilst not interfering with the regulation and supervision of the staff. Typewriters (unless of the silent type) and noisy office machinery are usually shut away from the rest of the office.

Light, ventilation, and sanitation are matters which should be carefully considered, especially when it is remembered that the greater part of the day's work will be done in the office. It cannot be expected that the best results will be obtained unless the conditions are favourable. Natural light should be available during the ordinary day time, as work cannot be done with the minimum of discomfort, and, therefore, the maximum of speed, where artificial light must constantly be used. The intimate connection between the eyesight and the brain must not be overlooked, and, similarly, the need for proper ventilation and sanitation in offices has an important bearing on efficient organization and the rapid transaction of work.

It is usually desirable that the telephonic instruments should not be in an open office where all communications can be heard by both the staff and the callers. There have been many instances of important business information leaking out because messages have been overheard in this way, although the modern "microphone" type of instrument now enables conversation to be much quieter. Where the telephone cannot be placed in a separate room, it is easy to encase it so as to ensure the desired privacy. It will be found desirable also that a place should be provided for the correspondence department where the click of the typewriters will not disturb the other clerks. Most of the makers now produce quiet models which, though usually more expensive, certainly make a return by way of extra comfort for the outlay involved. The Manager's confidential secretary should usually be located in an anteroom through which callers desirous of seeing the Manager must pass. This secretary should be in touch with his engagements, and should know what people he should see and who should be "diverted into other channels," this being by no means an unimportant duty in connection with large undertakings, as the expedients employed by enterprising travellers desirous of seeing the chief are both numerous and ingenious.

On the other side of the Manager's room is the most convenient place for the Chief Clerk or Principal Assistant who will overlook, as previously described, the general office. The arrangement of the latter will necessarily depend to a great extent on the size of the staff and the magnitude of the business, but, wherever possible, the various departments should be marked off, not, of course, by walls but by physical demarcation of counters, railings, or even low and glazed partitions. By this means, two objects will be served. The books and documents appertaining to each branch will have little chance of becoming mixed, and each sub-chief will have his "sphere of influence" properly defined. The chaotic appearance of many offices means more than untidiness. It is "the outward and visible sign" of the "inward" frame of mind which does not deal promptly with each matter as it arises. An untidy office implies waste of time. If books are not restored to their proper places when temporarily done with they have to be looked for when required. When letters and other documents are not properly filed, the time of the clerks and the Manager is wasted when these are urgently wanted for reference purposes. Many Managers get into a habit of keeping on their desks papers which they know they will want in the course of a few days in order to prevent the possibility of being kept waiting for their production. This is a habit which grows, and which should be fought against sternly. The correspondence clerks should be encouraged to pride themselves on the rapidity with which everything can be produced and the Manager should aim at an ideal in the shape of a clear desk. The Manager of a large engineering works in the Midlands employing several thousands of men makes it a principle never to keep on his own desk anything which requires dealing with, but refers every such letter to some one of his assistants, at the same time insisting on personally signing every letter which leaves the establishment. When there is an efficient system of "following up" such letters, there can be no doubt that this method of making each sub-chief responsible for matters affecting his own particular work has an excellent effect in developing a sense of individual responsibility.

The cash and book-keeping staffs should be adjacent, though the former should be partitioned off, so that there is no indiscriminate and unnoticed entry into their "sacred precincts," and the cashier should have his own safe distinct from the general office safe or strong room. Another portion of the room should be allotted to the orders and supplies clerks, another to the sales and invoice department, another to the wages, and yet another to the cost clerks and estimating assistants. It will be seen that this arrangement has reference to a manufacturing undertaking of a fairly extensive character. In smaller concerns, however, the same principle should apply, and if there is but one clerk dealing with each separate branch of the clerical work an effort should be made to give him his own fair share of the office accommodation, for the tidiness and the order of which he may be held responsible. It will not be found advisable, even if the drawing-office staff is limited to one, to house it in the general office. There is an amount of fascination in a drawing growing into shape which has a wonderfully time-wasting influence on some clerks, and it is well to limit temptations.

Similarly, the travellers should be assigned separate quarters of their own, for he is a poor traveller who does not amass—even in the course of one day's peregrinations—some amusing incidents which, if recounted in office hours, will be far from having an expediting effect upon the production of that Balance Sheet or those statistics which are anxiously awaited in the Manager's room.

Some take the view that counters to which inquirers and callers come should not permit of open inspection of the office beyond; that if the counter is an open one, a short partition should run behind it so as to limit the view of the public to the clerk in immediate attendance; or that the counter should be bordered with frosted glass, pierced with inquiry windows backed by a screen. There are obvious objections to outsiders being able to read documents that clerks are handling; but, subject to this, it is difficult to understand this passion for the mysterious. A well arranged, well kept office is a great asset on account of the favourable impression it produces.

At one time practically all modern office furniture was of American origin. Now our own manufacturers are second to none, but the design should always be carefully considered. If there is ample room for store cupboards, book racks, filing cabinets, etc., desks fitted elaborately with drawers should not be purchased—the drawers are too convenient, especially if the hour is nearing the end of the commercial day, for the receipt of books and papers which should be assigned other and more appropriate receptacles. There is no necessity for each clerk to have his own pile of letter paper, memo. forms, etc., getting crumpled and made useless in his drawer. A tear-off block is sufficient for ordinary purposes and printed stationery is an expensive form of scrap paper. The ordinary desk with a single line of drawers under it, mounted on spindle legs which will not harbour dust or prevent free access of ventilation, will be found to be the best, and two or three inquiries will bring in reasonable estimates for their supply. If, on the other hand, the office space is very cramped, desks with a set of drawers at each end will be found useful for store purposes, and, of course, correspondence clerks require a supply of stationery that is readily accessible. All drawers so used should have exterior labels giving the name of the main class of material to be found inside. If stationery and sundries are thus kept, they should not be placed loosely in the drawer, as, with its necessary opening and

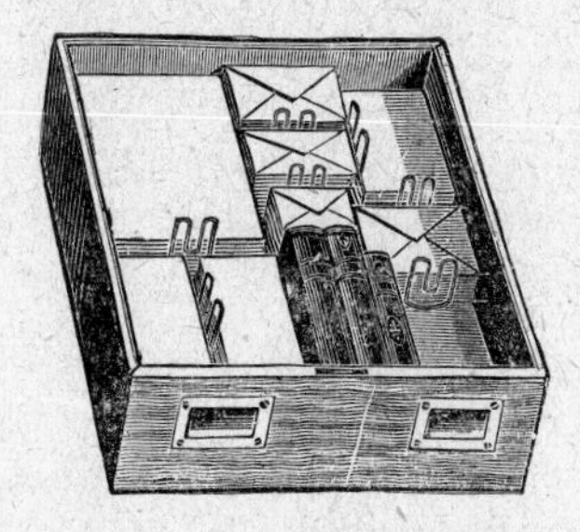

shutting, they will get intermingled and astray. Store drawers should be fitted with properly spaced wooden divisions. Some office supply stationers have for this purpose wire divisions which can be pressed down into their places by means of their sharp-pointed feet.

Drawers for keeping a temporary supply of different kinds of notepaper, etc., are now sometimes divided into "layers" by the provision of wooden slats which slide in sloping grooves cut in the side to the drawers, but generally speaking, storage in drawers is not satisfactory, and, as it is better to aim at the equipment of an office in a more modern manner, it may be of service to review briefly the principal points to be borne in mind. It is not desired in these pages to refer to individual manufacturers of office supplies, except in some one or two cases of useful specialities. There are many well-known firms of office fitters, all supplying goods such as are here described in general terms.

Stationery should have its own cupboard or store, divided off into spaces for the proper reception of letter paper, envelopes, foolscap, pencils, pens, blotting paper, etc., so that the stationery clerk can tell at a glance when his stock of any particular article is running short. Needless to say the issue of stationery should be controlled, and it should not be possible for the office staff merely to take whatever quantity seems to them good.

A catalogue file of a very useful and adaptable type is also obtainable, and is especially welcome in a large manufacturing undertaking,

where it is necessary to have prompt access to such trade requisites. The varying size and shape of trade catalogues render them somewhat difficult to file in any but a specially designed cabinet, which provides not merely a place for catalogues, but for each catalogue its own place.

Types of filing cabinets are dealt with in the chapter devoted to correspondence, but the card-index system may be mentioned here, as it is applicable to every department of office work, and not merely to correspondence.

If the card system is regarded merely in its indexing capacity in comparison with the old form of book index, it has several very distinct advantages. One of the difficulties in connection with the book index is that it is always being outgrown. It is not possible to substitute new entries for those which have ceased to be of use owing to the particular thing indexed being finished with. The indexing of one particular matter may, therefore, be spread over several index books. In the card system, everything appertaining to the one matter will always be found together, as another card can always be inserted. Dead matter can be removed with ease, as it only implies taking away a card. In some circumstances, however, this facility of removal is a distinct drawback; hence it is important to use discrimination. Being self-contained, the card system is capable of indefinite expansion with the growth of the business itself, as the drawer cabinets can be added to at any time. The cards can always be re-classified and re-arranged, and tabbed in different colours for urgent attention or any other

purpose. The arrangement may be alphabetical (by the names of customers or of articles dealt with, etc.); chronological (as in the case of bills to be met or accounts to be collected); geographical (corresponding with the routes of travellers' journeys); or on any other desired plan. While serving the purpose of an index better than any book, the system may be something more than an index. It is, in many cases, an index *plus* the thing indexed, as, for instance, where a literary man keeps a record of useful quotations. It may be adapted for recording particulars of customers' credit, for records of contracts, for employees' records, for advertising accounts and records, travellers' reports, etc.; and many firms are using it extensively in preference to book ledgers for customers' accounts. For the purpose last named, cards may be used as large as 8 by 5 inches, ruled on both sides. The use of cards or loose sheets as ledger accounts becomes essential where machine methods of posting are in use.

Card indexes so devised that the cards hang in slots and overlap are now sold in several forms. Their great advantage is that the essential information conveyed by each card can be typed or written on its uncovered portion, instant visibility without fingering the cards being thus obtained. The illustration is of a steel "Kardex" cabinet of twelve very shallow trays, in each of which some fifty or more cards can lie flat, and so overlapped that the

names or titles of all are visible at once as soon as the tray is pulled out.

The loose-leaf ledger is based on the same general idea as that governing cards, and many features are common to both systems. The advocates of the card ledger claim that it is even more mobile and easy of reference than the loose-leaf system, and, meeting possible objections, they hold that such a ledger is no more open to falsification than the ordinary book, and point out that a ledger is never used by itself but only in conjunction with other books. If desired, a rod passing through the cards and furnished with a locking arrangement may be had, and with reasonable care there should be no danger of cards being accidentally lost. One of the most important advantages of the card and loose-leaf systems is the saving of the time periodically consumed in the opening of new ledgers, with the consequent transfer of accounts from the old to the new books.

The loose-leaf or card ledger, once started, is practically perpetual. The position of an account in the ledger is always the same, rendering an index almost unnecessary; there is no need to estimate the space to be left for each account, as in the bound ledger, with the waste of stationery on the one hand and the over-running of the allotted space on the other, which is so characteristic of that method, because further sheets or cards can be added to any particular

account as they are required; filled leaves can always be removed, reducing the bulk of the ledger to what is absolutely necessary for current accounts.

The covers of a loose-leaf book are very substantially constructed, as might be expected of a "perpetual" system. The back of the book is telescopic to allow of a varying number of pages and may contain a lock to guard against accidental or fraudulent abstraction of the leaves. The latter may be had in various qualities and rulings, with either a paper or linen hinge which is pierced with holes through which the posts or straps in the back of the covers pass. Under this system, it is neither necessary nor desirable to have so long a page as in the bound ledger, and, as both debtor and creditor sides of an account fall on the same page, the shape of the leaf is somewhat different and the size generally smaller than in the old style. This contributes to convenience in handling, and compensates for the extra weight of the covers, which, with their leather covering and rounded corners, are by no means clumsy in appearance. As leaves of an account are filled, they can be transferred to a "Transfer

Binder" (constructed on the same principle but in a cheaper binding), in which the account takes the same position as in the original book. Whilst various methods of indexing may be employed, perhaps the most useful plan is to designate each account by its initial letter and a number, the index leaves (bearing lettered tabs and distributed throughout the book) being used to carry the names. The accounts under each section of the index would commence at No. 1, and the sheets belonging to a particular account would bear a subsidiary number. In other words, a number would be

allotted to each account placed under the several letters of the alphabet, and, to prevent any sheets getting astray, each sheet would bear a number commencing at unity for each account. Thus, the sheets of Allen's account might be A1-1, A1-2, and so on. The absence of any sheet would be at once noticeable. The fraudulent substitution of one sheet for another may be guarded against in several ways, viz.: (1) by the lock already mentioned; (2) by having a paper with a special water-mark; (3) by having the firm's name printed on each leaf; (4) by having each sheet machine-numbered, and a register kept of their exact whereabouts. The sheets should also be in charge of some responsible person. It is claimed for this system that, although the first cost is somewhat heavier than that of ordinary books, when the expense is spread over a number of years it compares favourably with the cost of any good account book, there being nothing but leaves to purchase after the first outlay. The advantages are incontestable, so long as the book-keeping staff is properly trained.

It will be readily understood that the advantages attaching to the loose-leaf system are not confined to ledgers. The increasing use of the typewriter and other book-keeping aids has made it convenient, for example, to create records relating to cash, sales, purchases, and other matters on loose sheets to be afterwards assembled into binders.

In connection with the card and loose-leaf systems, other labour-saving devices can be used with advantage in large offices. For instance, the name and address of every customer may be set up in type or be cut in a special stencil, and be retained in either form, so that it is available not only for stamping the heading of the ledger account but also for addressing purposes, or for stamping any document which requires the customer's name and address. The *modus operandi* is as follows: The stereotyped addresses are kept vertically in trays, like the cards of a Card Ledger; when

required, they are taken out and inserted in a machine of the type of the "Addressograph," which (practically automatically) prints them off at the rate of about 1000 per hour, repeating any that it may be desired to repeat, and skipping any that it may be desired to skip. The standard plate is in five lines, but any one (or more) may be blocked out if desired; and the machine can be adjusted to print names in consecutive lines on the same sheet, thus admitting of the rapid preparation of "skeleton" pay-rolls, lists of Ledger Balances, etc.

The great saving of time and tedious labour effected by the use of calculating machines is only now being sufficiently realized in commercial circles in this country, although for many years such machines have been in use amongst actuaries, astronomers, and others, and in general use in all large progressive businesses. The great bulk of business calculations are, of course, additions; accordingly adding machines are ordinarily the first to be introduced. These machines fall into two broad classes; there are those which produce a result on a dial without leaving any record of the quantities which have successively been put into the machine, and there are others which produce a list, on a ribbon of paper, of the quantities which have been added, together with an automatic total and sub-totals if desired. In the form in which they were originally introduced, both these types were actuated by keys arranged in ranks and files, each file containing the numbers from 1 to 9, and each rank consisting of the same number right across the keyboard. A more modern form, however, has done away with the ranks and files and has substituted an arrangement whereby one key for each essential figure plus a zero key is all that is required.

In many offices multiplication and division on a large scale are often necessary. Any adding machine can multiply, on the principle of repeated addition; adding machines can also divide, but this function is much more efficiently performed by specially made machines, of which there are several types. These machines can perform almost any mathematical calculation, but naturally they are, relatively, quite expensive. For special classes of calculations, slide rules are very useful indeed if handled with care and intelligence by a person well acquainted with the decimal system of notation.

Mention must here be made of the ingenious combination of adding machines and typewriters which has resulted in the development of ledger-posting machines. These are so arranged that when either a debit or a credit is posted to an account, the balance is automatically calculated and thrown out into a column provided for the purpose on the ledger card. Finally, a bare mention must be made of the facilities which are available in large offices through the utilization of suitably punched cards by specially designed machines (of which the "Hollerith" and "Powers" types are the outstanding examples), which sort the cards into any desired order, and then, by "feeling" the position of the punched holes, translate the information conveyed thereby into plain language.

If there is reason for saying that calculating machines are too little used, the same can hardly be said of typewriters. The office which nowadays conducts its correspondence by means of the pen is antiquated indeed. Not only on account of its speed (where the operator is worth having) has the typewriter an immense advantage, but several copies of the same document can be produced at one operation. The appearance of a properly typed letter is greatly superior to the general run of pen-written documents. The term "properly typed" is used advisedly, for perhaps in no other department of commercial life is the market so over-run with potterers. A badly typed letter, whose spelling is equalled only by its punctuation—or the want of it—is the reverse of creditable to the firm sending it out. It is well to bear in mind, too, that a typewriter is not a toy, but a somewhat expensive and intricate piece of machinery, and that it *pays*, therefore, to have an efficient typist even at somewhat above the minimum salary. As to machines, there is a sufficiently wide choice. There are now on the English market many makes, each claiming some peculiar advantage for itself. The combination of all the virtues in one machine is perhaps a "consummation devoutly to be wished" hardly obtainable at present. The general features of the type-writing machine are too well known to need description, though some remarks on the different types of machines may not be without service.

As regards the keyboard—the arrangement of the keys in relation to the letters of the alphabet—nearly all the machines adopt what is known as the "universal" arrangement of letters. At one time many patterns of typewriters had a separate key for each character, but the modern tendency is in favour of making one key do duty for two or more characters by means of a "shift" key, or keys. The use of shift keys permits of a more compact keyboard, a less number of working parts and a consequent saving in cost. The method of inking on most machines is by means of a ribbon against which the types strike and through which the impressions are produced. The Elliott-Fisher is specially constructed for writing in *books*, and will make a carbon copy of a letter in the letter-book or of an invoice in the day book at the same time as the letter or invoice is being written. Many machines are fitted with more than one style of type.

Noiseless typewriters were introduced into this country a few years ago, and electric typewriters which have recently been placed on the market are certainly worth attention, particularly when a large number of carbon copies is desired. All typewriters are inclined to be noisy, but if a rubber mat be placed underneath the machine it will be found to reduce this noise to a minimum. The typists will appreciate also the relief to the tips of the fingers obtained by covering the letters on the keyboard with rubber tips, which, duly inscribed with the name of the letter, can be purchased for a small price from any typewriter agent.

Another very useful adjunct to the office is the dictating machine into which a manager can dictate his letters, instructions, etc., in his own time, and at his own pace, leaving them to be reproduced by the typist (who meanwhile has been engaged upon other work) at whatever time may be found most convenient. The voice is made to produce an impression on a revolving wax cylinder which, having been placed into the "transcribing" unit of the machine, reproduces the voice of the dictator in a light speaking-tube which, the typist attaches to a headband. The dictator can, if necessary, "listen back" on his instrument and any corrections or directions which occur to him can be jotted on a specially prepared paper slip ruled to show the various positions on the cylinder. Each cylinder can be used over and over again if, after it is full, it be smoothed and polished in a specially devised "shaving" machine.

Not the least important feature connected with the remarkable growth of the use of the typewriter is the greater facility with which copies of an original document can be obtained by the aid of carbon sheets so that the old-fashioned press copy is almost completely out of date. For business purposes, the reproduction of hand-written circulars and similar matter is now practically obsolete. On the other hand, for the duplication—or, indeed, for the indefinite multiplication—of typewritten originals there is a wide choice of apparatus. Even lithography can be utilized in connection with the typewriter by using a lithographic ribbon and transfer paper. But the more usual method is that known as duplicating or mimeography. The paper used for the original has a prepared surface which is cut by the types of the machine (or by a stylo if done by hand) in such a way as to allow the ink supplied by a roller to pass through it. Ordinarily, the plan is to stretch the stencil in a movable frame, the paper for the copy being placed underneath; and where there is no great amount of copying work to be done this method answers well enough, especially if an automatic (self-lifting) frame is used. In that case the paper is placed under the frame, which is held down by one hand while the ink roller is passed over it by the other. When released, the frame rises, the printed copy is taken off and the process repeated. But where a large quantity of copying is required one of the rotary duplicators now on the market will be found more efficient and a great time-saver. One of the best-known of these machines (the Roneo) is thus described: "A metal frame supports a cylinder of thin, perforated steel. On the outer surface of the cylinder is stretched a linen ink pad, and over this is placed a stencil. In the earlier models, the pad is inked by a felt roller resting in an ink reservoir suspended between the two sides of the frame. . . . The ink is supplied automatically after the reservoir is once charged, and there is no risk of the ink coming into contact with the fingers, or of the paper getting soiled. . . . The cylinder is rotated by a handle, or motor if desired. The paper fed into the machine is gripped by a rubber impression roller, which presses it against the stencil as the cylinder revolves, and the sheet, perfectly printed, is then automatically discharged on the other side." Later developments of this machine make use of metal type set round the outer surface of the cylinder in lieu of a stencil. A cyclometer can be attached, showing the number of copies printed. Sixty copies per minute is a good average for the hand-worked apparatus. By using a self-feeding machine driven by foot, motor (connection with an electric lamp is sufficient) or other power, this speed can be greatly increased. It is claimed that anything up to five thousand copies can be produced from one original. It will be seen at once that such an apparatus is a great boon in many offices

for the rapid production of circulars, prices current, specifications, market reports, etc. In some respects, it is better than the printer. It is, generally speaking, more ready; and, if necessary, the work can be done under personal supervision. Circulars produced on the best machines, the names and addresses being inserted separately with ink to match, cannot be distinguished from original letters—an obvious advantage.

The rotary principle, so conducive to speed in the matter of duplication, has been applied with good results to ordinary press-copying, and is especially useful in cases where the system adopted is that of filing with each letter received a press-copy of the reply sent. The tissue, instead of being bound into a book, is placed in a continuous roll on the machine. The letter to be copied is passed through by a turn of a handle and the copy (automatically detached) is ready for filing. This entails a very considerable saving of time as compared with the old-fashioned style of lever or screw press.

No up-to-date office is complete without means of inter-communication between the Manager and the various sub-departments. There are several methods in vogue of which the least expensive is the provision of an electric bell in the outer office; this is connected with a small bell push on the principal's desk, there being a recognised code of signals, one ring being for the shorthand clerk, two for the principal assistant, three for the office boy, etc. If there are several chiefs using bell signals, each bell communicates with an indicator in the general office, on which indicator a disc drops which is assigned to the particular chief who has rung. This method is, of course, useful only as an indication that the chief requires someone to go into his room, and a good deal of time and unnecessary passing in and out will be saved by the adoption of a method which enables the message to be spoken. The old-fashioned speaking-tubes have now been superseded by various types of house telephones. A modern development of these enables the Manager, by means of specially sensitive apparatus, to converse with his subordinates so that neither party need hold the instrument to ear or mouth; an elaboration of this instrument enables several persons situated in different parts of a building to hold a conference without moving from their respective desks.

CHAPTER IV

Division of Responsibility—Principles underlying subdivision of work and arrangement of duties of Staff—Budgetary Control—Division into Departments—Branches—General Systems of Control and Internal Check—Cash Checks

In all except very small offices it is of paramount importance that there shall be a proper and defined division of responsibility. Even in small concerns, where the clerical staff is limited to two or three, care should be taken that each individual is held entirely responsible for certain portions of the work, rather than that any class of work should be done indiscriminately by whichever clerk happens to be disengaged. It may be urged that, in a small office, it is absolutely necessary that each member of the staff shall be able to take up any portion of the work in the absence of another clerk, but the experience necessary for this is better acquired by changing the work, say, at monthly intervals than by encouraging the slipshod arrangements which invariably result from a lack of proper definition of individual duties.

In large undertakings, this clearness of division of responsibility must commence at the very highest positions in the office. More firms than would acknowledge the fact, or are even aware of the fact, suffer appreciably from the results of friction and rivalry between heads of sub-departments, and it behoves the successful Manager to obviate justification for friction by laying down clear definitions of the work assigned to each of his immediate assistants, whose spheres should not be allowed to overlap.

Different businesses have different methods of defining the responsibility of their assistants or of organizing sub-departments, and the chart on the following page suggests but the general lines of a scheme suited to a medium-sized business. It is obvious, for example, that if the business were of very large proportions the "general manager" of this chart would need to be a veritable superman; in such a case it is probable that the supervision of different functions would be assigned to small committees of the Board of Directors, subject to the over-riding authority of the Board as a whole acting by the advice of its President.

Clerical Staff. It will be seen from this chart that the office clerical work is divided into three main sub-departments, the

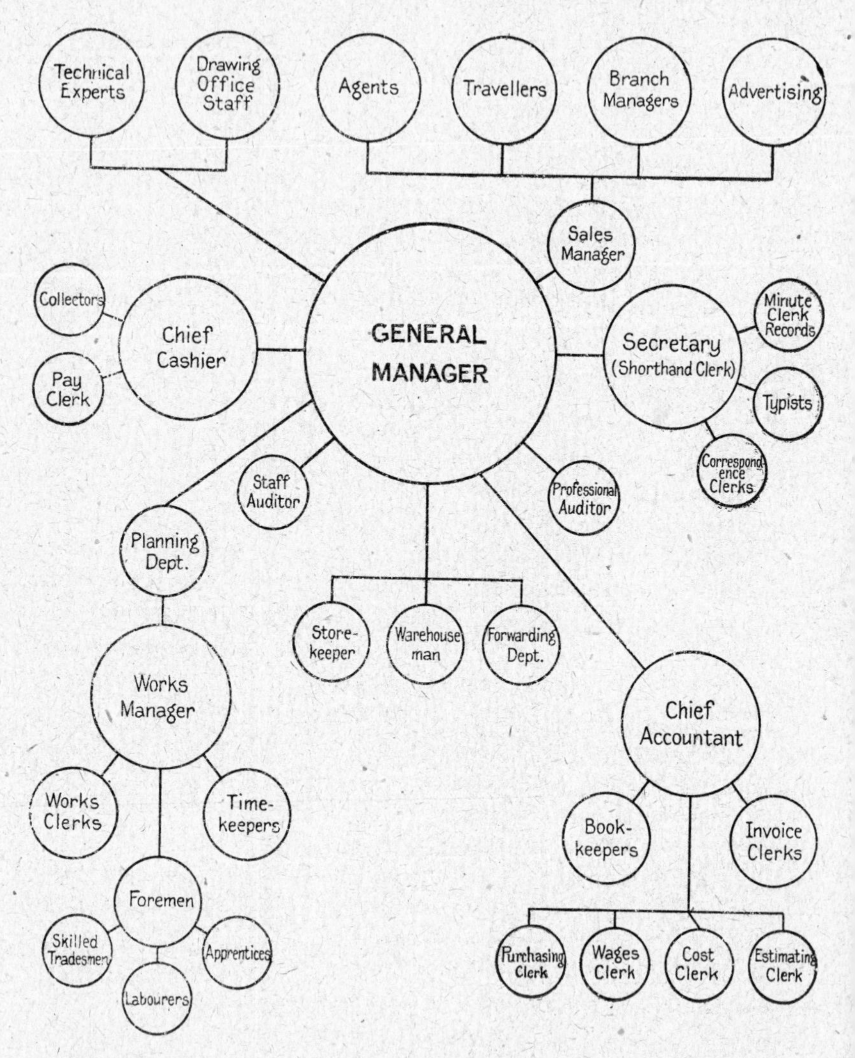

heads of which are here directly responsible to the Manager for the conduct of their particular portions of the work. The responsibility devolving upon each of these heads in nowise overlaps, and the Secretary, the Accountant, and the Cashier have well defined spheres and should have equally well defined office accommodation. If the undertaking is a Limited Liability Company, the Secretary will be responsible for certain statutory duties, more fully dealt with in the chapters devoted to Company work, and, in this case, he will be directly answerable to the Directors for the execution of such work. He will deal with the recording of minutes and other work connected with the meetings of Directors, the register of shareholders and the transfers of shares, and such portion of the correspondence as is purely secretarial. In this chapter and in the next, however, it is assumed that the business is one in which the Secretary is answerable solely to the Manager, and the chart shows that his subordinates take entire control of the correspondence and record work of the office. This work is dealt with in detail in Chapter V.

The Accountant holds a position of the utmost importance, and upon the accuracy and lucidity of the work of his department much depends. He is not merely responsible for "keeping the accounts" of the firm, but should also be of the utmost service to the Manager in collecting into systematic form all those multitudinous details which bear upon economical production and administration. It is his paramount duty to see that all the books are kept up to date, so that the most recent information on all details of the business is at hand for the Manager's information. It is not sufficient nowadays for the Accountant to be able to speak authoritatively and promptly as to the financial condition of the firm as a business undertaking; He must be in a position to advise as to the financial aspect of every important step, and this not from a theoretical point of view, but based upon actual experience of the results obtained from similar work which the firm has previously undertaken. Success in manufacture is obtained by careful study and improvement of each individual detail, and similarly the most successful Accountant is he who makes his figures illuminate the cost of production, administration, or distribution, so that the Manager or Technical Adviser can see at once where undue expenditure is taking place. Some Works Managers resent very much what they call undue interference in their province on the part of the Accountant, and it must be admitted that many Accountants are somewhat apt to look upon their work as the all-important part of commercial undertakings. Friction here is fatal, and the Manager must make every effort to see that his Works Manager shall realize the very great assistance his particular department will derive from the analytical figures of the Accountant, and how he will be helped to reduce his costs; whilst, on the other hand, the Accountant should be encouraged to carry out his work in a tactful manner, without any unnecessary treading on the corns of practical men. The Accountant of to-day is a very different individual from his predecessor, the old-fashioned double-entry book-keeper, and there are numerous examples of the new school taking an enthusiastic delight in the compilation of useful commercial statistics and assisting, by their scientific analyses of the minutest details of the firm's financial transactions, in guiding the Manager's decision on points of policy.

Books and forms are dealt with in the various chapters upon the financial arrangements, but it may not be out of place here to allude to the great usefulness of interim trading accounts and balance sheets. Where it was once customary for firms to continue trading for twelve months without having any very definite idea of how things were really going, the up-to-date Accountant has his books drawn up in such a manner as to be able to present quarterly and monthly statements, so that his Manager may see the drift of events. Many undertakings can have even weekly returns, and there are many businesses employing hundreds of hands whose Managers have, each week, a return showing estimated profits sufficiently accurate for all practical purposes.

The various systems known under the general title of "Budgetary Control" call pre-eminently for the services of the Accountant. Speaking very generally, they are based on the making of a forecast at the beginning of each productive season of the output which will be necessary to maintain the expected volume of sales at that level of prices which has been fixed as likely to produce the optimum return. A careful estimate is then made of the capital expenditure which will be necessary, of the materials which must be ordered from time to time, of the wages which must be paid and of all the manifold interdependent details which must be planned beforehand if the organization is to advance as one coherent whole. On the basis of this plan the Accountant can produce, subject to changes necessitated by unforeseen circumstances, schedules showing what are likely to be the movements of cash, goods, income and expenditure in each successive future monthly period. As time progresses, the results achieved can be compared with this forecast and the causes of any discrepancies can be instantly investigated and corrected. If the organization is at fault suitable remedies must be applied, and if the estimate itself proves to be defective then that portion of the figures which relates to future periods must be adjusted. The undertaking which is administered on a plan such as this is not helpless in the face of adverse conditions, for it is forewarned of the advent of trouble almost before it appears; the administration really does administer in the sense of exercising control over the factors which contribute to success or failure. All the sections of the business are enabled to pull together because any obstacle which impedes one section can be removed before the other sections are impeded by the existence of a laggard. Profits come because they are definitely earned; they do not accrue merely because conditions happen to be favourable, or because unlucky accidents do not occur. *Control,* in the full meaning of the word, is exercised through a specialized application of accounting.

The Accountant's staff consists of book-keepers or ledger clerks, who deal with the main books of the firm and into whose hands come the final results of the work of the other assistants in the Accountant's sub-department; the invoice clerks, who render accounts for work done or goods sold by the firm; the purchasing clerks, who deal with the ordering of raw goods or material used by the firm in its manufactures or works; the costing staff, who analyse the actual cost in material, labour, and establishment charges of each article manufactured; the estimating staff, who deal with the quotations and tenders which the firm sends out for work which is in the market; and the wages staff, who check the time sheets emanating from the Works Department, etc., and prepare the wages sheets for payment by the Cashier's staff.

It will be noticed that this scheme of division places under the Accountant some work which is, in many businesses, treated as entirely separate from the Accountant's Department, but, provided a man of the right stamp is the Accountant, there can be little doubt that the Manager will find great advantage in securing the assistance of a master of figures in the supervision of this work, upon which so much of the economy of the business depends. It should not be sufficient to extract a careful and accurate analysis of the result of each accepted quotation or tender, such result being divided properly into each item of material, labour, capital charges, forwarding, etc., so that the Manager can see at a glance wherein the profit lies, but every quotation or tender which has been unsuccessful, owing to more favourable offers having been made, should be re-examined to see whether a mistake in calculation or in principle has occurred, whether the margin of profit could not have been reduced so as to secure the order, or whether there is not some item in the quotation in which a reduction of the cost of production must be made if the competition, which has been successful this time, is to be beaten in the future.

The Cashier's position, though his staff may be small, is one of great responsibility, and its occupant must possess the absolute confidence of the Manager. All money except, of course, petty cash should pass through his hands, though the certificate of the Accountant should be necessary for all payments. In many firms, the position of Cashier is retained by a relative of the Principal, but, in any case, he should be guaranteed by one of the numerous companies dealing with this class of business. Similarly, it will be found advisable to guarantee every member of his staff, the premium being so small in comparison with the undoubted security thus obtained that there is no excuse for a Manager neglecting thus to protect his firm against the possibility of heavy loss through dishonesty. The Cashier will be in charge of any collector or collectors employed, and will also deal with the travellers in connection with the collection of accounts, if such work is done by them. Payment of wages and salaries will also be made by the Cashier's Department, after certified wages sheets have been received from the Accountant's Department.

WORKS MANAGER. The Works Manager must have absolute and undivided authority in the Works, and not even the Manager himself should give orders there except through the Works Manager. The necessity for this supreme control, so far as the outward issue of orders to employees is concerned, will be readily understood by all who have had the handling of large bodies of men, and the discipline of a Works has much to do with the quality of its productions and the rapidity of its output. It is not sufficient for the Works Manager to have a thorough and practical knowledge of his business so far as the methods of manufacture are concerned, to be thoroughly acquainted with the best and most modern types of labour-saving machinery, to be able to work out personally the numerous technical problems entailed in his particular branch, but he must be possessed of those special, yet unnameable, personal qualities which enable him to handle with successful results the workmen comprising his staff. He must be a strict, though scrupulously fair, disciplinarian—a slack Works Manager makes a slack Works, and that word "slack" with such a meaning spells, sooner or later, financial disaster. Workmen are quick to realize the temperament of their chief, and whether the old adage "Like master, like man" will be proved true in a particular Works depends entirely upon the force of personality. Smartness, activity, and punctuality are excellent examples and, in addition, it must be known that there is absolute reliability to be placed upon his word. A promise given *must* be kept, a warning uttered *must* have its threatened result. Effects of order and discipline in a Works are readily discernible. The physical aspect and cleanliness of the buildings, the personal appearance of the workmen, the very condition of the stores will speak with no uncertain voice. Just as it is necessary to take stock of materials in hand and to make sure that they are kept in such manner as to prevent their deterioration, just as it is necessary occasionally to shut down and clean boilers, just as it is necessary to keep machinery properly oiled to ensure easy running, or greased to prevent rusting when temporarily disused, so it is necessary that the intellectual and manual part of the manufacturing "machinery" should be properly catered for. The workmen must have proper hours, otherwise their work cannot possibly be of the best; they must have proper pay, otherwise their physical powers will be lessened; they must be in loyal co-operation with their chiefs, otherwise "scamping" will follow. All these are matters coming within the province of the able Works Manager, though it will be impossible, of course, to ensure that, even where the best conditions obtain, all the workmen will necessarily be of the highest grade. Still, that the conditions are good should be the aim, and every effort should be used to have a good understanding with the men.

The rules governing the Works should be carefully considered and clearly enunciated. Some urge that factory rules should be few, but it is much better for the desires of the management to be set forth clearly at the commencement of employment, than that foremen should be left too much latitude in this direction, or that new regulations should constantly be issued. The Works Manager has his own clerk, or clerks if the Works are large; timekeepers to record the time worked by each man; foremen in charge of the various branches of manufacture; together with the skilled and unskilled workman and the apprentices to the different trades. With the possible exception of the clerks or timekeepers, the Works Manager should be entrusted with all appointments in his department.

Engineering Assistants and Drawing Office. The Engineering or other technical assistants should, of course, be answerable directly to the Manager, but whether the same should be said of the work of the Drawing Office must depend upon the calibre of the Engineering and Drawing Office Staffs in each individual business. In a large Works, the Chief Draughtsman should be as carefully selected as the Works Manager himself, and harmony between the two officials is as greatly to be desired as harmony between the Works Manager and the Accountant. Even the most experienced draughtsman, with the most thorough acquaintance with workshop practice, will get many ideas from men in the Works, but no alterations in work should be permitted until these have been duly passed through the Drawing Office and incorporated in the drawings guiding the manufacture. Apart from the necessity of standardizing the new arrangement, and getting its exact dimensions recorded for future use, needless confusion will result from unauthorized departures from the official instructions conveyed by the drawings.

The Storekeeper and the Warehouseman should each be responsible direct to the Manager, except in businesses of such magnitude that it is quite impossible for the latter to give any supervision to these departments, in which case it will probably be found preferable to place them both under the Accountant. In some firms, it is preferred to place the Storekeeper under the Works Manager, but there are some marked advantages in these two departments being separate, and the Stores being, so to speak, the shop where the Works Manager makes his purchases. It is probable that lack of promptitude and attention on the part of the Storekeeper would be less likely to escape complaint if he were not one of the Works Manager's own staff, and there can be no playing with this work; as it has so great an influence on the regularity of completion of orders, with its resultant effects on the continuance of business relations. Again, if the Storekeeper is not responsible to the Works Manager, there is a better chance of his insisting upon all issues and returns of stores being duly made in the prescribed way.

Forwarding business should be a department by itself, and the work should be entrusted to a thoroughly reliable man, as it will entail not only a thorough knowledge of the technical details of transport but much absence from the office premises. Agents, travellers, and Branch Managers will deal directly with the Manager, unless their number justifies the appointment of a Chief Outdoor Manager. Even in this event, however, it will be found convenient that the Manager himself should devote some time to keeping in touch with this portion of the staff, as by this means he keeps himself familiar with the requirements of his individual customers in particular districts.

Similarly, where the business employs an Advertising Inspector, his work should be dealt with directly by the Manager, though his certificates will be passed on to the Accountant for use in connection with the Advertising Accounts.

It is unnecessary to say much under the heading of Internal Check in the present Chapter, as the subject is treated more fully in Chapters XVI and XVIII, which deal respectively with the division of responsibility and the functions of the staff and professional audits. On the subject, however, of the system of internal check provided by the undertaking itself, it may perhaps with advantage be pointed out at this stage that, whatever the precise nature of the business may be, the following fundamental principles must in all cases be complied with in order to render the system efficient—

(1) There must be a definite division of responsibility, so that in the event of any duties being improperly performed, or neglected, there may be no uncertainty as to who is at fault.

(2) No one should be allowed to perform duties which do not properly devolve upon him personally, save in pursuance of express instructions received from a superior who is prepared to assume responsibility for this departure from the general system of internal check.

(3) All clerical work should, as soon as possible after its performance, be checked by another member of the staff,

and no two clerks should check each other's work. Thus, supposing there are four clerks in a department, viz. A, B, C, D, the rule should not be for A to check B's work, B to check A's, C D's, and D C's, but rather should B check A's, C check B's, D check C's, and A check D's. The risks of collusion, it will be obvious, are far smaller if the latter plan is adopted.

(4) From time to time—as far as possible, not at fixed intervals, and not after previous notice—the duties of the various members of the staff should be changed, so that, if there are any irregularities in the books, they will, in the absence of collusion, be discovered by the book-keeper succeeding to the duties of that department.

(5) With a view to ensuring the efficiency of the above-mentioned safeguards, every member of the staff should be required to absent himself from the place of business for a minimum period of, say, ten days, and preferably longer, once at least in each year. The experience of the past has shown that frauds, which might otherwise have remained undetected for an almost indefinite period, are speedily discovered if the perpetrator is obliged to be absent, and is therefore unable to "explain" discrepancies as they come to light, and make unauthorized entries in order to secure the balancing of books, the double entry of which has been disturbed by previous fraudulent entries or omissions.

While this subject of systems of Internal Check is under discussion, it may be mentioned that there are numerous devices in the market designed to check automatically the money receipts of cashiers. These are of considerable value to tradesmen and others similarly situated, where the cashiers may be required to receive in the course of a day considerable sums, over which it is difficult to devise an efficient system of check by any system of pure accounting. For ordinary office purposes, however, they are unnecessary, as such receipts are practically non-existent. The best known instruments of this class are those supplied by the National Cash Register Co., Ltd., who manufacture several distinct types. For instance, one register is fitted with keys for recording amounts either paid in or paid out.

When cash is received, the appropriate keys are pressed and the amount is displayed in clear figures at the top of the register, and at the same time the printing and adding mechanisms record the same amount. There is space opposite the printed amount for any written particulars. An entirely separate adding mechanism will record the total of all money paid out, and the printings show the amount of each individual item, with written particulars as

required. The publicity of the amount indicated ensures accurate records.

A more advanced type of cash register is built to provide a number of separate totals which can be used to dissect transactions between a number of departments, or a number of assistants, or both. It will also record and dissect takings under Cash Sales, Credit Sales, Accounts Paid, and Money Paid Out. In each case it will issue either a printed receipt or will overprint the original and duplicate of an inserted bill or slip.

The fact that a printed record of the transaction is issued every time the register is operated and that the amount is publicly indicated and added, ensures the accuracy of the record. All added and printed records are under lock and key and therefore under the direct control of the Management. Separate counters check the number of times totals have been inspected.

Whatever the type of till-check adopted, it is very important to bear in mind that mechanical devices can only aid, not replace, human supervision; and in all cases it is necessary to set up rules of organization framed with a view to ensuring that the machines

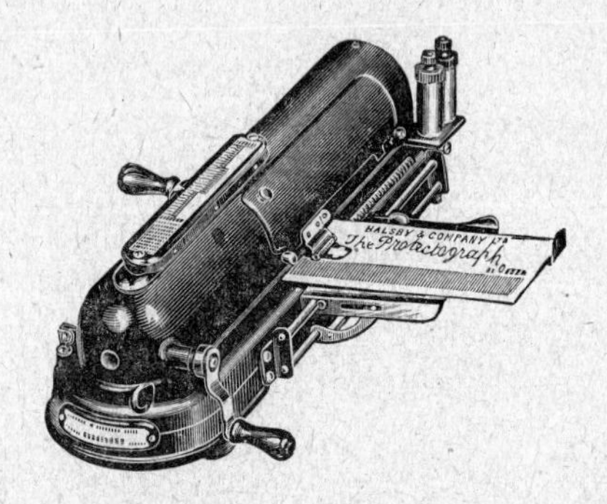

are worked under a proper routine. Indeed, one great advantage bestowed by machinery in offices and commercial houses may be said to be that it makes possible a greater regularity of routine and, consequently, a more even and certain flow of human activity.

Machines for counting money, for giving change, and for making up pay envelopes are now available. Machines for franking envelopes and wrappers do away with the cumbrous process of affixing postage stamps, and cheque-writing machines (of which one is illustrated above) protect those documents from fraudulent alteration by carrying an impression in indelible ink right through the thickness of the paper.

CHAPTER V

Correspondence, including Methods of Filing—Printed Forms, and Rubber Stamps for purposes frequently in use — Methods of following up Inquiries, etc.

THE Manager's Secretary or Chief Correspondence Clerk may be said to hold the key to the organizing side of an office, just as the Accountant holds the key to the financial side, and the proper organization of this department is of great importance to the personal convenience of the Manager as well as to the development of the business.

Unless dictating machines are in exclusive use, the Chief Correspondence Clerk must of necessity be an expert shorthand writer and one of first-class reliability as regards both his note-taking and his transcription. With a system of shorthand like Pitman's, there is no excuse for incapacity, but many commercial shorthand writers do not pay sufficient attention to the advanced stages of their art, with the result that there are still to be met with examples of those curious blunders which are the outcome of a failure to use the proper outline for a word easily confused with another. The speed required depends, of course, on the individual Manager, but a good reliable rate of 120 words per minute will, in most cases, be found sufficient for commercial purposes. The Correspondence Clerk should also be a capable typist, able to perform work which will give outside parties an instant good impression of the firm. The typewriter makes possible the duplication of circulars, etc., in a style and with an ease and rapidity which a few years ago would have been deemed almost miraculous. Some clerks are absurdly reluctant to learn shorthand and typewriting, particularly the latter, and it is largely owing to this that the lady clerk now holds so firm a position in the commercial world. It is foolishly suggested that the arts are mechanical. It is true that some manual skill is required; but the mere mechanical utilization of this manual dexterity produces nothing but disastrous results. It is the combination of the manual skill with a thorough knowledge of the two accomplishments—mixed, as Opie mixed his colours, "with brains"

—which makes the valued correspondent the Manager's right-hand man, the office assistant who becomes the confidential clerk and who, by reason of the knowledge which he acquires of every part of work which passes through the hands of his principal, makes himself one of the most important officials in the office. There is never any fear of a really competent shorthand clerk getting "side-tracked."

Where there are several departments in an organization it is very important to decide whether each departmental chief is to have his own typing service at his immediate call or whether, on the other hand, there is to be a common "pool" of typists, controlled by a "head of the typing room," doing whatever work may be called for. In a general treatise such as this it is possible to say only that where work is either technical or very varied and personal in character, the first scheme is probably the best; but where the work in a large organization is broadly of an average and consistent character, and particularly where dictating machines are in use, then the "pool" scheme is usually found to be more effective and economical.

Nearly every Manager prefers to deal first thing in the morning with the incoming mail, which has been opened and put in order for him by his Correspondence Clerk. Where possible—and it is astonishing how many things are possible when a really smart Correspondence Clerk is in question—a letter on which the Manager will want to see previous correspondence, or a copy of a contract, or the most recent quotation received from a manufacturer, should be brought in with the other documents annexed. Letters which have to be referred to a sub-chief to deal with should be endorsed to him for the Manager to initial. For this purpose, rubber stamps are best used, as time spent in writing frequent endorsements is wasted. For instance, the Correspondence Clerk will have stamps, each bearing the name of a sub-chief or department for use in referring letters. The manufacturers now make stamps bearing on the tops of their handles a clearly visible reduced facsimile of the stamp itself, and holder-frames of various types can be obtained in which to keep the stamps. Some Managers like to have a stamp for their facsimile initials, for use on such endorsements, and a stamp bearing a facsimile signature for signing orders, etc. These latter stamps should be kept carefully locked up.

All the letters should have the date of their receipt stamped upon them. A form of rubber stamp for the purpose is appended—

Earlham Manufacturing Co.
No. 890
Recvd. 17 Jan. '35
Ackd. B. 17 Jan '35
Ansd. 18 Jan. '35

The first date may be part of the stamp, the figures and month being movable. This line is changed the first thing each morning. The other two lines are written in by the clerk dealing with the acknowledgment or reply. The letter shown on the acknowledgment line refers to the type of acknowledgment sent. "A" may be a final acknowledgment which will not be followed by a letter, as shown on Form 1. "B" on the contrary will be followed by a definite reply (see Form 2); where there is no objection to the use of post cards they are to be preferred on account of the saving in postage.

All letters received should be entered in the "Letter Record Book" (Form No. 3) under their number. Telegrams should be dealt with in the same manner, except that red ink should be used for their entry in the Record Book and the acknowledgment should take the form of a confirmation.

Telephone messages wrongly recorded, or not recorded at all, are a frequent source of business errors and disputes. There should be an inflexible rule that every incoming message not immediately dealt with by a principal should be entered either on a specially tinted form (to be dealt with as an incoming letter), or should be entered in a Register such as that illustrated in Form No. 4.

The letter paper used should be good, though plain. Gaudy headings do not savour of business correspondence, and the following selection of note and letter headings will be found to answer most requirements (see Forms No. 5, 6, 7, and 8).

ACK. A.

Earlham Manufacturing Company.

TOXTETH WORKS

BOW, E.11

Partners
A. BEE
C. DEE

....*19*

Dear *Sir,* / *Madam,*

I have to acknowledge receipt of your *letter* / *postcard* *of the* ....*instant, re*..........................

....

....

for which I thank you.

Yours faithfully,

A. H. BLAKE,

Manager.

(*Form No.* 1)

ACK. B.

Earlham Manufacturing Company.

Partners
A. BEE
C. DEE

TOXTETH WORKS
BOW, E.11

.... *19*

Dear Sir, / Madam,

I acknowledge the receipt of your letter / postcard of the .... instant, re ....

....

....

which will receive attention.

Yours faithfully,

A. H. BLAKE,

Manager.

(*Form No.* 2)

EARLHAM MANUFACTURING CO.

LETTER RECORD BOOK

Date	Reference No.	Name and Address of Person from whom received	Nature of Communication	To whom referred with Instructions	Date Written to

(*Form No.* 3)

EARLHAM MANUFACTURING CO.

TELEPHONE BOOK

MESSAGES RECEIVED

Date		Time	Firm and Person Telephoning	Message	Signature of Official Receiving Message

(*Form No.* 4)

MESSAGES SENT

Date		Time	Firm and Person Telephoned to	Message	Signature of Official Telephoning

(*Form No. 4a*)

19

From

The Earlham Manufacturing Co.

Partners
A. BEE
C. DEE

TOXTETH WORKS

BOW, E.11

PLEASE REFER TO

IN YOUR REPLY.

To

We confirm Telegram *sent to / received from* *this day as follows:—*

(Form No. 5)

PLEASE QUOTE
REFERENCE No.

YOUR REFERENCE No.

Earlham Manufacturing Company.

Partners
A. BEE
C. DEE

Telephone—
No. 0341 EAST

Telegrams—
"EARLHAM, LONDON"

Typed

TOXTETH WORKS

BOW, E.11

Enclosure

(*Form No.* 6)

Please Quote Reference No.

Your Reference No.

Earlham Manufacturing Company.

Partners
A. BEE
C. DEE

Telephone—
No. 0341 East

Telegrams—
"Earlham, London"

TOXTETH WORKS

BOW, E.11

Typed

Enclosure

(*Form No. 7*)

Earlham Manufacturing Company.

Partners
A. BEE
C. DEE

Telephone—
No. 0341 East.

TOXTETH WORKS

BOW, E.11

.... 19

To ....

....

....

(*Form No.* 8)

Under the Registration of Business Names Act, 1916, every firm carrying on a business under a name which does not consist of the true surnames of all partners (or of the sole owner) must register with the Registrar the Business Names. The various necessary forms are set forth in the Business Names Rules, 1938. Further, the true names with Christian names, or initials, must appear on all trade catalogues, circulars, showcards, and business letters. Where the nationality is not British, the present nationality must be stated, and if an individual has changed his name the former name must be disclosed.

The Companies Act, 1929 (Sect. 145), enacts similar requirements in regard to all companies registered since the year 1916. Such companies must therefore print the names of their directors on all notepaper, etc., and must disclose foreign nationality and any changes of name.

In going through the morning's mail the Manager should immediately dictate replies to as many letters as possible, as this plan enables the correspondence department to deal with them during the day. Some Managers get into the bad habit of leaving their correspondence until last thing, which results in the bulk of the replies having to be written after ordinary office hours, and the letters go out without having been seen and signed by the Manager himself. Serious mistakes often crop up in this way, and the work of the correspondence clerks will not improve in quality unless proper consideration is given to the necessity for their having reasonable hours of labour; moreover, postage "late fees" may soon mount up to an appreciable sum.

When the Manager has gone through the mail and the letters have been either replied to or referred to the various departments, the Correspondence Clerk brings all out, putting those referred to each department in a special basket which he sends without delay to the sub-chief in charge. Having thus dispatched everything to which he is not personally attending, he should now take advantage of every opportunity to get his letters typed, either personally or by an assistant, and here again the importance of the use of correct shorthand comes in. There should not be the slightest difficulty in his handing on his note book to his typist to transcribe, and, where he desires to get together information required by the Manager, or to deal with other work, this is most useful.

In most offices, every letter which is typed has a carbon copy made simultaneously, and, after the original copy has been signed and any alteration made therein noted on the duplicate, the latter is annexed to the letter to which it is a reply and filed with it.

There are several methods of filing inward correspondence. The old plan was to file letters in order of receipt—whether by means of metal holders or by pasting into guard-books. This system was both time-wasting and inconvenient, for the letters had to be numbered, indexed, and cross-referenced in the same way as a press-copying book; and even then, if the Manager wished to go through the entire correspondence upon a given subject, he was obliged to turn over a large number of irrelevant letters, probably in several books more or less cumbersome. There was only this to be said in favour of such a system, that it easily allowed the letters received during any particular *period* to come under review. In this respect any system by which letters are filed in order of receipt has a certain advantage over those by which they are distributed under alphabets or numbers; but the Letter Register, already mentioned, will go a long way towards the same end so far as the inward correspondence is concerned, and a press-copy Letter Book, if kept, will perform a similar function with regard to the outward correspondence.

For rapidity of filing and readiness of reference, the alphabetical systems have much to recommend them. The earliest of these, the pigeon-hole system, was a stage better than the guard-book method, as it did keep all the correspondence from one firm together; and the soul of the "exact man" was surely gratified when he put away that neat cardboard-backed bundle in which every letter was duly docketed with its date, subject, etc. But the system was extremely cumbrous (involving, as it did, bundle after bundle being taken out until the right one was found), and it is emphatically out of date as a letter-filing system. It may, however, still serve for certain purposes, as where documents are required to be sorted alphabetically and placed in a temporary receptacle for further use. Sets of pigeon-holes can be purchased with revolving shutter fronts, as well as the more ordinary kinds.

Perhaps the simplest of the alphabetical systems is the expanding alphabet case having lettered pockets into which letters are simply dropped. The case is labelled on the back and within a somewhat narrow compass the system is convenient enough. Then there are systems, of which Stone's seems to have been the pioneer, consisting of boxes or drawers, with index sheets under which are placed the letters, a spring clip keeping them in place. For greater security, however, many of the systems in common use provide that the letters shall be pierced with holes at the side or top and placed over upright posts in the filing receptacle, whether in the form of book, box, or drawer. The Shannon may be mentioned as a representative of this class. The simplest form of the Shannon is a kind of glorified apron (hanging) file, with the addition of an index. Instead of a pasteboard back it has a substantial board to which is attached a perforator, a double spring arch over which the letters are placed, and a cover on which a spring presses to protect the letters from dust. With the addition of a drawer front (in which case the perforator is supplied separately), any number of these files can be arranged in a cabinet or cabinets. The index can be divided and subdivided as required and, as the file is filled, the contents are transferred to a "binder" or case marked with the dates on the back, the corresponding dates with the number of the case being recorded on the cover of the file from which the letters were removed.

Another method which has come into favour during the last few years is known as the "individual" system. The ruling idea of the system is a separate file for each letter of the alphabet, or for each correspondent or subject, or for a particular period. The letters are placed in a strong paper or linen jacket (which can be had in various colours to distinguish departments, subjects, geographical divisions, etc.), in the back of which are fastened metal strips which pass through corresponding holes pierced in the documents, the ends of the strips being bent down over the top letter and held in place by a clip. The files are stored in suitable cabinets. It is not intended that there should be any transfers, the files themselves being inexpensive. One of the advantages put forward on behalf of this system is that the files take up practically the same space as that occupied by the letters themselves, whereas it is necessary that a box or drawer should provide space for future as well as immediate needs.

In addition to these methods, there are two numerical systems which deserve consideration. The first has been for many years, and continues to be, largely used on railways, and may, therefore, be considered to answer fairly well even for a large correspondence. It has the advantage of requiring the minimum of equipment; indeed, this is probably the strongest feature in its favour. Each letter (or telegram), etc., coming in is stamped with the date of receipt, and is entered in a letter register; the date, writer's name, and subject being recorded thus—

Progressive No.	Name	Date	Subject	Sender's reference (if any)
1234				
5				
6				
and	so on			

The numbers start at unity and run throughout the year. As each letter is registered, the relative number is placed on it in the manner shown below. The letters are then sorted and handed over to the particular department to be dealt with, after which they are placed on edge (the paper used is generally octavo shape) in an ordinary drawer with the number showing in the right-hand corner, thus—

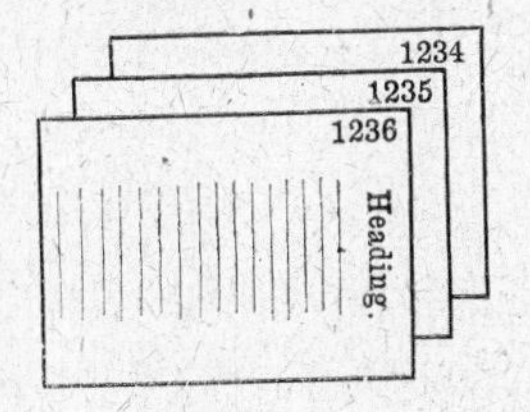

and afterwards tied into bundles and labelled.

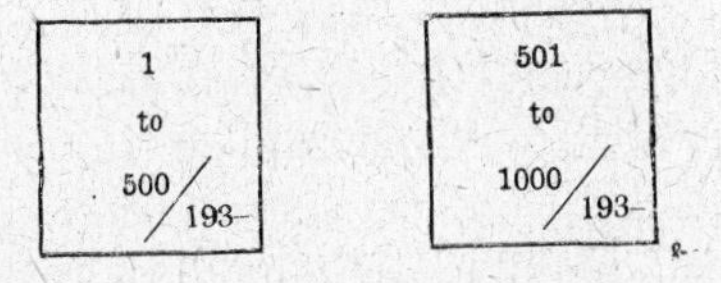

Each *reply* sent out bears the number of the inward letter in combination with the copying book reference, thus :—$\mathrm{A}2/\frac{16}{1234}$ "A" distinguishes the department, "2" the number of the letter (copying) book, "16" the number of the letter in the book (or the date may be used instead) and "1234" the progressive number under which the correspondence has been registered. This reference should be given on any further letter *received* from the sender of the original. Such further letter would not be registered (though its receipt might be noted against the original entry in the register), but would be attached by the filing clerk to the previous papers and sent to the party dealing with the matter. Should such a letter be registered in error, or should it be necessary to attach any letter or batch of letters to correspondence bearing a different number, the later number would be written off in the register thus : "6789—see 1234," the first and original number only being retained, and the number on the later letter being altered accordingly. To make this system at all convenient, an alphabetical index in the register is, of course, necessary.

There is one advantage possessed by the Letter Register, whether used in connection with the method just described or some other filing system, which is worth noting. It enables a Manager who has been absent from the office for any period to get a bird's-eye view of the correspondence which has taken place in his absence, and to call for any letters he may desire to see.

The second numerical system to which reference was made is of modern introduction, and, when used in combination with the card index, is probably the most scientific and the best all-round system extant. It is sold by the Library Bureau, Ltd., the Globe Wernicke Co., Roneo, Ltd., and many others, and is generally known as the Vertical system, the letters being placed upright in the drawer instead of being laid flat as in most of the alphabetical systems. The Vertical system is not, however, confined to a numerical classification, but can be used in connection with an alphabetical or geographical arrangement, and in such cases it would be possible to do without the index by making the system self-contained. In the numerical system with which we are now dealing, the correspondence with one firm or on one subject, etc., is placed in a stout manilla folder bearing a number. The folders are numbered consecutively from one upwards, and are placed upright in the drawer between guide cards numbered at intervals of ten and distributed through the drawer for the purpose of facilitating reference. Each

new correspondent is given a folder bearing the number next above the last one in the file. His name is entered on a card, together

with the date of the first letter and the number of his folder, the card being then filed alphabetically in the index drawer. Thereafter (until transfer is made) the folder will contain all the letters from that correspondent, and also the carbon or press-copies of the replies thereto as previously suggested. When, therefore, it is necessary to refer to the details of any matter dealt with in several letters, the folder containing the entire correspondence can be extracted without the slightest trouble. The drawers are fitted with an adjustable block or "follower" to keep the contents in position, and in the cabinets supplied by one firm the front of the file drawer is hinged at the bottom so as to fall slightly outwards at the top while the papers are being examined, and as the follower at the back of the letters at the same time recedes in the reverse direction (making a V-shaped space between them) the removal of a folder or the insertion of new matter is rendered extremely easy. The guide cards and block are kept in position by steel rods, and slides support the drawers when they are drawn out. The principle of the Globe Wernicke Company's well-known "Elastic" bookcases has been applied also to filing and indexing cabinets, allowing the necessary accommodation to be built up as required without looking ugly in the process. Steel has now largely superseded the use of wood in the construction of filing drawers and cabinets. Considerable space is thereby saved, and the life of the apparatus is appreciably prolonged.

What are known as "suspended files" are an improved form of folder and cabinet, folders being suspended from the top, thereby obviating the "sagging" which so often occurs in the case of ordinary folders that stand unsupported in the file drawer.

Different methods of transferring the contents from vertical cabinets when full may be followed. Periodical transfers of the entire contents can be made, or crowded files may be relieved from time to time by the transfer of single folders or of unimportant and out-of-date matter. While transfers at regular periods are not without advantage (as, for instance, keeping all the correspondence for, say, a year in one set of transfer cases), "piecemeal" transfers can be made at odd times without interfering with other work—an important consideration; while the plan of removing dead matter has the additional advantage of leaving in the cabinet all the correspondence that is likely to be wanted.

It is not difficult to understand that the alphabetical and numerical systems may be *combined*. For example, every correspondent (or subject) may be given a four (or five) figure number such that the first two indicate the letter of the alphabet with which his name begins, e.g. 01 would be A and 26 would be z. The other two (or three) numbers would be the progressive number under the particular letter of the alphabet assigned to the particular file. Further, a letter may follow these numbers to indicate a sub-file dealing with a related but subsidiary matter.

If there is one thing in connection with the numerical system which may be regarded as a drawback, it is the fact that it requires a separate index to make it workable. First of all, there is the writing and filing of the index card (for which purpose, however, an addressing machine may be used), and then, if it is desired to refer to the correspondence of a particular customer, that customer's number must (unless it happens to have been memorized) be ascertained from the card index before the reference can be made. It may, however, be said on the other hand that it does not follow that the index will be instituted for the sole purpose of recording the correspondent's number. As has been already shown, the card index can be made the means of recording *any* kind of information respecting a firm or subject, which information may be worth considerably more than the labour spent in compiling it; and the necessary reference to the index as a preliminary to finding the correspondence should be but a matter of seconds. There is also this advantage of a positive character, that correspondence with new business connections is placed *behind* matter already in the file; in other words, it comes in where there is most room for it.

An objection is sometimes raised against the card index on the ground that it necessitates the fingering of cards which, in course of time, begin to wear at the top and that, when this occurs, time is likely to be wasted. This objection has been overcome by the introduction of the "visible" type of record described in Chapter III. The cards are fastened lengthwise to hinged wires in such a way that the edge of each overlaps its neighbour. The headings of the whole series thus appear to the eye as a list and any particular card can be instantly selected.

Any card system can be improved by the addition of "signals," i.e. small metal clips which, by their position and colour, can be used to indicate, e.g. a subject classification, the date when the card should be re-examined, the fact that an account is overdue, etc.

According to taste or requirements, various modifications or combinations of the many filing systems in vogue can be made to an almost unlimited extent. It is almost unnecessary to say that, whatever system is adopted, there should be some provision for quickly tracing the reply to any letter when a copy is not attached.

Card indices should be turned to further use by the correspondence staff. If, for example, an inquiry has been received from a new correspondent for a catalogue of the firm's specialities, and the catalogue has been duly sent, an entry of the name and address of the inquirer and the nature of the inquiry is then made upon two cards, one being inserted in a card drawer referred to daily. The cards in this drawer are arranged between date guides, and by inserting the new card behind a certain specified date, the inquiry will be automatically brought under consideration again and a follow-up letter sent, the card being then inserted behind a later date. The second card is sent to the Travellers' Department, where it is filed in the drawer of a particular traveller, if in a town round, done regularly, or behind a guide card of its own town, if some distance away. By these means, the traveller when going over the particular ground can take out the cards within the area and follow up the inquiries personally. It is by such methods that the modern business Manager will neglect no effort to turn every inquirer into a customer, and the elasticity and adaptability of the card system cannot be over-estimated.

CHAPTER VI

Estimates, Tenders, Contracts, Orders, showing their connection with each other and with the Financial Books. Also discussing points in connection with Estimates, Standard Calculations, etc.

COMPARATIVELY few except those who have been engaged in some of the higher and more confidential office positions have anything but a vague idea of the manner in which estimates and tenders, particularly those of an important financial nature, are prepared. In firms where these documents are properly drawn up, after detailed consideration of the cost of production, the work involved in dealing with this matter is both considerable and intricate. Competition has quite killed the basing of estimates upon "general experience," and has emphasized the importance of substituting actual facts for mere imaginary figures and flights of the imagination.

There are four main items upon which estimates are based—

(*a*) Material
(*b*) Labour, and } known as Prime Cost.
(*c*) Direct chargeable expenses
(*d*) Indirect establishment and administration charges } known as Overhead

Although it is a simple matter to calculate the cost of so much raw material, or such and such parts bought complete, at certain prices, there is much consideration and experience required to settle the quantity of material necessary, the probability of a rise or fall in the market price of certain commodities, if the work will occupy a long period to execute, and the choice of a particular grade or quality of material which can be relied upon to give a satisfactory efficiency and life. Experience also is necessary for the reasonable and accurate computation of the labour cost of production of any given contract operation, and there are important matters, such as freight, etc., to be considered.

To deal *satisfactorily* with an estimate implies dealing with it *systematically*, and here comes in a most important test of the manner in which the organization of the undertaking has been carried out. If the business is a new one, the Manager must necessarily rely for his earlier estimates upon his own knowledge, and upon that of his principal assistants, as to the materials which will be required, the cost of labour involved, etc.; but, if the business has been established for some time, the estimating information should be of a most exact and accurate nature.

It should be the practice for the Estimating Clerk to deal with the estimating not merely for contract work to be performed for outside customers, but also for the production in the Works for stock purposes of all articles that may be manufactured by the firm. This gives him a good all-round knowledge of his work, and enables him to prepare expeditiously any information the Manager may require. He should have estimating information in tabulated form, so far as the cost of production in the firm's own Works is concerned, and should be in touch with the Orders Clerk's work, so as to be familiar with the sources of all classes of supplies likely to be required for contracts. Where the business is one for the supply of articles in which there are a number of small parts, most of which are made in the Works, the Estimating Clerk should have the cost of each of these; and, if (as in most cases) these vary according to dimension, it will be found most useful to provide a table or desk, the top of which is covered with a thick piece of glass. Under this can be kept the tabulated cost of the various sizes of parts, the standardized calculations used in the particular business, and any other data of constant service, in clean condition, and in a position of the greatest accessibility for consultation or copying purposes.

There is considerable difference between the methods employed in the preparation of estimates. It is well in the first instance for the Chief Draughtsman to prepare a dissection of the various portions of the work required, with a detailed statement of the materials to be purchased outside, if any. It is customary then for the Works Manager and the Estimating Clerk, separately, to price out each operation or item of manufacture, and then the Manager goes into the whole matter, in some cases even preparing his own estimate separately from the others. It is of distinct importance that the draft estimate should be prepared separately by several persons, and each material difference discussed, as in this manner only is due precaution taken against any serious omission. In large contracts, particularly with Public Bodies, very great care must be taken in the examination of the general conditions of the specification, which will be found to include full particulars as to the penalties for non-completion to time, the tests of efficiency which will be required, the terms of payment, labour conditions to be observed, etc. The terms of payment are important, because, although the firm tendering incurs its expenses (at all events in connection with labour) at once, it will be found sometimes that payment is made at a rate of only between 75 to 90 % of the total contract value (varying according to the nature of the contract) on delivery, and that the balance is retained for a certain specified period, in order to afford time to test the efficiency of the work. If the contractor is in a large way of business, it will frequently happen that he has many thousands of pounds outstanding under retention clauses, and, as his own expenses have to be met immediately upon the contract work being executed, he naturally has to allow for the financial arrangements which will be necessary to enable him to provide the large sums thus called for. The labour conditions imposed must also be carefully considered, as there are few Public Bodies now which do not attach heavy penalties, even to the extent of the cancellation of contracts, where the stipulated conditions as to labour have not been obeyed.

Having ascertained the cost of production in the Works, the cost of additional material which may be required and which must be purchased outside has to be ascertained. If such material is large, it is better to obtain special quotations, to include delivery either at the Works or at the site where the contract is to be completed, as and when required. Where the outside material is of a minor character, its price can be obtained from the lists already available in the office or from the catalogues which the Estimating Clerk will have duly filed.

The Prime Cost in connection with the estimate having now been obtained, there remains to be considered the matter of the Overhead expenses. The practice of dealing with these varies. This question is dealt with more fully in Chapter XIII, but it may be stated here that some prefer to work this out on *each item* and others on *each operation*, a similar difference prevailing in connection with the calculation of profit to be added.

In connection with contracts for work which has to be completed on a given site, it is often advantageous for that site to be visited, and its surroundings, facilities for local transit, local rates of pay for labour, etc., noted; and this should, of course, be done *before* the completion of the estimate. The cost of freight, or cartage, from Works to site must be ascertained and included; also cost of supervision during erection, which may involve railway travelling and maintenance for foreman and men.

In engineering firms, great use is made of the Slide Rule for rapid calculation purposes; conversion tables are frequently referred to, and constants and logarithms regularly utilized. It is surprising that the Slide Rule is not used to a greater extent in general office work, particularly in offices where much attention has been paid to labour-saving devices. It is true that its use requires a little

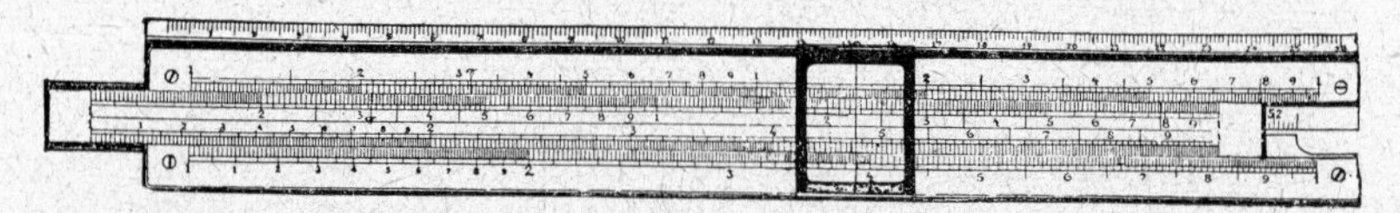

practice; but, given that, anyone with a knowledge of the decimal system will speedily become proficient. By its use, multiplication becomes, in effect, addition, and division becomes subtraction. The estimating clerk will also have an opportunity of making use of many standard calculations, and of referring to the various formulae applicable to the particular trade, such as are given in the reference books.

The prices being ready, proper attention must be paid to the form of tender. Many firms send this out in a very slovenly, slipshod style, on poor paper, and accompanied by badly designed drawings. Every tender should be typewritten on good paper, should be expressed in clear language, and any drawings sent should be carefully and neatly designed, and be properly numbered to correspond with the items in the specification. Too many provisions of a protective character should be avoided, but it is well to have some clauses of a nature which will protect the firm tendering against monetary losses owing to strikes, or causes over which it has no personal control.

The following is an example of such protective clauses—

Conditions of Contract

The Contractors shall be entitled to an extension of time for completion equivalent to any delay caused by Strikes, Lock-outs, or Combinations of Workmen, Accidents, Fires, or stoppages for want of material, either at their Works or at the works of any persons supplying machinery or materials to them for the contract work, or by any other delay caused by the purchaser in approving drawings, paying instalments, ordering alterations, or extra work, or otherwise howsoever.

Every effort will be made to secure sound material and good workmanship, and the Contractors will replace free of cost, and under the same conditions of delivery as the original contract, any material which proves faulty within six months of delivery or setting to work. Their responsibility shall, however, be limited to the above, and shall not include consequential damages, such as loss due to stoppage of machinery.

The following is another type of tender with protective clauses, and is very inclusive; but the Manager should carefully consider whether in this case the clauses are not of such a nature as to militate against chance of acceptance—

TENDER No. ...... (To be held open for.... weeks.)

This Tender for....................

is issued to........................

of ....

subject to the undermentioned conditions—

General (*a*) This Tender does not include the cost of any bricklayers', masons', smiths', or carpenters' work, which may be necessary when erecting the machinery or apparatus.

(*b*) It is to be distinctly understood that a proper leading-in way is provided by the purchaser as far as the door of the building which is to contain the material, together with all necessary cranes, lifting tackle, scaffolding, etc., suitable for the weights which have to be transported and handled.

(*c*) The cost of providing, fixing, and laying any cables or wiring, which may be required in connection with the machinery offered, is not included in the amount of this tender.

(*d*) The necessary lubricating material, waste, etc., which may be required when starting up the plant, or afterwards, must be provided by the purchaser.

(*e*) Our liability with regard to accidents that may occur during unloading, erection, or setting to work is limited strictly to the men in our own employment.

Prices

All prices given are strictly net, and include all the necessary packing and delivery to site (or elsewhere).

The cost of erection is included (or excluded).

Date of Delivery

We guarantee to deliver the material comprised in this tender and set to work within......weeks of the date of the purchaser's official order to proceed with the work. But it is to be understood that our responsibility in this respect ceases—

(*a*) If undue delay takes place with regard to the approval of drawings and arrangements, or if the necessary data for the execution of the work are not received in proper time.

(*b*) If extra work or alterations are ordered subsequent to the acceptance of this tender.

(*c*) In case the completion of the work has been delayed by strikes, accident, fire, stoppage of works, bad castings, failure of railway or other communication, both as concerns ourselves directly, or our sub-contractors for raw material, etc.

(*d*) If it is evident at the time the material in question is due for delivery, that the place destined for its reception, or the foundation for it, is not ready.

Terms of Payment

......% with the order.

......% upon the delivery of the material on the ground.

......% upon erection.

Balance......months after setting to work.

It is hereby assumed that the purchaser will be ready to take delivery of the material on order as and when same is ready at our Works; further, that the erection of the material can be commenced immediately after delivery, and that the plant can be set to work as soon as the erection has been completed. Should it happen, owing to causes beyond our control, that these stipulations are not fulfilled by the purchaser, payments must be made by him at intervals corresponding to the periods indicated above. In any case, payment is to be completed within. . . . . . months from the date of the completion of the material.

Guarantee The material comprised in this tender is guaranteed against defects of material, design, or workmanship, for a period of......months, fair wear and tear and carelessness or incompetence on the part of those handling the plant excepted. Any such defect showing itself during this guaranteed period will be remedied by us, at our expense, and in the shortest possible time, but our liability is strictly limited to this, and does not include consequential damages, such as loss through stoppages of machinery, etc.

Where the work is of an important nature it is usual to draw up a formal contract, after acceptance of the tender, and this should be carefully examined to see that no conditions have been included which are not contained in the form of specification upon which the tender was based.

CHAPTER VII

Packing and Unpacking, showing the methods of checking goods issued and received, and the connection between these records and the Financial Books—Mechanical Aids

THE location of the Packing Department is naturally governed by two main considerations—accessibility to the various departments and convenience for the ready receipt and dispatch of goods by means of railway trolleys or other conveyances. Of the two points, the latter claims first attention as being more dependent on structural conditions. The internal arrangements of a factory or warehouse may be assisted by the use of various appliances, such as lifts, trolley ways, or pneumatic tubes, which are capable of a wide degree of adaptation; but, if wagons and vans engaged in the collection and the delivery of goods are allowed to block each other in narrow streets and cartways, nothing but loss of time, money, and temper can result.

Before the actual receipt and unpacking of goods, certain operations must, of course, have taken place, at which it will be necessary to glance in order to show the method of checking. The buyers for the various Departments have made their selections, and orders have been given (possibly by a central Buying Department), care being taken to preserve carbon copies and to file them under a prearranged plan. On the receipt of the invoices, the latter, having been stamped with the date of receipt in the General Office or Counting House, are handed to the buyers concerned, or to the central Buying Department, to be checked. It is a safe precaution, however, before allowing invoices to leave the office, to have them entered in an Invoice Register to guard against loss of documents and subsequent trouble. This Register should show the supplier's name, the date and the amount of the invoice, and brief particulars of the relevant goods. A definite time should be allowed for the return of invoices from the Department. The buyer receiving an invoice checks the prices by his copy order, notes the receipt of the invoice thereon, and passes the invoice on to the Salesman or Storekeeper, who has to receive the goods, for his signature in acknowledgment of receipt.

If it is desired—and in many cases it is desirable—to withhold a knowledge of prices, etc., from the rank and file of the staff, the buyer enters the invoice into a Transit or Goods Received Book, substituting letters and quality numbers for the makers' names and prices. The person receiving the goods then signs the book instead of the invoice, and the buyer, having examined the goods as to their quality, returns the invoice to the Counting House with his initials. Where the business is conducted in Departments, it is a good plan to have a separate invoice for each Department concerned, marked with the name of the Department. The necessary instructions for giving effect to this arrangement will be stated on the order, the number of which should be shown on the invoice. It may be well also to have a Departmental Bought Book, containing particulars of all goods bought by the Department, not necessarily as a part of the system of book-keeping, but as a record for the buyer's information.

Similarly, as selling orders are received, it will be found advisable, before they are passed to the Department concerned for execution, to keep a record (Orders Received Book or Indent Register) in the main office, so that a general supervision may be kept over the work, and so that accidental omission to execute an order may be prevented. Nothing, probably, is more annoying to the would-be buyer, or to the firm at whose expense the order has been obtained, than to find that order overlooked. It may even pay to see that nothing of the kind occurs by appointing someone whose duty it is to look up any order for which the particulars (showing that it has been duly executed) are not forthcoming from the sale rooms in due course. If desired, separate registers may be kept for the orders from different travellers or branches, or for different departments of the business, for home and foreign orders, etc.

The order having been registered, the subsequent procedure will vary according to circumstances. Under the old-fashioned plan, that is to say before the use of machinery as an office aid became a commonplace, it was the practice to enter the orders into books, e.g. one for town, one for country, and one for export orders, and to pass the books into the sale room foı the necessary action. The goods having been placed together by an assistant were checked by the head of the department, who compared them item by item with the order, and called out the particulars to an Invoice Clerk. The latter entered them forthwith into the Sales Journal, and, to ensure accuracy, repeated the particulars as he put them down—goods, quantity, price—and also called out the "extensions," which were entered after being confirmed by the checker.

As some slight improvement over that rather cumbersome plan (which obviously opened the door to error in the course of copying and recopying) a Manifold Invoice Book was substituted for the Sales Journal, and, as the goods were called over by the checker, the particulars were entered in the form of a duplicate invoice, the calculations being made by the clerk and confirmed by the checker as before. One copy of the invoice was torn out to be sent to the customer, and the book containing the duplicate was used in the same way as a Sales Book, from which the customer's account was debited.

A drawback connected with the use of order books in the manner first described is that, if it should be desired to refer to any particular order (when writing to a customer, for instance) and it is necessary for the Order Book to be sent for, the salesman who may be dealing with another order in the same book will probably wait in idleness for its return to him; and the system is doubly inconvenient where the business is conducted in departments more than one of which is concerned in a given order, as one department has to wait until the other has completed its portion of the order.

The typewriter has revolutionized the routine of dealing with selling orders. Nowadays there are two preliminary steps which precede all others. First, a clerk in the sales office sees whether it is in fact possible to execute the order and, second, a "credit-authorization" clerk refers to the account of the customer with a view to seeing whether he is credit-worthy or whether cash should be demanded before execution of the order. These two points having been dealt with, the next step is to acknowledge the order (by using a "form" letter or postcard prepared for the purpose) and to mark on the order the prices to be charged, unless indeed these are "standard" and invariable. There is then brought into use one of the "sets" of stationery with which the office has furnished itself. These sets consist of a number of forms either attached together at the edge (by the stationer) in such a way that carbon paper can be interleaved or contrived in long ribbons (the units being detachable at perforations). There are typewriter devices whereby carbon paper may be mechanically injected into these ribbon forms with great rapidity. Adding registers may also be fitted to typewriters so that the invoices may be mechanically computed and added together. The reader will readily understand that once a "set" of these forms has been typed, all are identical, and, the top copy having been established as correct, all the copies may be distributed so that each serves a distinct purpose. For example, the top copy may be the invoice for the customer, the second may serve to build up the analysis of sales into departments, "lines," etc., the third may be the medium for debiting the customer, while the fourth and fifth (cut narrow so that no money value appears) may be respectively the advice to warehouse to dispatch the goods, and the delivery note to accompany the goods.

Whatever system is adopted, the goods should be checked before being packed, as, in regard to errors as well as other evils, "prevention is better than cure," or, as a humorist might say, "It is easier to rectify mistakes *before* they occur than afterwards."

Any "remainders" (goods to follow) are noted in the Order Book, or in a record specially set up for the purpose, and it should be seen to that these are not overlooked. The customer should be advised of any such temporary delay in carrying out part of an order, or of inability to supply certain goods ("omits"). Unless substitution is forbidden, it is usual, in some trades, to send the nearest "subs" (substitutes) which can be supplied, care being taken to explain that this is being done.

The necessary instructions as to packing, etc., must be sent with the goods to the Packing Department. Under the first system described above, the Invoice Clerk who enters up the goods in the Sales Journal makes out for each lot of goods a "packing slip," giving the description of the goods, customer's name and address, the method of packing, and the marks and numbers to be placed on the cases. Under any system where the order or invoice is manifolded, an additional carbon copy of the entry may be made for the same purpose. It will be better, however, as already stated, that no extensions should be made on this copy, although carried out on the others. On the completion of the packing, the slip, marked with dimensions and weight of the packages and the packer's signature, is returned to the Invoice Clerk.

When the goods are to be forwarded by carrier, a completed address label is usually sent with the goods to the packer, and in

SPECIMEN OF PACKING SLIP

Folio .... *Date* ....

Name.. *Address* ....

Date for dispatch .... *How pack* ....

Marks and numbers.	Goods	Measurements	Weights
B. & Co. # 1			
Cape Town 2			
3			
4			

Packer..

(*Form No.* 9)

some circumstances would be the only information which need be sent with such goods. The addressing machine (*vide* Chapter III) provides a useful means of completing a neat and correct label.

It will be the duty of the foreman packer to see that a stock of cases, wrappers, etc., sufficient to meet the ordinary requirements

SPECIMEN OF LABEL

Per................ *Date*..............19

Contents............ *Fol*.......*Sig*.([1])........*Packer*........

....

....

....

From..........................

(*Form No.* 10)

[1] Initials of Clerk who prepares the label.

of the business, without being unnecessarily large, is kept in hand; and, if the cases, etc., are of standard size designated by numbers, with a distinguishing letter for the *description* of the package (as C1, C2 for cases; W1, W2 for wrappers), it will be convenient for notifying the office as to the quantity of materials used in connection with any particular order. There is no need for the packing staff to know the charges made to customers for such articles.

Although the cost of packing obviously includes the packer's wages, it is usual to charge the customer with the cost of the replacement of materials only, wages being debited to General Expenses.

Sometimes, by the use of non-returnable cases, and by including cost of packing in the price of the goods, a separate charge is avoided altogether. Generally speaking, it may be said that the fewer special charges the better, as all extras are more or less irritating to the purchaser. All railway companies have special rates for returned empties. (See Chapter IX.)

The packing of goods for foreign markets deserves more consideration than has sometimes been given to it by British manufacturers and merchants. It has been said, with an appearance of some truth, that England has lost ground, as compared with her Continental competitors, through insufficient attention to the requirements and prejudices of customers as to the form in which goods are put up. If trade is to be retained, buyers' tastes must be gratified and the peculiarities of markets must be studied.

As regards the size of packages, the methods of transport in the country of destination must be kept in view. In some mountainous parts where railways are impracticable, merchandise has to be carried by mules or bullocks, or even on the shoulders of men. Inattention to these points will often mean serious inconvenience and expense to the purchaser, and the probable loss of his custom. Information of the kind indicated may be obtained, not only from the firm's own travellers and correspondents, but from Official Reports published by the Department of Overseas Trade and Consular Agencies, and from the various commercial papers and trade journals.

Instructions as to marking are generally given in the order or indent, and these instructions should be carefully followed. A mark usually consists of some design, such as a triangle, diamond, etc., made by means of a stencil, with the initials of the consignee and the port to which the goods are consigned. For example—

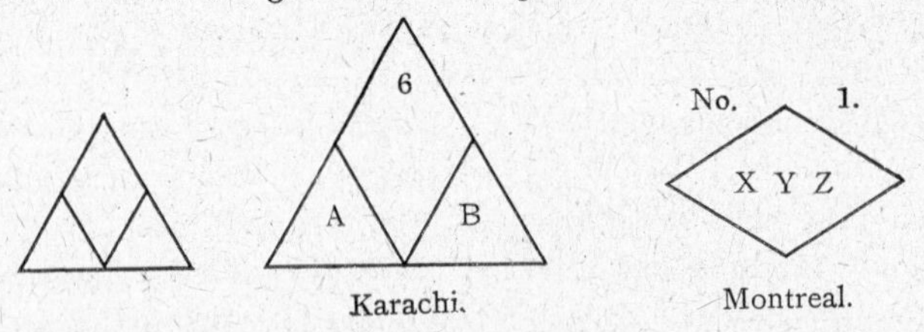

When there is more than one package in a consignment, the packages are numbered consecutively, and in the case of regular customers the numbers often run continuously for a year. Each package should also be marked with its dimensions and weight, and it may be necessary to give the latter in denominations other than British.

One advantage of consigning goods under mark is that trade competitors are less likely to get information of possible customers. It is also, generally speaking, quicker than addressing, and is more convenient in cases where the goods may be sold in their original packages by the person to whom they are sent. These remarks apply not only to goods exported, but also to large consignments sent by rail.

When the goods are ready for delivery, they should be entered in the Delivery Book kept by the Dispatch Clerk, and signed for by the carman receiving the goods.

If the business is a large one, it may be advisable to apportion the work of the packing staff in some definite way, in order to avoid friction. This allocation may follow the departmental divisions, or the various lines of railway, or the routes of different travellers, or any other suitable plan. In such cases, each packer should be assigned a number or some similar means of identification by which he may be known to the porters conveying the goods from the sale rooms, and for his own use on packing slips and other records of his individual work.

In conclusion, it may be pointed out that, in order to avoid the risk of goods being forwarded to customers without being first charged to the debit of their respective accounts, it is imperative that there should be some systematic connection between the Packing Department and the Sales Department. The systems which have been explained in this chapter are, therefore, no matter of mere theory designed to give an appearance of completeness, but a distinct link in the system of organization which should collect all the various departments of a large undertaking together, and which cannot in any circumstances be safely disregarded. In the case of a manufacturing undertaking, it will indeed probably be desirable to take the system even one stage farther, and require the Packing Department to advise the Cost Office of the quantities and description of all goods sent out from time to time. This will enable the Cost Office to complete its record by marking off the various goods as having been dispatched, and to advise the office of having so done, leaving it for the office to compare the advices it receives from the Cost Office with those it has received already from the Selling Department. Any discrepancy between the two should, of course, be very carefully inquired into.

CHAPTER VIII*

CUSTOMS procedure, dealing with the principal Regulations relating to the more important commodities on which Excise and Customs Duties are levied in this country, and the general procedure in connection therewith.

THE imposition of Customs Duties forms one of the most ancient methods of raising revenue for public purposes, while the word "Customs" itself seems to indicate the universality of its application. The traceable beginnings of our own Customs System are to be found in the "Prisage" and "Butlerage," the "Subsidies," the "Tonnage and Poundage," and other levies of the thirteenth and succeeding centuries. Some of these impositions were recognized as the hereditary right of the monarch, while others were under the control of Parliament, and granted to or withheld from the Crown according to circumstances. As a matter of fact, these taxes, often unconstitutionally levied, seem to have been a constant source of trouble between the King and Parliament, and formed one of the chief causes of the Civil War. By Acts of Anne and George I, the duties were made perpetual, and were mortgaged to the nation in return for the public adoption of certain obligations of the Crown.

In 1787, the year of the first Customs Consolidation Act, the customs duties, hitherto collected on the basis of a book of rates issued from time to time with the warrant of the Speaker of the House of Commons, were in a most chaotic state, some duties being levied according to bulk, others according to value, and in some cases by both methods on the same article. Pitt's Act considerably simplified matters, and was succeeded in turn by the Acts of 1825, 1853, and 1876. The Customs Consolidation Act of 1876, considerably amended by successive Finance Acts, is still in force. During the nineteenth century, the Customs Tariff was progressively reduced. In 1842 about 1,200 articles carried duty; in 1845 about 150, and in 1860 some 48. Before the end of the last century the list had been shortened to less than a dozen classes of goods—probably the smallest tariff in the world.

In the present century, the tendency has been reversed, and the

* The War of 1939 has entailed restrictions in every branch of importation and exportation but, as it is to be hoped that these circumstances are temporary only, no reference thereto is made in this chapter.

trend of the Customs Tariff has been steadily upwards. Since the legislation of 1932, very few goods are admitted into this country free of duty.

By the imposition of the Sugar Tax in 1901, the number of dutiable articles was considerably increased, owing to the large number of commodities containing sweetening matter as an ingredient, the list of subsidiary articles ranging from chutney to cattle food, and from chewing gum to blacking. The incidence of the tax on sugar is, therefore, very general and extensive, as it was perhaps intended to be. The year 1902 saw an export duty placed on coal (since repealed), while the import duty on corn imposed in the same year lasted only twelve months. By the Finance (No. 2) Act, 1915, motor-cars, cinematograph films,[1] musical instruments, and clocks and watches were subjected to import duty. These duties were, and still are, known as the "McKenna" duties. In 1916, matches, mechanical lighters, table waters, cider and perry became subject to duty. The Finance Act of 1920 increased the duty on imported cigars and sparkling wine. By the same Act, the duty on motor spirit was repealed as from 1st January, 1921, and a new system (i.e. according to horse-power) of taxing mechanically propelled vehicles was instituted on the same date. The Finance Act, 1928, reimposed a tax on imported motor spirit, but did not repeal the "horse-power" excise duty on motor vehicles.

In 1921 was passed the Safeguarding of Industries Act, designed "to promote and safeguard the development in the United Kingdom of industries of a special or pivotal character." These "key" industries were specified in a schedule,[2] and the Board of Trade was authorized to issue lists in accordance therewith; complaints as to inclusion or exclusion were to be referred to a referee appointed by the Lord Chancellor. Duties levied under this Act are known as "Key Industry Duties." The 1921 Act was amended in certain particulars by the Finance Act of 1926.

The "McKenna" and "Key Industry" duties are "*ad valorem*" duties, that is to say, the duty is calculated as a percentage on the value of the article, whereas duties levied under previous Finance Acts and other legislation were, in nearly every case, "specific,"

[1] Cinematograph films are now subjected to a specific duty.

[2] The "key industry" schedules originally included arc-lamp carbons. These articles are now subjected to a specific duty.

that is to say, they are based upon weight or bulk, or some other quantitative measurement.

The Finance Act of 1925 imposed heavy duties on silk and artificial silk. Specific duties were imposed upon raw silk, and on yarns and tissues of silk and artificial silk, while an *ad valorem* duty was imposed on manufactured articles. These duties were amended by the Finance Act, 1932, which imposed an *ad valorem* duty on raw silk, yarns and tissues, in addition to the specific duty, and increased the existing *ad valorem* duty on manufactured articles.

The *ad valorem* silk duties now range from 12 per cent to 43⅓ per cent, according to the percentage of silk in the manufactured article.

Before considering the numerous duties imposed by the legislation of 1932, we may summarize the articles subject to duty under the Statutes cited above as follows—

I. **Ad Valorem Duties.**

50 per cent **Ad Valorem**—

[1] Optical glass and component parts of optical instruments.

12 per cent to 43⅓ per cent **Ad Valorem**—

Silk and artificial silk articles.

33⅓ per cent **Ad Valorem**—

[1] Amorphous carbon electrodes.
Clocks, watches, and parts (20 per cent to 33⅓ per cent).
[1] Hosiery latch needles.
[1] Ignition magnetos.
[1] Certain rare metals (e.g. tungsten).
[1] Molybdenum, vanadium, and compounds.
Motor-cars and parts.
Musical instruments (10 per cent to 33⅓ per cent).
[1] Scientific instruments and parts of such instruments.
[1] Synthetic organic chemicals
[1] Wireless valves.

It must be remembered that derivatives or parts of the articles in the above named classes are dutiable, and the official list contains upwards of 7,000 entries.

[1] = Key industry duty.

Specific Duties—

- Arc lamp carbons.
- Beer.
- Cards, playing.
- Chloral hydrate.
- Chloroform.
- Cinematograph film.
- Cocoa.
- Coffee and chicory.
- Collodion.
- Condensed milk.
- Dried fruit.
- Ether.
- Ethyl bromide.
- Glucose.
- Hops and hop oil.
- Matches.
- Mechanical lighters.
- Molasses.
- Oils (hydrocarbon).
- Saccharine and similar substances.
- Silks and artificial silks.
- Spirits, and preparations containing spirits, or in the manufacture of which spirits have been used.
- Sugar and goods containing sugar.
- Table waters.
- Tea.
- Tobacco.
- Wine.

Composite goods containing any of these articles are dutiable, and some of them are assessed at specific rates. A schedule of current rates may be found in any good almanac. As regards the first levying or repeal of any duty of Customs, the time at which the importation of any goods is deemed to have effect is, under the provisions of the Finance Act, 1901, the time at which the entry for the goods under the Customs Act is delivered.

With a view to conferring a preference in the case of Empire products, the Finance Act, 1919, and subsequent Acts provided for the charging of lower rates of duty on certain goods which are shown to have been consigned from, and grown, produced or manufactured in the British Empire. Empire goods are entirely free of Key Industry Duty. The preferential rate must be claimed at the time of passing the import entry for the goods, and the claim must be supported by a certificate of origin, in one of the approved forms. Full information as to the qualifications for and method of claiming the preferential rates are given in notices issued by the Commissioners of Customs and Excise. Copies can be obtained free of charge at any Custom House, and importers and agents who deal with Empire goods should obtain a copy, and become conversant with its contents.

Until 1931, the element of protection in the Customs Tariff was small. The duties set out above covered a relatively limited range of articles, and the United Kingdom remained, by comparison with others, a Free Trade country. The year 1931 was, however, a period of unparalleled financial strain. The world-wide depression had led almost every country in the world to erect high tariff barriers, and, in consequence, the export trade of this country was declining at an alarming rate. Imports, on the other hand, declined much less rapidly. The resulting strain on our financial resources was increased by the loss of investment income from abroad. A large proportion of the imports of this country is, taking a general view of economic organization, paid for by dividends received by persons residing in the United Kingdom who hold foreign investments. The general depression had caused dividends to fall off everywhere, and in many instances obligations were even repudiated. The financial strain reached breaking-point when a widespread panic on the Continent led to heavy withdrawals of foreign funds invested in Great Britain. This was in July, 1931. In August, the Government was forced to suspend the obligation of the Bank of England to pay its liabilities in gold, and the effect of the adverse balance of trade became immediately visible in the rapid depreciation of the foreign exchange value of the pound sterling. It was clear that the country as a whole was importing more goods than it could afford to pay for at the existing level of exports, and taking into account the foreign investment situation. The Government at once took drastic steps to reduce the volume of imports, and the Abnormal Importations (Customs Duties) Act was hurried through Parliament. This Act, and the Orders made thereunder, imposed heavy, and in many cases, prohibitive duties on imports covering a wide range of articles. It is not, however, necessary to consider the provisions of this Act in detail, since it was repealed in the following year, when the financial situation had considerably improved. The Act of 1931 was replaced by the Import Duties Act of 1932, by which the United Kingdom became definitely a protectionist country.

The main provisions of this Act are as follows—

(*a*) For the first time, a general *ad valorem* tariff of 10 per cent was imposed. This duty applies to *all* goods, unless specifically exempted.

(*b*) The Treasury is empowered to impose additional duties (over and above the general duty of 10 per cent) upon—

1. Articles of luxury.
2. Articles which are being produced, or are likely to be produced within a reasonable time, and in sufficient quantities, within the United Kingdom. Thus, in effect, the Government is at liberty to impose new and prohibitive tariffs without further legislation.
3. The Board of Trade may impose supplementary duties (not exceeding 100 per cent of the value of the goods) upon goods imported from a country which, in their opinion, discriminates by its import regulations against British goods.

The exemptions from the general 10 per cent tariff may be classified as follows—

1. Goods which are already dutiable under other statutes. Thus the goods included in the two lists above (of *ad valorem* and specific duties) are exempted from the 10 per cent duty.
2. Goods for re-export.
3. Empire goods: manufactured articles are not entitled to preference unless a prescribed proportion of their value is derived from expenditure of a prescribed kind which has been incurred in the British Empire or the United Kingdom in respect of materials grown or produced or work done in the British Empire or the United Kingdom.
4. The Free List. Goods in the Free List are exempted from the 10 per cent duty (though this does not necessarily imply that they are not liable to duty under other statutes). For example, wheat in grain is on the Free List, but is subject to a specific duty under the Ottawa Agreements Act, 1932 (see below).

The more important items on the Free List are as follows—

Gold and silver bullion.
Wheat in grain.
Maize in grain.
Meat other than meat in airtight containers.
Live quadruped animals.
Fish of British taking.
Raw cotton and cotton seed.
Raw wool and animal hair.
Raw hides and skins.
Wood pulp.
Raw rubber.
Metallic ores.
Iron pyrites.
Copper unwrought.
Sulphur.

Coal and coke.
Newsprint.
Cork.
Potassium salts.
Certain oils.
Scientific films.
Wooden pit-props.

The additional duties at present in force (see (*b*) page 83) cover a very wide range of articles, which cannot be enumerated in full, but the principal classes are as follows—

Shell fish.
Certain preserved fruits and condensed milks.
Pottery and other clay products.
Glass and glassware.
Certain classes of furniture.
Certain iron and steel products.
Articles manufactured of certain metals, including aluminium, copper, and lead.
Cutlery.
Electrical goods.
Machinery.
Certain articles manufactured of wool, cotton, linen, and jute.
Clothing.
Boots and shoes.
Certain chemicals, paints and colours.
Candles and soap.
Leather and leather goods.
Paper.
Cycles.
Certain rubber products.
Arms and ammunition.
Toilet preparations.
Furs and skins.
Jewellery.

The additional duties range from 5 per cent to 23⅓ per cent *ad valorem*. Empire goods, including manufactured goods complying with the prescribed regulations, are exempt from the additional duties.

The Customs Tariff was further extended as a result of the Imperial Conference at Ottawa. By the Ottawa Agreements Act, 1932, duties (some specific, and some *ad valorem*) are levied upon certain classes of food. Imports from countries within the British Empire are exempt. The levying of duties upon imports of food may be said to complete the transition from Free Trade to Protection.

The principal classes are—

Wheat in grain.
Butter, cheese, and eggs.
Condensed milk.
Fresh fruits.
Preserved fruits.
Honey.
Rice.
Linseed and linseed oil, and certain other oils.

Where these duties are charged, the general 10 per cent duty is not levied (see above), but any additional duties, for the time being in force under the Import Duties Act, 1932, may be charged. If any goods in the above classes are liable under the ordinary Customs Tariff, both duties are charged. Thus, condensed milk is liable to duty under three heads, viz.—

(*a*) The ordinary Customs Tariff (under sugar).
(*b*) The Import Duties Act, 1932 (additional duty).
(*c*) The Ottawa Agreements Act.

To complete the survey of the Customs legislation of 1932, mention should be made of the Irish Free State (Special Duties) Act, 1932. Under this Act, which was occasioned by a regrettable financial dispute between the two governments, duties are levied on the following classes of imports from the Irish Free State.

Live cattle (from £1 5s. to £6 per head).
Live sheep (10s. per head).
Other animals (40 per cent *ad valorem*).
Meat.
Poultry.
Butter, eggs, and cream.

These duties are superimposed upon all other duties for the time being in force (even including the general 10 per cent duty).

Some articles which are liable to duties under the ordinary Customs Tariff are charged with Excise duties if produced in the United Kingdom, but no Excise duties are charged on goods liable to duty under other enactments (viz. Safeguarding of Industries

Act, the Import Duties Act, the Ottawa Agreements Act, and the Irish Free State (Special Duties) Act).

Board of Trade Orders are issued under the Acts in the *London Gazette* and in the *Board of Trade Journal*, and the regulations made by the Commissioners of Customs and Excise are issued as notices to importers and agents.

In addition to the comprehensive scheme of duties which has been outlined above, the importation of the following goods is either prohibited altogether, or is subject to special restrictions—

Copyright works.
Coin : imitation British, foreign bronze, etc.
Fictitious postage stamps or any instrument for making them.
Lottery advertisements.
Extracts or essences of coffee, chicory, tea or tobacco.
Indecent or obscene publications.
Snuff work, tobacco stalks, or stalk flour.
Explosives or materials or apparatus used in their manufacture.
Gold and silver plate, not of standard quality.
Dyestuffs.
Tobacco, sweetened or compressed.
Foreign prison-made goods.
Infected carcasses or parts of animals, etc.
Goods bearing marks infringing the Merchandise Marks Acts.
Tobacco, adulterated.
Dogs and other canine animals.
Certain fish.
Frozen meat, not produced in the British Empire.
Musk rats.
Articles bearing devices implying any government guarantee.
Horses, asses and mules.
Live animals, (i.e. cattle, sheep, goats and other ruminating animals, and swine).
Plants of various kinds.
Fish illegally caught.
Sealskins of certain kinds.
Matches made with white phosphorus.
Shaving brushes from Japan.
Opium and preparations thereof.

The *exportation* of arms, ammunition, military and naval stores, etc., may be prohibited by proclamation or Order in Council.

Finally, mention must be made of the various quota systems now in force, by which quantitative limitations are placed upon the importation of certain classes of goods, notably wheat. Under the Wheat Act, 1932, every importer of flour must, in addition to paying any customs duties due, produce to the customs officer a receipt from the Wheat Commission showing that the prescribed quota payment has been made to that body in respect of the flour imported. The subject of quotas in general is, however, beyond the scope of this chapter.

With reference to British marks on foreign goods, further consideration of the regulations is desirable in view of the fact that they apply to *all* goods and not merely to particular articles, as is the case with most of the other prohibitions. Under the provisions of the Merchandise Marks Acts, 1887 to 1926, goods bearing marks in any way suggesting British origin require, in order to legalize their importation, some counteracting qualification, such as " Made in Germany," etc. Government Departments are further empowered to submit to a special Committee the question whether it is expedient that given classes of imported goods be marked to show their country of origin. Upon an affirmative reply His Majesty may, by Order in Council, make an appropriate Order, and penalties are thereafter laid on all persons offering unmarked goods for sale.

The following are some of the classes of goods which must at present be marked to indicate the country of origin—

Rubber tyres and tubes.
Pottery.
Insulated electrical cables and wires.
Electric incandescent lamps.
Fresh apples.
Cutlery.
Eggs.
Oat products.
Raw tomatoes.
Wrought hollow-ware.
Fertilizers and feeding-stuffs.
Rubber boots and shoes.
Clocks.
Dead poultry.

Goods not produced in the United Kingdom, such as wine and tea, and some special forms of manufacture which cannot be mistaken for home-made goods, such as Dutch cheese of the kind well-known to be made in Holland, are exempt from the provisions of this legislation. Thus, certain marks which might be passed in respect of these goods would render other goods liable to detention. Besides marks suggesting British manufacture, however, there are other grounds of prohibition, such as a false trade description, whether as to place of production (as between one foreign country and another), or as to quantity, mode of manufacture, material, etc. A wine produced in Germany, for instance, should not be described simply as "Sherry," which suggests Spanish origin, but should be described as German Sherry. The description "Port" or "Madeira," applied to wines other than those which are the produce of Portugal or Madeira respectively, though the description is accompanied by an indication of the actual country of production, is a false trade description. Wine from Portugal described as "Port" must be accompanied by a certificate showing that the description is valid under Portuguese law. When the name of a place in a trade description is indicative merely of the character of the goods and is not misleading, no objection is taken. The description "Brussels Carpet" is an instance of this. Amongst the marks suggesting British origin are included, of course, the names and trade marks of manufacturers, dealers, or traders in the United Kingdom. The Board of Customs has established a system of registration so that any person interested may register his name or mark at such port or ports as he desires, with the object of preventing the importation of goods bearing such marks, or a colourable imitation thereof, without his authority. It must be understood, however, that the use by any manufacturer, etc., even of his own name or other mark indicating production in the United Kingdom is prohibited as regards foreign made goods unless such name or mark is properly qualified by a definite indication of foreign origin.

When any goods are detained on account of names or marks which have been registered at the Customs, notice is sent to the owner of the mark, and any detention beyond 48 hours is at his risk unless the marks are illegal apart from the question of registration. If prolongation of the detention is desired, security may be required by the Customs Authorities. Under the powers conferred by the Act, the following regulations have been made by the Commissioners—

(1) Goods prohibited to be imported as hereinbefore recited having applied to them forged trade marks, false trade descriptions, or marks, names, or

descriptions, otherwise illegal, which upon examination are detected by the Officers of Customs, are to be detained by them without the requirement of previous information.

(2) In giving information with a view to detention, an informant must fulfil the following conditions, viz.—

(*a*) He must give to the Collector or Superintendent, or the Chief Officer of Customs of the port (or sub-port) of expected importation, notice in writing, stating—

The number of packages expected, as far as he is able to state the same:

The description of the goods by marks, or other particulars, sufficient for their identification:

The name or other sufficient indication of the importing ship:

The manner in which the goods infringe the Act:

The expected day of the arrival of the ship.

(*b*) He must deposit with the Collector or other officer, as aforesaid, a sum sufficient, in the opinion of that officer, to cover any additional expense which may be incurred in the examination required by reason of his notice.

(3) If, upon arrival and examination of the goods, the officer of Customs is satisfied that there is no ground for their detention, they will be delivered. If he is not so satisfied he will decide either to detain the goods, as in a case of detention upon ordinary examination, or to require security from the informant for re-imbursing the Commissioners or their officers all expenses and damages incurred in respect of the detention made on his information, and of any proceedings consequent thereon.

(4) The security thus required must be an immediate *ad valorem* deposit of £10 per cent on the value of the goods, as fixed by the officer from the quantities or value shown by the entry, and also, subsequently, a bond to be completed within 4 days in double the value of the goods with two approved sureties. The *ad valorem* deposit will be returned upon completion of the bond, and will not be required if, as an alternative where time permits, the informant prefers to give a like bond before examination upon estimated value of the goods declared to by him under statutory declaration. If the security is not duly given as above required there will be no further detention of the goods.

(5) In the above regulations the words "Officer of Customs" mean an officer acting under general or special direction of the Commissioners, and the words "value of the goods" mean value irrespective of duty.

(6) The "Notice" and "Bond" required, as above, shall be in the forms contained in the schedule to these regulations, or in such other forms as the Commissioners may from time to time order and direct.

(7) The security taken under these regulations will be given up at the times following; that is to say,

Where given before examination, and, if no detention, forthwith.

Where given on detention—

If the forfeiture is completed, either by lapse of time, or ultimate condemnation by a Court of Justice, then on such completion of forfeiture.

If the forfeiture is not completed, then

If the goods are released by the Commissioners, and no action or suit has been commenced against them, or any of their officers in respect of the detention, then at the expiration of three months from the time of detention; or if the goods are released for failure of proceedings taken for the forfeiture and condemnation thereof, upon information under Sect. 207 of "The Customs Consolidation Act, 1876," and no action or suit has been commenced against the Commissioners, or any of their officers, in respect of the detention, then at the expiration of three months from the trial of such information.

If, within such periods, as aforesaid, any such action or suit, as aforesaid, has been commenced, then upon the ultimate conclusion of such action or suit, and the fulfilment of the purpose for which the security was given.

(8) These regulations apply to transhipment and transit goods, as well as to goods landed to be warehoused, or for home consumption.

While existing primarily for the collection of revenue, the Customs organization is utilized for many purposes in no way connected with the receipt of duty. These functions, undertaken for the common weal, have been thus described in a public lecture by a former Deputy Chairman of the Board of Customs: " We collect the Trade Statistics, though they are published under the name of the Board of Trade. We also undertake the duty of registration of ships and of collection of light dues, besides other important duties for the Board of Trade under the Mercantile Marine Acts. We perform the duties of Coast Police in reference to public health, preventing the introduction into the country of certain diseases, both of men and of animals, and of unwholesome food, as well as the moral pollution of vile literature. We are entrusted with the administration of the Merchandise Marks Act, so far as it prohibits the introduction of goods with misleading marks. We guard the copyright privileges of authors and artists. We prevent the importation of dangerous explosives without due precaution. We keep guard on the exportation of ships or other *matériel* of war to foreign belligerents, which might involve us in breaches of the laws of neutrality." To these duties have since been added the administration of the Aliens Acts, 1905 and 1919.

It is not proposed (indeed it would be impracticable) to give here detailed information respecting the transaction of Customs business, such as must be acquired by the clerk whose special work it is. This can be better obtained by inquiry at any Custom House, and from the official and semi-official publications issued from time to time. It is desirable, however, for the Manager of a business with an Import or Export Trade to have a general knowledge of the Customs System of the United Kingdom, so as to be able efficiently to control this branch of his undertaking.

By an Order in Council made under the Finance Act, 1908, the management of the Excise duties was, on 1st April, 1909, transferred from the Commissioners of Inland Revenue to the Commissioners of Customs. The amalgamated Customs and Excise Department is controlled by a Board of four Commissioners appointed by the Sovereign under the Great Seal on the nomination of the Treasury, to whom the Commissioners are directly responsible. The rules regulating the conduct of business within the Department are issued by the Board from time to time, and those affecting the business of traders are communicated to them orally, or in the form of public notices, or as Statutory Rules and Orders, which may be purchased from H.M. Stationery Office or through any bookseller. Memorials and representations on matters not dealt with in the General Regulations, or appearing to require special treatment, should be addressed to the Board, who are, as a rule, ready to consider any case on its merits, and to grant special concessions within the limits of the law, provided good cause can be shown. Personal interviews can also be had on occasion. The Superintending branches, together with the clerical staff of the Port of London Establishment, are located in the principal Custom House of the Kingdom, situated in Lower Thames Street, City, on the left bank of the Thames below London Bridge. A Custom House will be found in every port, the status of the officer in charge varying according to the amount of trade and the size of the staff. At the principal outports (i.e. ports other than London) the chief official is styled a "Collector." Ports of less importance are in charge of "Collector-Surveyors" or "Surveyors," and the minor ones are in charge of "Officers," "Preventive Officers," or "Assistant Preventive Officers." In London, the "Collector" is head of the Port Clerical Establishment, the Outdoor Department for landing, shipping and warehousing duties being in charge of the Collector, London (Port). The Department employs several thousand persons, a large proportion of them being stationed in London.

The Outdoor Department consists of two branches: "Landing" and "Waterguard." In the former, the various grades of officers are entitled Inspectors, Surveyors, and Officers. These are usually engaged on "Landing and Shipping" and "Warehousing" duties. The Waterguard Branch is controlled by an Inspector-General, assisted at headquarters by an Inspector and two Assistant Inspectors, the staff are graded as Superintendents, Chief Preventive Officers, Preventive Officers, and Assistant Preventive Officers.

Let us now consider the means by which the objects of the Customs System are achieved, although our description must necessarily be brief.

In the first place, every ship coming into a port of the United Kingdom from "beyond the seas" must "bring to" at the appointed "Boarding Station" in order to take on board the Customs Officers whose duty it is to make the first inquiries as to the ship, her cargo, and crew, to collect dutiable stores and place them under seal in some secure place on board, to make a record of these particulars. The Boarding Officer inquires as to the health of the passengers and crew, and if satisfied there is not, and has not been, any case of cholera, yellow fever or plague on board, he issues a Certificate of Pratique, permitting the vessel to proceed to her place of discharge. In doubtful cases the vessel is held for the inspection of the Medical Officer of Health. The passengers and their baggage are then landed, the former being interrogated by the Aliens Officer when necessary, and the latter examined by the Waterguard staff. The landing of any cargo whatever from foreign countries is prohibited except at places which have been approved by the Commissioners. Further, tobacco and plain spirits (as merchandise) can be imported only in ships above a certain tonnage, and in packages of a fixed minimum content. The importation of tobacco is further restricted to approved ports, a restriction which applies also to wine in casks. Trade samples of tobacco, etc., are subject to special regulations. Saccharine, including substances of like nature and use, can be imported only at approved ports and in packages of not less than 11 lb. net weight.

Within 24 hours after arrival, and before bulk is broken—except by special permission—the master of every ship must present at the Custom House an account in proper form of the cargo, giving the number of packages, marks, etc. In this "Report," high-duty goods, such as spirits, tobacco, and saccharin, have to be specifically described. They cannot be reported simply as "merchandise," as may be done with other goods. This business is usually performed by agents, but the master (or a ship's officer appointed by him) attends personally to answer certain questions and make the necessary Declaration.

The discharge of the cargo is subject to certain limitations as to hours, and the goods are usually landed into sheds for the Customs examination. Some of these sheds are specially approved by the Commissioners as "Transit Sheds," which have certain privileges. One of these is that they may be used for the reception of goods from a ship prior to report, the shed thus taking the place of the ship.

Before the goods can be "cleared" by the Customs, an "Entry" must be passed by the importer or his agent. In the case of dutiable goods, to be delivered for home use direct from the ship, the law requires that the Entry shall be passed before the goods are landed, except into an approved transit shed. These Entries are of various kinds according to the description and destination of the goods; but the object of all is to obtain from the importer an account of all goods, with particulars of their description, quantity in some cases, and value in all. The particulars enumerated are declared to be true. The Entries and Report are afterwards compared and checked one against the other, and any discrepancies have to be accounted for by the agent for the ship or the importer as the case may be.

Goods exported are dealt with in a somewhat similar fashion. The agent for the ship is required to deliver to the Collector an account, in the form of a "Manifest," of all goods sent in the ship, while the exporter himself must deliver, within six days, a "Specification" of the goods exported by him. The total of the Specifications must agree with the Manifest.

To render possible the classification and tabulation of our import and export trade, the Entries and Specifications referred to in the preceding paragraphs, in addition to giving the commercial designation, must describe the goods in accordance with headings set out in the official Import and Export List, which may be obtained through any bookseller or direct from H.M. Stationery Office, London, W.C.2. This list, which came into use on 1st January, 1920, superseded the old Import and Export Lists and Appendices. Goods are divided therein into the following classes—

(1) Food, drink and tobacco.
(2) Raw materials and articles mainly unmanufactured.
(3) Articles wholly or mainly manufactured.
(4) Animals, not for food.
(5) Parcel Post, non-dutiable articles.

The first three classes are subdivided into numerous groups. Throughout the list the headings marked "I" apply to imported goods and re-exports thereof; headings marked "E" apply to; exported goods of United Kingdom produce and manufacture and all other headings apply to both imports and exports. There is an alphabetical index to assist in finding the correct heading for the various kinds of goods.

Where any denomination of tale, weight, or measure is affixed to an article in the list, the *quantity* of such article in that denomination is required in addition to the *value*, which is to be given in every case. Import values are "c.i.f."; export values "f.o.b." For imports, the name of place (or country) of consignment must be given, and for exports the country of destination. Foreign goods re-exported are to be described according to the Import headings and entered on the foreign (red) forms of specification.

The officials whose duty it is to check these entries naturally become expert in comparing quantities and values, etc., and in case of doubt have power to call for documentary evidence of correctness. This power is pretty freely used, and instances of frequent or gross inaccuracies are met by fines, which it is in the power of the Commissioners to impose. This matter of fines touches the question of staff. Occasional errors are human and inevitable, and in dealing with incorrect declarations, the Customs Authorities take into account the general reputation of the firm as well as the magnitude of the particular offence. There are some firms which, in the course of time, pay an appreciable amount in fines of this kind. In some concerns, it is the practice to charge the clerks responsible for the errors with the monetary consequences of their mistakes; but this does not seem a very desirable or magnanimous proceeding. It would be better to take a little extra care in the selection of the men assigned to this branch of the work, and thus avoid, as far as may be, the causes of the trouble.

Special care should be taken to avoid the entry of dutiable goods on a "free entry" form, as this irregularity is regarded seriously. Forwarding agents have the greatest need to be on their guard in this respect, and they cannot be too careful in dealing with goods advised by foreign shippers under some general description. It is wise in such cases for agents to obtain a definite declaration from the actual importers that the goods are free of duty before passing a free entry, so that any penalty inflicted for a revenue offence can be charged to them. The offending firm has to prove its *bona fides* in such a case, and even then is not, as a rule, let off scot free.

When any doubt exists as to the exact nature of the goods or as to their quantity, etc., a way out of the difficulty is provided by the form of entry known as a " bill of sight." This enables the importer to describe the packages as " contents unknown," and the goods may then be landed and examined in the presence of a Customs Officer. The entry must be " perfected " within three days by endorsement on the back, the document being thus made equivalent to one of the forms mentioned below.

Provided sufficient particulars of the goods have come to hand there need be no difficulty. A " Free Entry," as the name implies, is used only for goods free of duty; a " Warehousing Entry " is required when goods liable to duty are to be placed in a bonded warehouse; while a " Home Use " Entry enables the importer to pay duty immediately, and to take delivery from the ship's side. Saccharine, however, and similar articles *must* be warehoused on importation. Cavendish and negrohead tobacco must be warehoused on first importation, and may not be delivered for home use until the duty has been paid and the tobacco packed, wrapped and labelled according to law. Foreign gold and silver plate must on first importation be entered for warehousing, and sent to an approved Assay Office to be assayed and stamped before delivery is allowed.

The bonded warehouse system, which has existed in some degree since 1700, serves to mitigate to a considerable extent the inconvenience of the Revenue restrictions, and very great use is made of it. The regulations applying to warehouses under the charge of the Customs and Excise respectively are identical. The proprietor of each warehouse is under bond to the Crown for payment of duty on any goods illegally removed therefrom—this, of course, in addition to his responsibility to the owner of the goods placed in his charge. Any building which complies with certain conditions laid down by the Customs and Excise Authorities, and is approved by one or other of them, may be used for the purpose. It must be shown that the accommodation is required by the trade of the port. These warehouses, except when open for receipts and deliveries, are kept under Crown locks.

Warehoused goods can be either duty paid for home consumption or exported under bond. Some goods, such as tea, coffee, cocoa, and saccharine are charged on delivery for home consumption with duty at the landing weights, in other cases on the quantities found at time of delivery, with certain allowances for alterations in bulk or weight arising from natural causes while the goods are in the warehouse. Operations such as sampling, sorting, and blending are allowed on request and under proper supervision, and the ownership in the goods may freely pass from one person to another by means of a negotiable instrument known as a Dock Warrant issued by the Warehouse Keeper. The goods may also be removed from one warehouse to another under bond. Certain goods liable to Key Industry Duty may not be warehoused. This regulation compels the importer to pay the duty immediately.

The Home Consumption Entry mentioned in the above paragraph must be distinguished from the Home Use Entry referred to above. The latter is frequently called a Prime Entry from the fact that, should the quantity entered be found to be short of the actual amount, a Post Entry on a similar form must be passed for the shortage. On the other hand, should the quantity entered be too much, the excess duty is returned to the importer by an Over Entry Certificate. Such discrepancies as are here referred to are recognized as a part of the system, and are not in the nature of irregularities. Free, Warehousing, and Home Use Entries are required in duplicate. One copy goes to the Landing Officer, and serves as a warrant for the clearing of the goods. The other, known as a *Bill*, is used for statistical purposes. Warrants are periodically transmitted from the Custom House to the Docks by official messengers, but importers will sometimes find it advantageous in cases of urgency to employ their own messengers for the purpose. Amendments of entries within certain limits are allowed by the local officers.

The forms used for these entries, and some others, have to be supplied by the merchant at his own expense. They are officially printed and are obtainable from agents appointed for their sale, usually stationers in the proximity of the Custom House. The forms may, however, be printed privately, so long as they conform to the official style. It will depend on the number used which method of obtaining supplies is the more economical. Merchants using a large number of forms may effect a great saving of labour by having the name of port, name and address of importer, and other frequently used particulars printed on their own privately printed forms.

If it is desired to re-import dutiable goods previously duty-paid and afterwards exported, a "Bill of Store" must be passed and, on verification of the export particulars, importation will be allowed without a second payment of duty. This privilege is confined to British goods and to foreign cinematograph films, motor-cars, musical instruments, and clocks and watches. Other foreign goods, if re-imported, whether duty has been paid at a previous importation or not, are liable to the same duties, rules and regulations as if imported for the first time. If Drawback (see page 100) has been paid on exportation, this must, of course, be refunded.

Bullion, diamonds, and coin must be entered in a special form within 72 hours of arrival, under a penalty of £20. They are allowed to be landed and cleared upon a printed request (addressed to the Examining Officer), carefully made out, stating the true weight and value, and upon production of a Bill of Lading. Every separate address, or mark, should be given, with the number of the packages on the back of the request, which should be ruled as follows—

Mark.	No. of Packages.	Weight Ozs.	Value £.	Description.	Whence.

Sometimes bullion and coin are cleared at the Mint or the Bank of England. When the importer desires this, he must pay for the officer's attendance.

Goods in transit deserve special consideration. By taking advantage of certain facilities offered by the regulations, the expense and delay of a full examination of the goods will be avoided. These regulations apply to (1) Transhipments within the same port, and (2) Goods for removal by rail in transit between ports in the United Kingdom.

Transhipments are allowed only at eighteen approved ports, and the goods must be reported specifically as "in transit." A

Transhipment Bond in an approved form must be entered into and a Transhipment Bond Warrant, containing a full description of the goods, must be passed. A Transhipment Delivery Order and a Shipping Bill are then issued, when the goods may be conveyed from the importing to the exporting vessel by a licensed lighterman or carman. The importer may have to pay for the attendance of an officer to accompany the goods. If not shipped within a reasonable time, the usual entries (free or warehousing) have to be passed.

Goods imported in transit for removal by rail between ports in the United Kingdom, to which the privilege of removing goods under the transit regulations have been conceded by the Board, must be reported "in transit." The consignee, exporter, or agent receiving the goods for conveyance must enter into a standing bond for the delivery of such goods into the care of the proper officers at the port of exportation; if an officer is sent in charge, a return railway ticket, or pass, together with an insurance ticket for £500, must be provided, and a deposit made to cover expenses; the goods must be delivered without delay from the importing vessel into the railway vans (which are placed under Crown locks, and also, when not accompanied, officially sealed) and delivered into Customs charge at the port of shipment within 48 hours thereafter, excluding Sundays and holidays.

Goods removed under these conditions are ordinarily exempt from examination. A further form of procedure—in which the goods are subject to examination—is provided for free goods in transit on through Bills of Lading when it is not desired to give bond. The following regulations apply to any port—

(1) The importer hands in a special (green) form of entry (No. 15, Sale).
(2) If the importer knows the name of the exporting vessel, he may hand in a green specification (Sale Form No. 16), which will take the place of the duplicate entry.
(3) If the goods are exported by more than one vessel separate Specifications for each are required, giving only number of packages, with their marks and numbers, quantities and values being given by a Covering Specification, corresponding with the Entry.
(4) If not shipped by the vessel named, Specification to be amended within six days from the date of ship's clearance.
(5) If the exporting ship or ships cannot be named the entry (No. 15) will be passed in duplicate, and the Specification (No. 16) will be required when the goods are exported.
(6) Goods to be described according to the Official Import List, and quantities to be fully stated.

It should be understood that all opening and closing of packages required for Customs examination, whether on importation, transhipment, or exportation, must be done by the proprietor (or his agent) and at his expense.

Some remarks on the Exports Regulations must close this chapter.

With free or duty-paid goods generally, all that is necessary is to hand in a specification, as already stated, but certain goods are restricted on exportation. No unclean or unseasonable salmon, and no salmon caught during the time at which the sale of salmon is prohibited in the district where it is caught, may be exported or entered for exportation from the United Kingdom to any ports beyond the seas. Penalty: £5 for *each salmon* exported or entered for exportation. Salmon, explosives, arms and munitions of war must be entered before shipment. In the case of arms and munitions, the final or actual destination of the goods is to be clearly established to the satisfaction of the Export Clerk.

In the case of goods exported in vessels carrying cargo for several ports or places, and also of goods destined for different countries or places beyond those to which the vessels in which they may be exported are bound, being subsequently transhipped into other vessels, or sent by some continuous system of water and land carriage, the Commissioners of Customs have directed that the actual and ultimate destination of such shipments shall be stated in the specification, and the Commissioners request the co-operation of all shippers in furnishing such information, so as to secure the publication of correct statistics.

A ship built in the United Kingdom, and not registered as a British ship, when she departs on her first foreign voyage is treated both as goods (the builder or owner being the exporter) and as an exporting ship.

The regulations with regard to warehoused or drawback goods are naturally more exacting than those for free or duty-paid goods. The expression "drawback goods" refers to goods upon which duty has been paid and upon the exportation of which (or deposit in warehouse) drawback—i.e. the return of the duty—is allowed.

The fact that duty has been paid upon goods upon importation does not of itself automatically entitle the exporter to drawback.

Drawback is allowed only upon goods of certain classes, and the list is a much shorter one than the list of goods liable to duty.

Under the ordinary Customs Tariff, the percentage of dutiable goods upon which drawback can be claimed is fairly large, and the list includes foreign beer, coffee, chicory, cocoa, cinematograph films, clocks, watches, motor-cars, tobacco manufactured in the United Kingdom, stalks, shorts, or other refuse of tobacco, sugar (British refined), British-made goods containing sugar, molasses, glucose, saccharine, dried fruit, silk and artificial silk, hops, and hydrocarbon oils.

All Key Industry goods are entitled to drawback.

Under the Ottawa Agreements Act, drawback is allowed in respect of one class of goods only, viz. agricultural and horticultural seeds.

The drawbacks allowed on goods which are liable to duty under the Import Duties Act, 1932, are relatively few, in comparison with the very wide range of goods subject to duty. The drawback list includes manufactures of cotton or vegetable fibre, clothing, boots, shoes, dressed fur skins, machinery, leather, paints, linoleum, stainless steel sheets, bullets and sporting cartridges.

No drawbacks are allowed on goods liable to duty under the Irish Free State (Special Duties) Act, 1932.

Excise drawback is allowed in respect of British beer, British spirits, sugar, glucose, molasses, saccharine, and artificial silk made in the United Kingdom, tobacco grown in the United Kingdom, and matches and molasses made in the United Kingdom, in consideration of loss caused by the Excise regulations. The drawback is payable on a "debenture" (see page 101) issued by the Customs. The declaration on the left of the form (and, of course, the receipt at the foot) must be signed on behalf of the exporting firm, and the document can then be negotiated through a bank if desired.

A drawback is not, of course, in the nature of a bounty. It simply puts the exporter in the same position as he would have been had no duty been payable on importation.

The following is an extract from the Customs Act—

No warehoused or drawback goods shall be shipped, put off, or water-borne to be shipped for exportation from any port or place in the United Kingdom on Sundays or public holidays except by special permission of the Commissioners of Customs, nor from any place not being a legal quay, wharf, or other

DEBENTURE FOR GOODS EXPORTED AS MERCHANDISE

No. ________

Port of ____________________

This is to Certify that ____________________ of ____________________ (*a*) Licensed Manufacturer, (a) Delete when not applicable

did enter on the ________ day of ____________ 19 ___, to be exported to ____________ *viâ* ____________

____

in respect of which Bond has been taken, as directed by the Act 39 & 40 Vic., cap. 36, and that ____________

____________ thereof were shipped and exported on board the ____________ at ____________ the ______ day of ____________ 19

____________ *Surveyor.* ____________ *Officer.*

____________ 19 ___

I ____________
____
do hereby declare that the goods mentioned in this Debenture have been actually exported as Merchandise, and have not been re-landed, and are not intended to be re-landed in any part of the United Kingdom, and that ____________ at the time of Entry and Shipping w____ and continue to be entitled to the Drawback thereon.

Signed and declared this ________ day of ________, 19 ___, in the presence of

____
pro Collector.

	£	s.	d.
The Drawback on the Goods above specified, amounts to ____________ ________ Pounds ________ Shillings and ________ Pence.			

____________ *Collector.*

____________ 19 ___

Examined & Entd. ____________ *Accountant and Comptroller-General.*

____________ 19 ___

RECEIVED this ________ day of ____________ 19 ___ of the Honourable Commissioners of His Majesty's Customs the sum of ____________ pounds ________ shillings and ________ pence, in full of this Debenture

NOTE.—This Debenture must bear an impressed stamp of the value
of 1*s*. 0*d*. if the amount does not exceed £10.
of 2*s*. 6*d*. „ „ „ „ £50.
of 5*s*. 0*d*. „ „ exceeds £50.

place duly appointed for such purpose, nor without the presence or authority of the proper officer of Customs, nor before due entry outwards of such ship and due entry of such goods, nor before due clearance thereof for shipment.

A ship exporting drawback, warehoused, or transhipment goods must not be of less than 40 tons register. By law, a ship must be *cleared inwards* (an operation performed by the officers on completion of the discharge of inward cargo) before shipment of outward cargo; but in practice, at the larger ports, the entry outwards is allowed to be deposited (by the master or his agent) at the time of the ship's report inwards, and export officers take care that no outward cargo is shipped until complete separation between inward and outward cargo is assured. Vessels discharging inward cargo at one or more ports in the United Kingdom may be entered outwards for a foreign destination, and may take on board export cargo provided it can be separated from the inwards cargo to the satisfaction of the officers. On the same conditions, goods may be carried coastwise in a vessel from foreign parts before the discharge of the whole of the foreign cargo, the prohibition in the Customs Consolidation Act having been repealed.

Form of Request

To the Surveyor or other proper Officer at the Port of ....

I request to ship on board the.............from.................

now bound for....................viâ[1] ....

the undermentioned goods to be discharged at.........................

Marks	Number of packages, etc.	Description of goods

[1] To be filled in when the vessel is to discharge at more than two ports.

Before the exportation of goods deposited in a bonded warehouse, or on which drawback is claimed, a bond for due exportation must be given by the exporter with sufficient sureties. A bond for this and other purposes may be in respect of a single transaction only, or it may be a General Bond to cover any number of transactions of the same kind. In the latter case, a Notice of Exportation only is required on each separate occasion.

A bond having been given, a Bond Warrant must be passed in order to release the goods from the warehouse. Spirits and unmanufactured tobacco are generally accompanied by a permit—a form describing the goods and stating number of packages it covers, a sort of voucher attached to the goods themselves. For direct exportation (i.e. shipment at the same port), the proprietor must prepare and hand in a Shipping Bill (Customs Form No. 64), and (in London) when the goods are conveyed wholly or in part by lighter this is supplemented by a Shipping Note (an advice to the Shipping Officer, Customs Form No. 58). In London, goods from the Customs warehouses carried by cart or lighter for direct exportation must be conveyed to the ship by a carman or a lighterman holding the licence of the Commissioners, or be accompanied by an officer at the proprietor's expense.

If the goods are removed for shipment at another port, they are advised officially by Dispatch. On this document the exporter or his agent (at the shipping end) makes a request to ship and prepares a Shipping Bill with (in London) a Shipping Note if required.

Any undue delay in conveying goods from warehouse to vessel renders the goods liable to an extended examination. and duty is claimed on any deficiencies.

A vessel must be *cleared outwards* at the Custom House before she can legally sail. For this operation, a Victualling Bill, containing a statement of all dutiable stores taken for use on the voyage, must be prepared. To this document a clearance label is affixed and is the authority for departure. A Bill of Health is issued to the master when required, certifying that the port he is leaving is free from epidemic diseases. For a British ship, the following documents have to be produced at clearance : Ship's Register, Outward Lights Receipt, Load Line Certificate, and Board of Trade Certificate.

For statistical purposes, even coasting vessels—vessels engaged in trade between ports of the United Kingdom—have to comply with certain requirements as to documents, but these are comparatively slight and can be easily ascertained on inquiry.

CHAPTER IX

Means of Transport: Canals, Railways, Tramways, Carriers, Ships, Aircraft —Rates of Carriage—Insurance, etc.

RAILWAYS of a kind have existed since 1759. Before that date, the only practical means of conveyance for merchandise were, in the then state of the roads, the great river systems of the country, and, early in the 17th century, in order to facilitate the haulage of goods to the waterways, the practice of laying down slabs of stone or blocks of timber flush with the surface of the roads began to be adopted. In this rough and ready method of overcoming the difficulties occasioned by the ever-deepening ruts our modern railways were foreshadowed. With the introduction and promotion of canal systems (as distinguished from river navigations) this method of making roads became more general, and in 1776 the Canal Companies themselves were being granted powers to make railways in connection with their properties. Iron was being substituted for wood and stone, and the broad level surface began to be abandoned in favour of grooved or flanged metals. The adoption in 1789 of a flanged *wheel* was a great step forward—probably the greatest improvement until the substitution of steam for horse haulage.

The connection between railways and canals has thus been close from the first. The growth of canals caused a corresponding growth of railways, and with the development of steam engines the infant soon outgrew the parent and became a powerful and successful rival. Indeed at one time there seemed to be cause for fearing that the relations would approximate to those existing between the lion and the lamb—with the lamb inside. In the years 1845-7 (the three mad years of railway speculation, when Parliament sanctioned no less than 580 new railways, many of which were never begun), nearly a thousand miles of canals passed under railway control. The railway policy is fairly obvious, and it has been the more successful owing to the fact that the canal proprietors, frightened by the prospect of impending bankruptcy as the result of railway competition, were only too glad to sell or to lease their systems to the railway companies.

In 1888 Parliament intervened with the Railway and Canal Traffic Act of that year, which empowered the Railway Commission, on being satisfied by an interested person that the canal rates levied by the railway companies were such as to divert traffic from the canal to the railway, to order the rates and tolls to be amended in such a way as appeared to them to be reasonable. This power is necessarily limited in effect, and as a matter of fact smacks somewhat of locking the stable door after the steed has gone, for by this time nearly a third of the four thousand miles of our inland waterways were owned by railways. To realize the full effect of this fact, it should be remembered that these railway-owned canals, some of them but "little better than ditches of mud and stagnant water," form parts of systems which should give through-communication between the great centres of commerce.

The advantages of canal transport—cheapness, immunity from risk of damage by shunting, etc.—when time is not of prime importance, need no demonstration. They were long ago recognized in France, Germany, and other Continental countries to such good effect that "it costs less to bring sugar from Hungary, thousands of miles across Europe to London, than to carry the same sugar over our own rails from London to Manchester." Even with the disadvantages our inland navigations have at present to contend with, they have carried in a single year as much as 40,000,000 tons of goods, and, although this may seem a small figure compared with the 300,000,000 tons carried by railways in the same period, it is a remarkable total when the difficulties are considered.

One of the greatest drawbacks connected with the canals is the manner in which they were constructed. Each navigation was undertaken as a purely local concern, and without regard to other systems of which it was destined to form a part. The consequence is that, even when there is through-communication, the gauge, capacity of locks, and depth of water vary in different sections, and it is, of course, the lowest capacity which sets the standard for the whole. As an illustration, a single instance may be given. One of the most important of our waterways is that between Liverpool and Hull, formed by the Liverpool and Leeds Canal, the Aire, and the Calder. The latter part of the route will accommodate vessels 120 feet long and drawing 7 ft. 6 in., while the earlier part can accommodate only boats of half that length and draught. Much interesting information on this subject will be found in Bradshaw's *Canals and Navigable Rivers of England and Wales.*

At present, the direction in which, exactly, reforms will take place, is but a matter of surmise, but, with the revived interest in the subject, with the advent of the motor boat on the one hand and motor road transport on the other, the pre-eminence of railways seems to be threatened, and it is hardly too much to say that the next few years will see considerable changes in the means of transport for merchandise. It is somewhat curious to note that, although railways were originally intended only for the carriage of goods, it was found, soon after their coming into general use, that the greater part of the revenue was derived from passenger fares. At the present time, however, about three-fifths of the receipts are derived from the carriage of goods.

For many years, a process of amalgamation of railway companies has been going on, and the railways of Great Britain were, under the Railways Act, 1921, organized into the following four groups : the Southern Railway, Great Western Railway, London Midland and Scottish Railway, and London and North Eastern Railway. If the time for nationalization comes, the change will be the simpler for this process. One important effect of this change is seen in the greater facilities for through-traffic, and, by the Railway and Canal Traffic Act of 1854, the duty of providing these facilities is laid upon the companies whenever possible, as well as that of avoiding undue or unreasonable preference in favour of any particular person or class of traffic. This prohibition of undue preference does not, however, prevent the Company from quoting special rates (*a*) to traders sending large consignments of goods at regular intervals (provided they are ready to give the same terms to any other person under the same conditions), or (*b*) between certain places when it can be shown that this is in the public interest.

The power of enforcing compliance with the provisions of the Act is vested in the Railway and Canal Commission, consisting of five Commissioners, two of whom are appointed by the Board of Trade, the other three being Judges who act *ex officio*. Any person receiving or sending, or desiring to send, goods by rail, who considers that he is being treated unfairly, or unreasonably, may apply to the Commission or lodge a complaint with the Ministry of Transport.

The earliest railways were apparently formed with the intention of common use in the same manner as high roads, and by law anyone can claim the use of a railway for his own engines and carriages—subject to conditions. That right has for many years been a dead letter, except for such instances as the provision of private wagons by the proprietors of collieries and similar undertakings. Any person, too, may lay down a branch railway or siding to communicate with the main line, and the Company are bound to make (at the cost of the person requiring the same) the necessary connections. This right is also subject to many qualifications, and private sidings are nearly always put in under agreement between the trader and the Company.

The power to act as carriers, and to charge for their services, was conferred by the Railway Clauses Consolidation Act of **1845**, which also provides that the Company shall not bear a greater liability than that of a common carrier. The Company may refuse to be common carriers of any particular class of goods, and, on their giving notice to the public to that effect, the procedure is governed by the provisions of the Traffic Acts under which "reasonable facilities" for the conveyance of such goods must be given. The goods are then carried under a special contract, the terms of which must be "just and reasonable." When the goods *are* accepted by the Company as common carriers, the acceptance implies insurance against loss or damage. When the loss or damage is due to natural causes, and could not have been prevented by any foresight, pains, or care reasonably to be expected, the carrier is not liable. Railway Companies are now obliged to provide facilities for the carriage of perishables by passenger train, subject to "reasonable regulations."

With reference to the question how far the notices published by railway companies with the intention of exempting themselves from liability in certain cases have the effect of special contracts, the position seems to be that the mere issuing of such notices does not exempt the company from liability as common carriers, but that, if notice is specifically given to the sender of the goods, it is binding in the same way as any other contract or agreement. The terms of such special contracts are generally printed on the consignment note which is signed by every person sending goods by rail, and it has been held that he is bound by such conditions thus brought to his notice whether he reads them or not. The following statement of the present position is from Preston's *Manual of Railway Law*—

"Railway Companies are bound to carry goods which they have facilities and appliances for carrying. Those goods which they profess to carry as common carriers they become insurers of. Those goods which they do not profess to carry as common carriers they become liable for, if lost or damaged through the negligence or default of their servants in receiving, forwarding, or delivering them, unless the goods are carried under a special contract. No mere notice is now held to be valid, or to operate as such special contract, but conditions may be incorporated into any contract between the Company and the owner or sender which is in writing, and signed by the latter; and to the extent to which these conditions are held to be just and reasonable the liability of the Company for the negligence or default of their servants is qualified."

Carriers have a lien on goods at common law in respect of charges for carriage. This does not, however, imply that they may dispose of such goods, but where goods are carried by special contract a clause is sometimes inserted giving the Company further powers, including the power of sale. Traders doing a regular business with a line of railway frequently open a Ledger Account with the company, and in such cases the agreement generally includes a clause giving the company a lien on goods for any money due on the account.

It is important to distinguish between the duties of railway companies as common carriers and as warehousemen. Where the company contract to deliver to the consignee, liability continues until delivery is effected, but where the Company do not undertake to deliver, the practice is for them to issue to the consignee an Advice Note stating the time within which the consignee is expected to take delivery of the goods. On the expiration of that time, the company cease to be carriers and become warehousemen with warehousemen's liabilities. That is to say they become liable only for loss or damage resulting from the negligence of themselves or their servants, and in the event of goods being (say) accidentally destroyed by fire, the loss will fall on the owner.

At any time during the transit of the goods, a consignor has the power to stop delivery to the consignee and to require that the goods shall be returned to himself. This right is termed "stoppage *in transitu*," and is exercised in the event of the insolvency of a buyer becoming known to an unpaid seller after the goods have been delivered to the carriers. If, however, the buyer has in the meantime sold the goods to a third party the consignor loses his right.

In the case of loss or damage on the railway, the proper person to apply for compensation is the owner of the goods, whether this be the consignor or the consignee, except that where the goods are carried under a special contract the right of action lies with the person with whom the contract was made. When goods are booked at through rates over the lines of more than one Company, the Company to whom the goods were delivered for conveyance can be sued for loss or damage, whether such loss or damage took place on their own line or not, unless the goods are carried under a special contract specifically exempting that Company from responsibility for the goods when they have passed off their system. In that case, an action would lie against the company on whose line the loss or damage occurred. When goods are consigned for a special purpose —such as a particular market, or for exhibition—it will facilitate the recovery of damages in the event of undue delay if notice of the special circumstances is given to the company at the time of the consignment. Special contracts frequently contain a condition to the effect that claims shall be made within a certain time. It is important, therefore, that examination of the goods should be made as soon as possible after delivery. In the case of certain animals, the liability is, in the absence of a declaration and the payment of insurance rates, limited to specified amounts laid down in the Railway and Canal Traffic Act of 1854.

For many classes of goods, two rates are quoted by railway companies, one of which is the ordinary common carrier's liability rate, and the other the "owner's risk" rate. As to which it is to the owner's advantage to employ must, of course, depend on the circumstances, the difference in the rates, the character of the goods, and their inherent liability to damage or otherwise, the exact conditions of the O.R. rate, and so on. The owner's risk rate does not imply the exemption of the company from the consequences of the wilful misconduct of their servants, but whether it would exempt the Company in the case of mere negligence would depend partly on the conditions of the contract and partly on the view taken by the Court. In the specimen on page 110 liability for wilful misconduct only is accepted (if proved).

L. M. S. RAILWAY

Consignment Note for Goods to be carried at Reduced Rates at Owner's Risk

The L.M.S. Railway Company hereby give Notice that they have two rates for the carriage of the undermentioned Goods, at either of which rates the said goods may be consigned, at the sender's option; one, the ordinary rate, when the Company take the ordinary liability of a Railway Company; the other, A REDUCED RATE, adopted when the Sender agrees to relieve the Company and all other Companies or persons over whose lines the goods may pass, or in whose possession the same may be during any portion of the transit, from all liability for loss, damage, mis-delivery, delay, or detention (including detention of Traders' Trucks), except upon proof that such loss, damage, mis-delivery, delay, or detention arose from wilful misconduct on the part of the Company's Servants.

To the L.M.S. RAILWAY COMPANY, ...*Station*, ...19

Receive and forward the undermentioned Goods, to be carried at the Reduced Rate, below the Company's ordinary rate, in consideration whereof I agree to relieve the **L.M.S.** Railway Company and all other Companies or persons over whose lines the Goods may pass, or in whose possession the same may be during any portion of the transit, from all liability for loss, damage, mis-delivery, delay, or detention (including detention of Traders' Trucks), except upon proof that such loss, damage, mis-delivery, delay, or detention arose from wilful misconduct on the part of the Company's Servants. And I also agree to the Conditions on the back of this Note. This Agreement shall be deemed to be separately made with all Companies or persons parties to any through rate under which the Goods are carried.

***Signature** of Sender or his Representative*.................................... *Address*....................................

Owner and Wagon No.	To what Station and Railway to be sent.	CONSIGNEE.		No. of Articles.	Description of Goods and Marks.	WEIGHT.				Charges paid on.			Who pays the Carriage.
		NAME.	ADDRESS.			T.	C.	Q.	lbs.	£	s.	d.	

Goods which may be required " To wait order " at any particular Station, must be so consigned.

A railway company cannot be compelled to carry aquafortis, oil of vitriol, gunpowder, lucifer matches, or any other goods which the Company may deem to be dangerous, and anyone sending such goods without distinctly marking the packages containing them, or otherwise giving notice of their nature to the Company, is liable, under the Railway Clauses Act of 1845, to a penalty of £20 to be forfeited to the company. The Explosive Substances Act, 1875, requires every railway company to make by-laws, subject to the approval of the Board of Trade, for the loading, conveyance, and unloading of the explosives named in the Act, and the Company is liable to penalties for irregular dealings with such goods; but the liability may be transferred to the consignor or consignee if it can be shown that the fault lies with either of them.

The Companies have given public notice that certain articles, such as acids, oily substances, gunpowder, matches, and products of petroleum, are, in the judgment of the Company, of a dangerous character, and "that they are not and will not be common carriers of any of them, and that they will carry them only at owner's risk, by special agreement and under special conditions."

The Companies have further given notice that certain goods, such as bisulphide of carbon and nitro-glycerine, are, in the judgment of the Company, dangerous, and that they will not carry them on any terms whatever.

For many articles included in the first-named class various special forms of consignment notes are provided, each with its special set of conditions, such as (1) that the company accept liability only for *wilful* misconduct, and (2) that the consignee removes the goods from the station within 24 hours after he has received the company's advice note of arrival.

By the Carriers' Act, 1830, common carriers are exempted from liability for the loss of or injury to any package containing certain specified goods, arranged in four classes, when the value exceeds £10, unless the nature and value of the contents are declared, and, if demanded, an increased charge paid. In consequence of a report by a Parliamentary Committee published in 1877, most of the principal railway companies bound themselves to charge uniform rates for such insurance. These rates apply whether the goods are conveyed by goods or passenger train, but parcels up to 28 lbs. in weight are insured only when sent by passenger train.

Under the Railways Act of 1921 a new tribunal, called the "Railway Rates Tribunal," was set up, and nearly all the powers of the old Railway and Canal Commission were transferred to it. It was also given many new powers, notably the settlement of the schedules and charges of the amalgamated companies. The tribunal consists of three persons; a lawyer is chairman, and the other two members have, respectively, railway and commercial experience.

The Act laid down an entirely new principle as governing the basis of charges for carriage. Under Section 58, the charges are to be based so as to yield an estimated amount of net revenue (called the "standard revenue") equal to the total net revenue in 1913 of all the companies now amalgamated, plus allowance for interest on new capital coming into use since 1913. The charges are to be periodically reviewed, and if the Tribunal finds that the actual net revenue of any company is substantially in excess of the standard revenue the excess is to be allocated, as to 80 per cent in reducing charges and as to 20 per cent to the company as profit. The standard revenue is then automatically to be increased by the 20 per cent mentioned.

To the Tribunal was also delegated the very important duty of reducing the complexity of the old rate books, which were alleged to contain more than 80,000,000 exceptional rates, many of them being obsolete. Since the passing of the Act, the Tribunal has been engaged in ascertaining the standards, and in hearing representations by organizations and by the railway companies as to traders' rates. Meanwhile the old book rates (which had been increased up to 100 per cent from September, 1920) have been successively reduced, subject to variation in numerous particular instances, so that many cases now approximate to pre-War levels.

As from 1st January, 1928, the Tribunal substituted an entirely new scheme of rates. New rate books were issued to every station in the United Kingdom, showing the mileage between pairs of stations. With a view to reducing the number of "exceptional" rates the old eight classes have been replaced by 21, and the actual rate can be found by applying the appropriate "class" scale to the ascertained mileage. The books show exactly how the rate is made up, the standard rates being "station to station," but there is a standard rate of cartage charges to be added whenever cartage is performed by the railway companies. A standard classification of goods, revised to meet modern conditions, has been officially published in these volumes.

The new charges are uniform throughout Great Britain, and for a given mileage the charge is the same irrespective of locality or direction. The plan on which the rates have been built up is interesting; formerly the charges on each railway were separately computed, but now a "zone" system is substituted under which for each mile over twenty miles the average charge per ton per mile decreases as the distance increases. All rates were increased by 5 per cent in October, 1937.

Exceptional rates have been drastically reduced in number, although it has been found impracticable to abolish them altogether. Where, however, an old exceptional rate is within 5 per cent either above or below the standard it has been cancelled and the standard charge applies. As a general rule those 5 per cent or more below the standard are being continued, and have been entered in the new books as actual chargeable figures, but those more than 40 per cent below the standard were referred in detail to the Tribunal for special decision in each case. Exceptional rates in excess of the standard have been reduced to standard.

The Tribunal has also arranged standard conditions fixing the liabilities of the companies respecting loss of, and damage and delay to, goods.

Where goods are sent by rail to a port for shipment, it is generally necessary to employ an agent there, to whom an advice is sent. The agent attends to the shipping of the goods, complies with the Customs and Dock or Harbour Board requirements, effects insurance on the goods when desired, and takes out Bills of Lading, which he sends to his principals with an account of charges, commission, etc. In order to prevent delay, trouble and expense, great care should be taken that sufficient and accurate information is given to the agent to enable him to perform the services required of him.

The rates for water carriage (freights) are liable to no such restrictions as apply in the case of railway transport, and the liabilities of a shipowner are not necessarily the same as those of a railway company or other land carrier. At the same time, the cargo is liable to risks which do not exist during carriage by land. It may happen, for instance, that, in consequence of war, or from some other cause, it is impossible to land the goods at the intended destination, and it may be necessary to sell them at some place other than that originally intended, for which purpose the captain becomes the agent of the owner of the goods—and, as such, bound to do the best he can. Or the goods may be lost altogether. If, through stress of weather, the captain finds it necessary to throw the cargo overboard, he incurs no liability by so doing. It is, therefore, a practically invariable rule to insure all goods sent over sea. Some questions connected with insurance will be dealt with in a later chapter; for the present, we concern ourselves with the relations between the shipper and the shipowner, but we may note in passing that, by the Sale of Goods Act, 1893, it is provided that "unless otherwise agreed, where goods are sent by the seller to the buyer by a route involving sea transit, under circumstances in which it is usual to insure, the seller must give such notice to the buyer as may enable him to insure them during the sea transit, and if the seller fails to do so the goods shall be deemed to be at his risk during such sea transit."

It is a very common thing now for railway companies to own steamboats. When this is so their liability does not differ, as regards the sea portion of a journey, from those of shipowners, even though traffic may be booked through partly by rail and partly by sea; and where a contract is made by a railway company to carry by sea, its liability is the same whether the goods are carried in vessels of its own or not. The land portion of a through journey is subject to the usual conditions of land carriage.

When a merchant hires the whole cargo space of a vessel, the agreement between himself and the shipowner is known as a Charter Party. This document (which presents some analogy to a lease of land) describes the vessel, the purpose for which she is let, and the terms of the letting, the first condition being that the ship is seaworthy and fit for the voyage. The terms of the contract may be such that the ship passes under the control of the charterer for the time being; but more usually it remains in the possession and under the control of the owners. A charterer is not bound to fill a ship with his own goods. He may sub-let a part of the space to another person, or may accept cargo from all and sundry who may present it, or the original owner may, of course, offer the ship for general freightage in the same way. In these latter cases, the

Bill of Lading is brought into use, and sometimes the two forms (Charter Party and Bill of Lading) are used in combination. Either form of contract is liable to a stamp duty of sixpence, which, in the case of a Bill of Lading, must be embossed before execution. The chartering of vessels is usually done through a ship-broker, whose business it is to negotiate and effect such contracts, and the Charter Party often contains a note of the commission payable to the broker by the owners. The Charter Party, when signed, is usually retained by the broker, who issues certified copies as may be required.

The importance of a Bill of Lading is largely due to its three-fold character, for it serves as a receipt for the goods, it fixes the terms of carriage, and it is a convenient and ready means of transferring the property in the goods while they are in transit.

Under the Carriage of Goods by Sea Act, 1924, the carrier is made responsible for the proper loading, stowage, and discharge of goods, and must issue to the shipper a bill of lading stating the apparent order and condition of the goods. The leading marks, the number, quantity, or weight, etc., must be stated as furnished by the shipper, and the latter is deemed to have guaranteed to the carrier the accuracy of the details furnished, and to have indemnified the carrier against loss, damage, or expense resulting from inaccuracies in such particulars.

When goods are sent for shipment, the document which takes the place of the railway consignment note is the Shipping Note addressed to the ship or dock company. This is accompanied by a form called the Mate's Receipt, which is signed by an officer of the ship and returned to the shipper. This is a necessary preliminary to the signing of the Bills of Lading by the captain or his agent—usually at the office of the latter. If the Mate's Receipt is signed without any remark thereon as to damage, it is understood that the packages are accepted as being in good external condition. Any note as to damage or imperfect condition is transferred to the Bill of Lading, unless the shipper, in order to obtain a " clean " bill, gives a letter of indemnity to the shipowner by which the latter is insured against claims for damage by the consignees. Forms of Bills of Lading, stamped or unstamped, can be obtained from a commercial stationer; but most steamship companies have their own forms which must be used for goods shipped by those lines. They are always drawn in sets of three or four, two of which are sent to the consignee by different routes, so as to provide as far as may be against the consequent trouble should one copy fail to reach its destination, for, unlike goods sent by rail, the goods will not be delivered except on production of evidence of ownership which the possession of the Bill of Lading supplies. Both of these copies must be stamped, and the discharge of one of them renders all other copies void. An unstamped copy is retained by the agent and handed by him to the captain with the ship's papers, and a fourth copy (which must be on stamped paper if it is to be available for use in any way except for reference) is usually retained by the shipper.

Freight is charged in various ways. It may be by weight, by measure, by the package, or by the lump, according to the character of the goods; and a " ton " may be a ton of 20 cwts. or of forty cubic feet. Cases of ordinary merchandise are generally charged by the last-named method.

An interesting judgment of Lord Ellenborough contained the following sentences: " The shipowners undertake that they will carry the goods to the place of destination unless prevented by the dangers of the sea or other unavoidable casualties; and the freighter undertakes that if the goods be delivered at the place of their destination he will pay the stipulated freight; but it is only in the event of their delivery at the place of destination that he engages to pay anything. If the ship be disabled from completing her voyage, the shipowner may yet entitle himself to the whole freight by forwarding the goods by some other means to the place of destination; but he has no right to any freight if they be not so forwarded, unless the forwarding of them be dispensed with, or there be some new bargain upon this subject. If the shipowner will not forward them, the freighter is entitled to them without paying anything. One party, therefore, if he forward them, or be prevented or discharged from so doing, is entitled to his whole freight; and the other, if there be a refusal to forward them, is entitled to them without paying any freight at all."

Unless the shipper has received notification from the shipowner to the contrary, the shipper is entitled to assume that the master is authorized to receive payment of freight.

When the consignee is drawn upon for the price of the goods, the Bill of Lading is handed to the banker with the draft and is attached to the draft with the other documents which go to make up a "Documentary Bill" (of Exchange). The foreign banker receiving such a Bill usually lands and warehouses the goods pending the discharge of the Bill.

A Bill of Lading is passed from one holder to another in the same manner as a Bill of Exchange; but whether it is "negotiable," in the same sense as a Bill of Exchange or a bank-note is negotiable, is a doubtful point. Some authorities hold that it is not, that the property therein is *assigned* by endorsement, but that the holder for the time being can have no better title, even though he may have given good consideration for it, than any previous holder have had; while many others describe the document as a negotiable instrument, provided the goods named in it are deliverable to the "order or assigns" of the shipper or consignee. A safe view to take would be that, although the rights under the contract may be *transferred*, no right can be *created* by a wrongful holder.

On the presentation of the Bill of Lading, the goods named therein will be delivered by the master of the importing ship, without risk to himself so long as he acts in good faith. Goods for which no Bill of Lading is presented may be landed and placed in the custody of some person at the discretion of the master. Goods arriving in England in so damaged a condition as to be worthless to the importer may be abandoned to the ship in lieu of freight.

The principal Customs requirements on importation have already been dealt with. The Merchant Shipping Act of 1894 empowers a shipowner to *enter* and *land* goods on arrival in the United Kingdom if the importer fails to do so within a specified time, and may give notice to any person as wharfinger or warehouseman in whose custody they are placed that they are subject to a lien for freight or other charges, and the wharfinger or warehouseman is bound to retain them until the lien is discharged; or, if he fails to do so, make good to the shipowner any loss thereby occasioned to him. If the lien is not discharged, and no deposit is made as prescribed by the Act, the wharfinger or warehouseman may—and if required by the shipowner shall—at the expiration of ninety days (or, if the goods are perishable, at such earlier period as he thinks fit) sell the whole or part of the goods, the sale having first been advertised and notice sent to the owner if his address is known. The proceeds, if any, after payment of all charges, are to be paid to the owner.

The same Act provides that the owner of a British sea-going ship shall not be liable to make good any loss or damage happening without his actual fault or privity in the following cases, viz.: (1) where any goods or merchandise, or other things whatsoever, taken in or put on board his ship are lost or damaged by reason of fire on board the ship; or (2) where any gold, silver, diamonds, watches, jewels, or precious stones, the true nature and value of which have not at the time of shipment been declared by the owner or shipper thereof to the owner or master of the ship in the Bills of Lading, or otherwise in writing, are lost or damaged by reason of any robbery, embezzlement, making away with, or secreting thereof.

The liability of a sea-carrier is limited by law to an aggregate amount of £15 for each ton of the ship's tonnage in respect of loss of life or personal injury, and an aggregate amount of £8 for each ton of the ship's tonnage in respect of damage to vessels or goods.

The law relating to shipment of dangerous goods is pretty much the same as in the case of similar goods sent by rail. The packages must be marked, and notice of their contents given to the master or owner at or before the time of shipment, and "for the purpose of this part of the Act, the expression 'dangerous goods' means aquafortis, vitriol, naphtha, benzine, gunpowder, lucifer matches, nitro-glycerine, petroleum, any explosives within the meaning of the Explosives Act, 1875, and any other goods which are of a dangerous nature." Any such goods sent or carried on board ship in contravention of the law may be thrown overboard by the master who incurs no responsibility by so doing. Grain and timber are subject to special provisions as to loading and carriage.

During recent years a means of transport which has come rapidly to the front is the commercial motor van. In many cases the costs of running are less than railway rates (including terminal charges), and where speed is an important factor the advantage is altogether with the motor van. Probably, however, its advantages are most apparent in connection with those business houses where definite deliveries at fairly frequent intervals are required between one branch and another, or between branches and headquarters; or where goods of small bulk have to be transported over relatively short distances.

Under the Road Traffic Act, 1930, Section 19, the hours worked by drivers of goods vehicles are limited and under the Road and Rail Traffic Act, 1933, Section 16, there is an obligation to keep a record, in prescribed form, of the work performed, journeys, loads, etc. Further, under the last-named statute all motor goods vehicles used in connection with trade require special licences. These fall into three classes according to the class of trade and area to be covered and are granted (subject to appeal to a special Tribunal) by Traffic Commissioners constituted under the 1930 Act. Further, under the Road Traffic Act, 1934, drivers of heavy goods vehicles must be specially licensed. Attention is directed to the remarks on page 308 as to third party insurance.

Transport by air is now rapidly developing for both passengers and light goods when speed is of great importance. The number of air routes in operation is increasing, and there has been a steady advance in the annual value of goods carried by this new form of transport.

The railway companies have taken power to engage both in road and in air transport, whether by direct action or by the means of acquiring share interests in operating companies.

CHAPTER X

Publicity through Posters, Newspapers, Mail Order Schemes, Prize Competitions, Free Samples, Exhibitions, Window Dressing, and by other means

THE inventive ingenuity of engineers and the organizing skill of industrial technicians appear, in these days, to have solved the problems of industrial production. That is to say, there are indeed few commodities the production of which cannot be expanded far beyond the limits of potential demand. The trouble from which the modern world suffers is not shortage of the power to produce, but lack of that effective means of demand called purchasing power. The consequence is that sellers in all markets are in a constant and intense state of competition. We must not forget that success in this struggle to find purchasers depends fundamentally on the sterling quality of the goods which are offered for sale, but the purpose of the present chapter is to offer some remarks on one of the weapons, to wit publicity, which modern organization has put into the hands of those whose business in life is salesmanship.

Before describing the various forms which publicity may assume, we must lay down two conditions which are to be regarded as governing the whole subject. First, publicity must be honest. A very wise man created the aphorism that it is possible to fool some of the people all the time, and all the people some of the time, but not all the people all the time. Advertisements which put forward dishonestly untrue statements about the goods advertised defeat themselves, certainly in the long run and possibly even in the short run. A dishonest claim which is "found out" is apt to create "bad will" as distinct from goodwill, and no commercial house can long survive if it is founded on a policy of thrusting into the hands of consumers goods which do not come up to the claims made for them. Secondly, publicity for goods or services must be backed by an efficient organization capable of meeting the demand which the publicity stimulates. All the efforts of advertising men are likely to be brought to nought and to be of no avail if, after they have put purchasers into a mood to buy, those purchasers are met with unwilling service or slip-shod execution of orders. It is true that "publicity pays," but only on the footing that the payee is willing to return good consideration for the payment.

Granted, therefore, that any given commercial organization is ready to "deliver the goods," it becomes necessary to consider how public demand may be stimulated and sustained. For present purposes we take for granted that a sufficient force of trained travellers is at disposal and that the potential territory of the sales is systematically mapped out amongst them; we also assume that the article offered for sale has a potential national, as distinct from a local, demand. The very first consideration is that there should be a plan, first formulated and then consistently followed. The fundamental basis of any plan must necessarily be financial and it follows that the directors, or other financial authority, of the business concern must decide at the beginning of the year (or other business "season") on a sum of money to be appropriated to the purposes of publicity, this sum not to be exceeded unless further authority is obtained beforehand. The next matter is to appoint an advertising manager who must, needless to say, work in close collaboration with the other departments of the business, especially the sales department.

The advertising manager will probably make it his first business to see that the goods themselves are presented to the public in a form so acceptable as to give advertising its maximum opportunity. The most important point here is the *description* of the goods, for, unless they can be described in such a way as to effect an instant and certain identification, the value of advertising must be largely lost. This is the underlying reason why "branding" is so popular. Under this system the goods are usually given a catchy name, self-descriptive of their quality; they are packed in an attractive and distinctive container so that the eye, even of the most careless person, can recognize them at a glance; the price of each size of container is standardized. If the brand can once be impressed on the public mind, retailers will find themselves being asked not simply for (say) "a pound of sugar" but for "a packet of Sweet-heart." Success along these lines results in the customers being saved trouble, the business of the retailer being easier to carry on and the sales of the wholesaler or manufacturer being increased and made more certain. Hence branding is a most important principle depending for its success on the choice of a suitable name and on clever bringing together of convenience and attractiveness in the general ensemble under which the goods are sold.

The various forms of publicity may conveniently be considered under separate headings as below but the reader will realize that, speaking generally, in practice more than one method is commonly put into force at the same time. We shall consider—

(*a*) Bill posting.
(*b*) Newspaper display.
(*c*) Mail order.
(*d*) Prize competitions.
(*e*) Free samples.
(*f*) Exhibitions.
(*g*) Window dressing.
(*h*) Miscellaneous.

(*a*) Bill Posting. There can be little doubt that this method (as well as newspaper display) can best be practised through the agency of a reliable firm of publicity agents. Advertising is now a regular profession which is in a position to attract the best artistic and literary ability and to employ these according to the best commercial skill as developed and informed by experience. In regard to poster display, and in regard to the formulation of matter to be included in newspaper publicity, the remuneration of the agent is usually by a negotiated fee; but for the actual placing of newspaper advertisements the agent usually looks for his remuneration to the newspapers concerned, from which (if he is a recognized practitioner) he will receive a special discount personal to himself. Needless to say, if a professional agent is employed, his advice (after due discussion) should be implicitly followed, for the agent himself cannot give his best service unless his ideas are allowed full scope.

If, on the other hand, our undertaking should decide to do its advertising wholly through its own paid advertising department, the following remarks will apply. First and foremost, poster advertising is suited only to articles which have a really popular appeal. Posters are looked at by the "masses" and it is unfortunately true that the average income per family in this country is much lower than the ordinary person imagines. Hence if posters are displayed in the attempt to sell articles which are either very expensive or which have an appeal only to a limited class of persons, then a large proportion of their address must be wasted since a great many of the people who read them cannot accept the invitation to buy, no matter how strongly they may wish. Further, if the article to be sold has a limited appeal in the sense that its number of uses is small, then again poster advertising would be of doubtful utility. For example, the manufacturer of a special tool, to be used in one small branch of the engineering trade, would obviously be ill-advised to spend money on posters to be displayed outside the geographical area of the particular trade. It is the same principle as that which dictates the foolishness of sending travellers to the tropics to sell fur coats.

There are many points about the production of the posters themselves which are worthy of mention. First and foremost, their message should be capable of being instantly conveyed without any ambiguity whatever. The ideal is that a glance out of the tail of an eye should convey very nearly as much as a prolonged inspection. Hence a general similarity of all matter issued by the same firm is indicated; for repetition of a similar appeal assists the public, almost unconsciously, to receive the suggestion which is offered. Posters should be bold and striking, and there is no reason why that quality should not conform with real beauty and artistic excellence; in fact, the public is becoming steadily more and more educated in the appreciation of artistic form and any offence against the principles of beauty is likely to react unfavourably on the popularity of the article advertised. Instant visibility is a matter of colour combination as well as of form. The wasp is a dangerous insect and Nature has protected it by boldly striped markings in black and yellow so that every other animal can recognize it at sight. It is not surprising that it is now found that black print on a yellow ground is well seen in almost any light and it is certainly for this reason that, for instance, the Automobile Association prints road direction signs in these colours. The Royal Automobile Club has chosen another effective scheme in blue letters on a white ground.

"Style" in advertising counts for very much, and the poster advertiser should aim at achieving distinctive individuality. A "slogan" or a "mascot," if happily conceived and if persistently associated with an advertiser's goods, may have almost unlimited publicity value. Examination of successful posters usually shows that they are so designed, in the pictorial sense, as to lead the eye to a representation of the goods or to something calculated instantly to suggest an idea associated with the advertised goods and with those goods only.

The appeal of the poster should be calculated to recall pleasurable ideas rather than to create repulsion and inhibition. We are all cowards in the respect that we would rather think of pleasure than of pain, and, just as it is better to reward a child for cultivating virtue than to punish him for following evil, so it is well for a salesman to emphasize the pleasure given by his goods rather than the displeasure entailed by not buying them. The moral is, for instance, that if we are selling an article beneficial to health it is better to emphasize its positive quality than to mention the disease from which it may protect. We would all rather see a picture of the (impossibly) lovely teeth of a beautiful girl than be reminded of the dentist's drill; and even a bottle of disinfectant, if wrapped like perfume, will attract a purchaser who might be repelled if reminded of microbes.

The actual posting of bills is usually undertaken by bill-posting contractors who, in most cases, rent hoardings and other sites in various localities. Their charges naturally vary with the size of the matter to be posted and it will accordingly be useful if we now mention a few of the technical terms which describe the various sizes of printing paper. Examples are—

Crown	20 in. × 15 in.
Double Crown	30 in. × 20 in.
Post	19¼ in. × 15½ in.
Double Post	31½ in. × 19½ in.
Double Large Post	33 in. × 21 in.
Demy	22½ in. × 17½ in.
Double Demy	35 in. × 22½ in.
Royal	25 in. × 20 in.
Super Royal	27½ in. × 20½ in.

Very large sheets are described as containing such and such a number of one or other of the basic sizes. Not all the bill-posting contractors are equally reliable and it is usually found advisable by advertising firms to appoint inspectors whose duty it will be to go round actually to see the posters displayed and to ascertain that the terms of the various contracts have been faithfully observed.

Modern conditions have brought into prominence the importance of public conveyances as advertising stations. Inside the vehicle the passengers are perforce seated for a considerable period with the announcements displayed right in front of them, while advertisements placarded on the outside are paraded up and down the streets, being thus displayed before many more people than would be likely to study a stationary poster.

(*b*) Newspaper Display. Publicity by means of displayed advertisements in newspapers involves three considerations. These are (1) the choice of the medium, (2) the positioning of the advertisement in the newspaper and its general lay-out, and (3) the writing of the textual matter, usually known as the "copy."

With regard to the choice of the newspapers to be patronized it is necessary to consider their total circulation, their class of circulation, and their charges. Total circulation was at one time a matter of considerable mystery but the tendency of modern newspaper ethics is now to make a frank disclosure of the circulation attained. It is now almost a commonplace for the larger newspapers to publish the precise terms of a certificate by their auditors showing the average daily (or weekly, monthly, as the case may be) circulation. The reader ought perhaps to be warned that the terms of these certificates should be looked at carefully; every newspaper has a "free" list and it is, also, inevitable that many of the copies sent to newsagents should afterwards be returned. The ideal certificate of circulation excludes all these free copies and deducts the returns as and when they come back.

Of much more importance than mere aggregate figures of circulation is the class of readers amongst whom the particular publication is current. It is obvious, for example, that there would be no point in advertising ladies' wear in a journal addressed exclusively to men. This is a matter on which it is difficult to lay down any very precise rules and perhaps it is here sufficient to say that the important matter of the choice of the right class of medium should engage the very anxious attention of the expert who is in control of the publicity.

The charges made by the various newspapers should be considered more in their relative than in their absolute aspect. That is to say, it is obviously better to spend one hundred pounds from which results accrue than ten pounds on an advertisement which brings forth no business. We shall be referring below to the important matter of "keying" but we remark here on the desirability of ascertaining by any possible means the results which accrue from every separate advertisement. The cost of the advertisement is then to be considered in relation to the profit which has been earned as a result. Under this head, of course, repeat orders are of particular significance.

When we refer to the "positioning" of an advertisement in a newspaper we have in mind the situation in which it is printed in the columns and pages of the publication. Almost without exception people buy newspapers in order to read the news and the consequence is that the most valuable advertising position is that which closely adjoins reading matter. The technical description of this position is "next matter." Clearly, the description "next matter" has varying degrees of value according to whether the advertisement is, as it were, an island entirely surrounded by news or is merely contiguous to news on one or other of its four sides. Thus an advertisement may be technically described as "under and next matter" or "next, under, and over matter." Further, the juxtaposition of news and advertising is especially valuable when it occurs in the top half of a page, for the reason that the eye is naturally first attracted to the headlines of the news matter. There is general agreement that the right-hand page of a newspaper is more valuable than the left-hand page and, in any case, the top outer corner is usually regarded as one of the best possible positions. Next to this the lower outside corners are regarded with favour. A position which cuts across the natural folding line of a newspaper is to be avoided. A "solus" position is one on a page which contains no other advertising matter. Sometimes certain pages are peculiarly adapted to receive advertisements of particular classes of goods; for instance, athletic goods may be well advertised on the pages reporting sporting events.

With regard to the "lay-out" of a newspaper advertisement there is a good working rule to the effect that an illustration of the goods should not occupy more than about one-third of the available space. Further, the elements of any picture should not exercise a "dispersive" effect; that is to say, human figures should be looking inwards and the various components of the goods should be so drawn as to lead the attention from one to the other. It is a great mistake to try to cram too much into the available space; it is far better to say a little in a compelling manner than to risk wearying the reader's attention by calling upon him for too great an effort. There is no doubt that "every picture tells a story" and, if every illustration issued by a particular advertiser can include a common component, the effect of its message is obviously increased to a very substantial degree.

Where the advertisement is to be printed on inferior paper any illustration should be produced in "open" effect. In this sense a drawing is "open" when the lines or dots of which it is composed are fairly wide apart. The reproduction of such drawings on common paper does not involve a blurred and smudgy effect. Where, however, the paper to be used is of better quality then half-tone or other blocks can be employed. The preliminary drawings should be executed in a size much larger than that ultimately to be used, as the photographic processes to be employed will achieve a much better sharpness of line in reducing than in enlarging.

Most pictorial advertisements are printed from "blocks." These may be either "process-line" or "half-tone." A process-line block is manufactured from a drawing. If desired this drawing can be done on a photograph, the latter being afterwards dissolved away by chemical means. The resultant drawing is then photographed and the negative is printed on to a sensitized surface of zinc. The zinc block is then immersed in acid which eats away the whole of the unprotected surface. An effect of tinting may afterwards be added by the cutting of dots and lines on that portion of the surface which has not been acted on by the acid. A half-tone block is manufactured in very much the same way except that the original drawing is photographed through a "screen." This screen produces small dots on the negative and, in consequence, by choosing carefully a suitable mesh for the screen different intensities of shading may be produced.

Where it is necessary to issue duplicate blocks to a number of publications simultaneously, it becomes necessary to produce "stereos" or "electros." A stereo is made by pressing a block into papier-mâché. Molten type metal is then poured into the mould thus produced. An electro is made by pressing a block into a wax mould which is then black-leaded and immersed in a chemical bath which has the effect of plating it with a very fine film of copper. This copper shell is then filled with molten metal and the effect is to produce a type face with a very high degree of durability and sharpness.

Colour printing is usually effected by the "three-colour" process. Blocks are made by taking three different photographs of the subject, respectively through yellow, red and blue filters. Printings from these three blocks, in the colours indicated, are then very carefully superimposed one upon the other. For certain classes of advertisements lithography is used. This involves drawing upon a prepared surface of stone in a greasy pigment. The stone is then flooded with acid which eats away the stone wherever there is no grease. Printing is then effected by pressing paper between the stone and a roller.

It remains to consider the textual matter which accompanies pictorial advertisement. There is more skill in the composition of this than is generally believed. One golden rule is that "brevity is the soul of wit," and one of the marks of amateur composition is that it runs to prolixity. The head-line is probably the most important part of the copy, for its purpose is to attract the interest of the reader. As far as possible the head-line should concentrate within itself the essence of the matter which follows. The body of the copy must maintain and, if possible, increase the interest created by the head-line, and the design of the writer must be to carry the reader with him to the very last word, for it is at that point that the final decision whether or not to buy the goods is formed in the reader's mind. It is hardly necessary to add that the appeal should be directed to the very person of the reader himself and an effort should be made to leave him in no doubt upon any of the vital points connected with the goods and his need therefor. The price should certainly be mentioned and where this is subject to variation for special qualities, etc., the advantages attaching to the higher priced goods should be indicated.

Modern printers describe the size of their type on the "point" system. A "point" is one 72nd part of an inch. Hence 18-point type is that of which the face is attached to a body one-quarter of an inch deep. Tables are available which show the number of words of the various type sizes which may be expected to occupy one square inch of paper. Thus a square inch will take something between four and seven words of 18-point type, the variation being due to the amount of space allowed between lines. The actual printing surface of type is known as its "face," and there is a very large number of different varieties of design, each having a technical name, in common use. Much depends on the choice of a suitable face for displayed matter and the advice of a skilled printer on the point should be obtained.

It is highly desirable, where possible, to "key" an advertisement. A key is an indication which enables the advertiser to connect a particular inquiry or sale with a particular advertisement. The object in view is twofold; first, the advertiser desires to judge the comparative values of different pieces of copy and, second, he desires to assess the drawing powers of the various newspapers in which he advertises. Keying devices are legion. The advertiser may be requested to write to department 1 or department 2 or to such a number in a building; or, again, he may be requested to send for booklet A or pamphlet B. Another common method is to publish an application form or "coupon" with the advertisement. This coupon will contain a key mark and, if the inquirer uses the form, it is perhaps the most effective device known.

Where newspaper advertising is practised it is necessary to set up a careful system whereby the charges made by the newspapers may be checked. It should be the duty of the publicity department to see that they obtain a specimen copy of all advertisements. One means of effecting the necessary check is to prepare, at the moment when an order is given to the newspaper, a card somewhat as illustrated in Form No. 11 on page 130. The head of the card (which is signalled for the month of insertion) contains particulars of the newspaper and of the advertisement, and it is possible for the clerk to see from the specimen copies that the advertisement ordered has duly appeared. When publication has been completed in accordance with the contract, the invoice received by the accounting department can be certified from the card and a suitable note be made on the latter.

(*c*) Mail Order. Another distinct use of newspaper publicity is the creation of "mail order" business. Under this scheme goods are advertised at a clearly stated price and purchasers are asked to send their money by post, in return for which immediate dispatch of the goods is promised. There are several points about this method of trading which require serious consideration. Obviously it can be practised only where the goods are capable of very specific

FEB

Date order	Quantity	Grade	Begins	Expires	Amount	Rebate	Am't P'd	Date P'd

(*Form No.* 11)

description indeed, and it is therefore usual to give a picture (often bearing a number or symbol) as part of the announcement. The main point in mind, however, is the necessity of setting up the most careful routine for dealing with the orders when received, for any failure in prompt delivery must necessarily create suspicion in the mind of the person who has remitted the money, and even if this is later removed the damage has been done and the probability of a repeat order will often have been destroyed. Further, there is always a danger of peculation within an office where hundreds or thousands of letters containing heterogeneous forms of remittance are received by every post. Hence, rigid routine must be the order of the day, and every effort must be made to secure a constant and uninterrupted flow in dealing with the orders. Form letters must be prepared for dealing with cases where, for one reason or another, it is not possible to supply the goods, but, obviously, it is highly desirable that this necessity should not often arise. A very important point is to set up an organization for dealing with queries. Experience shows that a surprisingly large number of people will send money yet omit their address, or enclose cheques which they have forgotten to sign or misunderstand the price or write in a confused way about the goods they really want. Every one of these cases demands the instant attention of an intelligent member of the staff because, obviously, each one must be dealt with according to its particular circumstances and, what is more, be so dealt with as not to destroy the trading connection which the would-be purchaser desires to set up.

This form of trading involves the necessity of paying particular attention to the packing of the goods in such a way that they will receive no damage from the method of transit chosen. Further, with regard to the transit itself, it is very important that proof of dispatch should be preserved, lest any dispute should afterwards arise. It is worthy of mention that the arrangements made in recent years whereby the Post Office will accept, subject to certain conditions, parcels under the "pay on delivery" plan, have greatly facilitated in many instances the practice of mail order trading.

Finally, the mail order plan lends itself in a very marked degree to the practice of "keying" advertisements. Needless to say, a very careful record should be kept, in all possible cases, of the results from advertising in any particular newspaper. In this connection it is most important to observe that a repeat order is far more significant than a first order. It is highly probable that a first order does not yield sufficient profit to cover the cost of the relative advertisement but, if a customer follows this up by entering into a regular course of dealing, the advertising may be regarded as the sowing of very fruitful seed.

(*d*) Prize Competitions. Most of us like to think that we are above the appeal of "something for nothing" but many of us must admit that, when it comes to the point, we find difficulty in refusing offers where the promise is more prominent than the price. The purpose of prize competitions is really to take advantage of this weakness of human nature and clever advertisers induce consumption of their goods by holding out an expectation of a lucky reward following a relatively insignificant effort. The particular kind of competition proposed has usually some clear connection with the goods which are being advertised. The competitor is asked to suggest a slogan, or to colour a picture of the goods or of a mascot, or to place several different advertisements of the goods in order of popularity, etc. It is usually a condition of entry that a voucher should be sent which can be obtained only on purchasing the goods, or, if this method is not adopted it will usually be found that the entry must be sent in on a form clipped from one of the newspaper advertisements of the goods. The competition itself is usually widely advertised and the conditions are often cleverly devised so as to allow a judicious time-interval between entry and the announcement of the result; the theory is that during that period the entrant has the goods in mind and is probably talking about them to his friends. It is necessary under this head to add a word of caution. In every competition there must be an element of real skill in order that a contravention of the Gaming Acts may be avoided.

(*e*) FREE SAMPLES. One means of bringing new and special goods to the notice of potential consumers is the offer, through the newspapers, of a free sample to applicants fulfilling certain conditions. The most general form of these conditions is the filling up of a coupon clipped from the advertisement and (needless to say) bearing a "key" indication. In other cases the offer made is to supply the applicant or his friends with free samples on surrender by the applicant of a voucher included with the goods which have been purchased. A trader undertaking this form of publicity obviously runs considerable risk and, generally speaking, the practice should be adopted only where the trader is certain that his goods are so special that they will carry an instant appeal. There is, of course, the risk that an intelligent applicant may reason that if the trader can afford to give goods away they cannot be of much real value and he will be bound to make a comparison with their presumably low cost, and the price charged to him in the shops. There is also the possibility that persons may obtain a continual supply of goods through the simple device of employing fictitious names or of using the good offices of their intimate friends. For this reason "free sample" offers are usually made for short periods only and are best made in newspapers appealing to a very "likely" class of persons.

(*f*) EXHIBITIONS. In the publicity of some trades, exhibitions occupy a position of the very highest importance. It is traditional that if the mountain will not come to Mahomet then Mahomet must go to the mountain. To take one example only, motor car manufacturers have seen the force of this dilemma and, by combining together to give an exhibition at a stated time of the year, they save the potential consumer the trouble of perambulating scores of widely separated showrooms by bringing together under one roof prepared specimens of their newest models. There are similar manifestations in the engineering, shipbuilding, and other "heavy" trades.

There can be no doubt that this method of publicity is really effective both in stimulating trade and in enabling manufacturers mutually to profit by comparison of one another's products. From the retailers' and distributors' point of view, however, there is one very grave drawback. The exhibition takes place only at one stated time of the year or season and it is natural that consumers should defer their purchases until they have had an opportunity of inspecting the exhibition. The method of publicity accordingly induces all the evils of "peak periods" and certainly tends to kill business at other times.

A variant of the exhibition plan, calculated to avoid the objections cited above, is the appointment by manufacturers of exclusive distributing agents. The showrooms of these agents then constitute a kind of perpetual exhibition and it is, of course, to the interest of the manufacturer to offer to the distributor financial and other inducements to take into stock, for window display and demonstration, the newest models as and when they are produced by the factory.

(*g*) Window Dressing. The modern shopkeeper has discovered that he cannot expect his customers to ask for goods which the customer cannot see. As the converse of this proposition he has further discovered that if goods are suitably displayed in the sight of the potential customer then sales will very probably follow. It is hardly necessary to add that effective display is one of the real forms of art, a form moreover where the expert is easily superior to the amateur. It is inevitable that the small shopkeeper should have neither the personal skill to display goods in the most effective form nor the financial power to employ an expert of the first order. In consequence a very effective plan has come into common use whereby the manufacturer co-operates with the retailer. At the inception of such a scheme the retailer is informed that the manufacturer proposes to undertake a special campaign of publicity in the retailer's district. The manufacturer then carefully prepares the ground by local newspaper or poster publicity (or by both). At an arranged date this publicity begins to announce that Mr. Blank, retailer in the selected town, stocks the particular goods. At this point of time the manufacturer sends an expert window dresser to the retailer and the result is a very prominent display of the manufacturer's goods. Under such a plan it is obvious that both the retailer and the manufacturer may, given suitable conditions, derive mutual benefit.

(*h*) MISCELLANEOUS. The forms of publicity which have above been described do not, of course, exhaust all the possibilities. One modern development is collective advertising. For example, there are good professional reasons why individual members of the Stock Exchange should not advertise; nevertheless, the Stock Exchange itself takes steps to warn investors that they should deal only through members of the Exchange. Similar steps have been taken in recent years by opticians, photographers, and architects. Other examples in a similar field might be cited in the "beer is best" and "eat more fruit" campaign. The (now defunct) Empire Marketing Board was a governmental attempt to stimulate, through publicity, trade between the component parts of the Empire.

Mutual advertising is a pleasing modern development. Thus a very well-known Oxford Street store occasionally devotes space to mentioning the names of its friends and neighbours. Not far from the place where these words are being written there are two departmental stores, traditionally fiercely competitive; the tradition has not prevented them from arranging to place on each building flood-lights which illuminate the other. The obvious result is that the whole street is brightly lighted and the public has been quick to recognize a "shopping area." The recent technical advance in, and cheapening of, electric light has popularized illuminated displays of many kinds. Down to a short while ago these mostly took the form of ordinary bulb lamps arranged so as to form letters or pictures and from this it was an easy development to produce apparent motion by making the separate lamps successively appear and disappear through the medium of clockwork switching mechanism. This scheme has now been superseded to a great extent by the invention of the Neon light which produces brilliantly coloured displays in tubes charged with a suitable gaseous content. Although the voltages required are very high (and careful protection is therefore necessary), running costs are quite low and the illumination is so brilliant that the advertising value continues even during sunlight. A later invention which supplements, but does not supersede, the Neon light is the principle of flood-lighting. Artistic posters can now be arranged so that they can be seen both by ordinary daylight and by white or coloured flood-lighting after darkness has set in. Enamel plates have their usefulness in such confined places as railway stations, public passage-ways, etc., but they require periodical renewal because in course of time they become dirty or defaced by rust, etc., and obviously a disreputable tablet is a very poor form of advertisement. Attempts are now being made to adapt poster advertising to the medium of the aeroplane. On cloudless days daring pilots climb very high and write in smoke upon the face of the firmament. Others in all weathers drag banners at the tail of their machine which can be read from below. It is perhaps a matter of opinion, but doubt may be expressed whether these forms of publicity are really valuable. On the calmest day the smoke writing can last but a limited period and it is questionable whether its novelty will not quickly wear off. There are persons, too, in whom is aroused a feeling of resentment at the flaunting noisiness of the low-flying "banner" aeroplane, and here again it is distinctly doubtful, from the point of view of the advertiser, whether the game is worth the candle.

Advertising by broadcasting is excluded from the British stations but is freely practised on the continent of Europe and in America. Many British firms take advantage of stations radiating from continental places and they presumably consider that this form of publicity pays. There is, however, a widespread impression that the practice can be overdone and it seems doubtful whether radio advertising, for the British market, has any real future.

CHAPTER XI

Systems of ascertaining amounts due for Wages and Salaries—Various modes of checking time and the like, including Mechanical Accessories

THE accurate recording of time worked by the employees of a firm is of importance not merely from its financial aspect, but also because doubts cast upon it are amongst the most fruitful sources of irritation, and oft-times are the commencement of serious trouble with workmen. The larger the Works, the greater the preparations which must be made, and it behoves the up-to-date Manager to study carefully the various methods which have been adopted and to select that which seems most suitable to his own particular requirements.

To treat the office staff first—many Managers dislike the institution of an Attendance Book, and it must be confessed that it is disagreeable to have to impose such a check upon a staff, each member of which should be capable of being trusted in such a matter. Stern experience, however, calls for such a book in every well-organized office, and the book in itself has a helpful effect in encouraging punctuality, as well as in furnishing at times necessary information with reference to periods of absence through illness, holidays, etc. The specimen on p. 137 will be found to be a very general form adopted for such book.

In many offices, it is the custom to allow a certain number of minutes' "grace," generally five or ten, after which a red line is ruled, and later entries require explanation. The Attendance Book should be inspected and initialed *every* morning by some appointed officer, generally the Chief Clerk or Principal Assistant, and in large offices a weekly summary is made out of the time lost by each clerk after the "grace" period. On these summaries, the name of a regular offender becomes prominent, and he attains the unwelcome privilege (in such circumstances) of an interview with the Manager. This will be found to have the necessary effect in all except unusual cases, in which it may become necessary to dismiss a gross offender as an example.

Some Managers, where the clerical staff is large, prefer that the recording of time should be automatic so as to obviate any chance of favouritism, on the one hand, on the part of the clerk entrusted

ATTENDANCE BOOK

....19

Signature	Arrived	At Lunch		At Tea		Left	Remarks
		From	To	From	To		

(*Form No.* 12)

with the booking of the time each clerk puts in an appearance, or, on the other hand, of inaccurate times being put down where the system is that each clerk " signs on " and records his own time. There are several clocks of an inexpensive nature which enable each clerk to write his name and which automatically print the time the signature is affixed.

In the case of a large Works or Factory, any system either of *personally* signing attendance books or of autograph recording is, of course, quite impracticable, and the general practice is to record the time either by automatic time clocks or by the tally system.

This latter method is still used in many Factories and Works in this country, and is operated in several different ways. One of these consists in each workman having a distinctive number assigned to him on the books of the firm and being supplied with four brass tallies of different sizes, each bearing his number, thus—

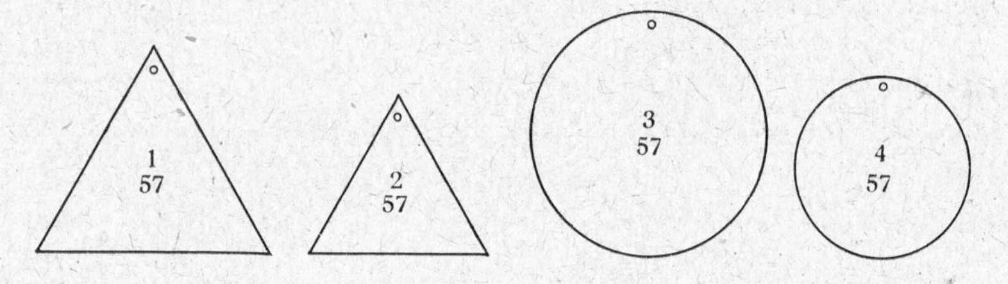

The first tally is dropped by the workman, whose distinctive number it bears, into a slit in a box which is placed near the gates when these are opened prior to the hour for commencing work, say 8 a.m. When all the workmen present by 8 a.m. have deposited their tallies, a spring controlling a shutter over the slit is released, the slit is closed and only the key held by the Wages Clerk can re-open it. The box is then sent to the Wages Department.

The second tally is used by those workmen who are too late for the first box and who are allowed to enter the Works at a subsequent time, which varies in different shops, some admitting them half an hour later, others making them " lose a quarter " (of a day). The slit in this second box is just sufficiently large to admit the second tally, and this slit is again closed at the expiry of the allotted time exactly as in the case of the first box.

In some Works, in which late comers may be the cause of expensive

COMBINED WEEKLY TIME AND WAGES SHEET

Reduced facsimile from Dey Time Register showing four registrations per day for six days. Any number of records per day can be provided.

No.	Friday Mrn IN	Friday Dinner OUT	Friday Dinner IN	Friday Even OUT	Saturday Mrn IN	Saturday Dinner OUT	Saturday Dinner IN	Saturday Even OUT	Monday Mrn IN	Monday Dinner OUT	Monday Dinner IN	Monday Even OUT	Tuesday Mrn IN	Tuesday Dinner OUT	Tuesday Dinner IN	Tuesday Even OUT	Wednesday Mrn IN	Wednesday Dinner OUT	Wednesday Dinner IN	Wednesday Even OUT	Thursday Mrn IN	Thursday Dinner OUT	Thursday Dinner IN	Thursday Even OUT
1	758	1232	127	534	58	1233			59	1232	128	531	759	1234	130	530	758	1235	130	533	757	1231	128	531
2	758	1233	127	535	58	1233			59	1232	130	534	758	1234	130	531	756	1235	130	533	757	1231	128	531
3	759	1231	129	537	58	1232			57	1231	128	532	756	1237	130	532	758	1234	130	535	757	1232	128	531
4	757	1233	128	535	57	1231			59	1233	129	535	758	1234	128	533	759	1237	127	535	757	1236	130	534
5	758	1234	130	535	00	1234			00	1236	130	537	758	1237	128	535	758	1239	129	537	759	1234	130	536
6	757	1232	129	536	00	1231			57	1237	127	535	756	1238	130	536	758	1236	130	535	758	1233	129	538
7	755	1231	127	538	59	1233			55	1234	128	534	754	1235	130	535	759	1233	130	534	758	1236	127	536
8	758	1232	130	536	801	1234			57	1237	128	532	756	1238	129	534	758	1231	129	538	759	1238	129	535
9	758	1233	130	537	58	1233			59	1238	129	532	759	1235	128	537	758	1233	127	534	759	1236	130	534
10	759	1231	129	537	59	1231			00	1238	130	533	759	1234	130	538	759	1232	128	534	800	1235	128	534
11	759	1231	130	538	00	1234			59	1237	128	535					932	1235	128	536				
12	800	1233	127	536	00	1235			57	1238	129	535	758	1237	130	538	758	1233	130	537	759	1233	127	536
13	800	1234	130	732	58	1233			58	1238	130	534	758	1231	130	537	800	1231	130	537	800	1236	129	535
14	800	1232	129	537	59	1235			759	1233	129	531	756	1234	128	535	800	1234	130	535	800	1238	129	534
15	757	1232	130	734	57	1234			00	1235	130	534	754	1235	127	536	800	1236	129	536	758	1237	130	533
16	759	1235	130	735	58	1236			59	1233	129	536	756	1233	128	537	757	1236	127	538	759	1238	130	535
17	800	1233	131	535	59	1237			57	1232	129	534	759	1235	130	539	758	1238	126	538	759	1239	130	534
18	800	1235	128	732	58	1235			59	1235	129	532	759	1233	128	535	758	1234	132	534	759	1237	129	533
19	800	1236	130	537	59	1233			59	1238	130	535	758	1233	127	537	757	1233	126	536	759	1235	128	531
20	758	1235	130	537	59	1235			800	1234	128	536	756	1235	129	535	759	1233	130	538	759	1237	130	534
21	757	1234	128	733	00	1236			802	1232	127	534	758	1236	130	537	759	1231	129	538	759	1239	130	532
22	759	1232	130	732	00	1234			59	1234	129	536	800	1236	129	538	759	1235	127	536	759	1240	130	534
23	758	1232	130	734	58	1232			00	1235	130	534	758	1237	127	537	758	1237	130	535	800	1240	130	534
24	758	1235	128	538	58	1234			00	1233	130	538	800	1235	128	535	759	1237	130	539	800	1238	130	533
25	757	1233	127	536	58	1236			58	1232	132	533	800	1233	130	538	758	1238			758	1236	128	531
26	758	1232	129	538	801	1234			56	1230	128	535	758	1231	128	539	759	1236	128	539	759	1238	128	533
27	757	1233	130	538	59	1232			58	1232	126	538	757	1233	127	538	759	1233	127	537	759	1240	130	534
28	756	1230	130	538	59	1234			59	1235	127	535	758	1234	125	534	757	1232	127	535	758	1241	128	534
29	758	1234	129	536	58	1235			59	1232	129	534	758	1232	127	537	801	1232	127	535	759	1242	127	533
30	759	1232	130	534	59	1233			00	1231	130	537	759	1230	129	538	759	1234	128	539	758	1238	129	536
31	800	1233	128	538	58	1235			58	1233	128	539	757	1232	127	536	800	1238	130	537	758	1238	130	536
32	757	1232	126	538	57	1233			57	1231	129	536	759	1145			800	1232	132	535	759	1240	128	533
33	759	1234	128	536	59	1235			58	1233	128	538	757	1232	129	536	800	1237	129	538	759	1242	127	531
34	757	1234	126	534	00	1236			59	1234	129	536	756	1234	130	538	759	1233	128	536	758	1240	128	534
35	756	1233	125	537	59	1233			58	1236	129	539	758	1232	130	536	800	1231	127	535	755	1238	129	536
36	758	1235	127	533	00	1233			56	1233	128	539	758	1233	128	534	800	1231	129	534	757	1236	129	534
37	759	1233	128	532	58	1231			758	1231	129	537	756	1234	129	533	800	1233	130	536	758	1239	129	531
38	757	1233	130	535	00	1234			756	1233	130	540	758	1232	128	531	801	1231	128	536	757	1240	130	534
39	758	1235	128	533	00	1236			758	1234	129	538	755	1235	126	535	758	1232	127	533	758	1238	129	535
40	757	1235	126	536	58	1233			759	1235	129	535	757	1233	128	532	757	1234	129	531	757	1236	127	533
41	755	1234	124	537	56	1231			758	1233	130	537	756	1231	129	534	759	1231	130	531	758	1235	126	531
42	757	1235	122	534	59	1234			759	1231	129	538	755	1233	127	535	759	1230	129	533	759	1233	128	534
43	758	1233	126	532	00	1233			758	1233	127	533	801	1231	126	533	759	1232	127	535	759	1235	129	537
44	756	1232	129	535	58	1232			800	1235	129	535	756	1233	127	531	757	1233	129	534	757	1238	129	533
45	757	1234	130	537	59	1234			800	1232	130	531	758	1232	129	534	800	1231	127	532	758	1234	129	531
46	758	1236	127	534	58	1232			758	1234	129	533	758	1234	127	532	759	1233	126	534	758	1233	127	532
47	758	1237	130	537	59	1234			756	1235	128	536	758	1239	125	534	759	1234	129	535	757	1235	126	535
48	800	1235	128	538	58	1235			758	1233	130	534	758	1236	129	536	757	1231	132	533	755	1233	127	532
49	758	1234	129	535	56	1233			759	1231	130	537	800	1231	130	534	759	1230	129	532	756	1231	129	531
50	757	1232	130	537	59	1231			800	1233	130	534	758	1234	130	532	757	1232	130	533	758	1233	127	533

No.	NAME	Ordinary Time	Overtime	Pay on	RATE	£	S	D	Less Ins	Nett Wages £	Nett Wages S	Nett Wages D	No.
1	Shanks C.	47		47	1/8	3	18	4	6½	3	17	9½	1
2	Oldfield J.A.	47		47	1/8	3	18	4	6½	3	17	9½	2
3	Wale J.	47		47	1/6	3	10	6	4	3	10	2	3
4	Jones C.	47		47	1/8	3	18	4	6½	3	17	9½	4
5	Blake M.	47		47	1/6	3	10	6	4	3	10	2	5
6	Bone Geo.	47		47	2/-	4	14	:	6½	4	13	5½	6
7	Miles A.E.	47		47	2/-	4	14	:	6½	4	13	5½	7
8	Clarke S.	46¾		46¾	1/7	3	14	:	6½	3	13	5½	8
9	Masters F.	47		47	1/8	3	18	4	6½	3	17	9½	9
10	Richardson E.	47		47	1/8	3	18	4	6½	3	17	9½	10
11	Collins F.F.	28¼		28¼	1/9	2	9	5	6½	2	8	10½	11
12	Alexander E.	47		47	1/9	4	2	3	6½	4	1	8½	12
13	Abbott T.H.	47	2	49½	1/8	4	2	6	6½	4	1	11½	13
14	Patey W.S.	45		45	1/8	3	15	0	6½	3	14	5½	14
15	Lee C.	47	2	49½	2/-	4	19	0	6½	4	18	5½	15
16	Dawson P.	47	2	49½	1/7	3	18	5	6½	3	17	10½	16
17	Cook T.	46¾		46¾	1/7	3	14	0	6½	3	13	5½	17
18	Hooper H.	46¾	2	49¼	1/7	3	18	0	6½	3	17	5½	18
19	Squire J.	47		47	1/8	3	18	4	6½	3	17	9½	19
20	King A.	47		47	2/-	4	14	0	6½	4	13	5½	20
21	Bowman L.	46¾	2	49¼	1/8	4	2	1	6½	4	1	6½	21
22	Bolton F.	47	2	49½	2/-	4	19	0	6½	4	18	5½	22
23	Lloyd L.	47	2	49½	1/7	3	18	5	6½	3	17	10½	23
24	Hopkins A.	47		47	1/7	3	14	5	6½	3	13	10½	24
25	Blanchard V.	42¾		42¾	2/-	4	5	6	6½	4	4	11½	25
26	Parsons P.	46¾		46¾	1/8	3	17	11	6½	3	17	4½	26
27	Rowbotham K.	47		47	1/8	3	18	4	6½	3	17	9½	27
28	Repton B.	47		47	2/-	4	14	0	6½	4	13	5½	28
29	Benham D.A.	46¾		46¾	1/8	3	17	11	6½	3	17	4½	29
30	Hughes H.	47		47	2/-	4	14	0	6½	4	13	5½	30
31	Vickers Geo.	47		47	1/7	3	14	5	6½	3	13	10½	31
32	Andrew A.	42		42	1/7	3	6	6	6½	3	5	11½	32
33	Barrett M.	47		47	1/8	3	18	4	6½	3	17	9½	33
34	Cunliffe L.	47		47	1/8	3	18	4	6½	3	17	9½	34
35	Moore Geo.	47		47	2/-	4	14	0	6½	4	13	5½	35
36	Jerome C.	47		47	1/8	3	18	4	6½	3	17	9½	36
37	Steventon G.	47		47	1/8	3	18	4	6½	3	17	9½	37
38	Turner K.	46¾		46¾	1/9	4	1	10	6½	4	1	3½	38
39	Chamberlain F.	47		47	2/-	4	14	0	6½	4	13	5½	39
40	Ankin A.	47		47	2/-	4	14	0	6½	4	13	5½	40
41	Murphy H.	47		47	1/9	4	2	3	6½	4	1	8½	41
42	Goodman B.	47		47	1/8	3	18	4	6½	3	17	9½	42
43	Boston G.	46¾		46¾	2/-	4	13	6	6½	4	12	11½	43
44	Hook J.W.	47		47	2/-	4	14	6	6½	4	13	5½	44
45	Smith J	47		47	1/8	3	18	4	6½	3	17	9½	45
46	Parker I.	47		47	2/-	4	14	0	6½	4	13	5½	46
47	Brown Wm.	47		47	1/9	4	2	3	6½	4	1	8½	47
48	Cheeseman V.	46¾		46¾	1/8	3	17	11	6½	3	17	4½	48
49	Tomkins K.	47		47	2/-	4	14	0	6½	4	13	5½	49
50	Edwards E.	47		47	1/8	3	18	4	6½	3	17	9½	50
	TOTAL									202	11	6	

WHEN ORDERING PLEASE QUOTE REFERENCE NO. 2829

Week ending February 5th 1934

The time of late-comers, employees leaving early or working overtime, is automatically printed in red ink, regular time records printed in blue.

(Form No. 13)

(B.1545)

machinery standing idle, there is a system by which a dilatory workman, who is perhaps only a few minutes late, may purchase a ticket from the gatekeeper, which ticket is dropped with his second tally into the second box. This tells the Wages Clerk that, although the man has been too late to deposit his tally in the first box, he may be booked from the first hour as he has paid to be admitted.

"An International Dial Recorder"

The third and fourth tallies are used similarly for the second part of the day. The morning boxes are dealt with by the Wages Clerk prior to the men going off duty, so that they are able to collect their tallies from a numbered board on their way out.

In the majority of factories, clock registration has been adopted for time-keeping, and there are several well-known makes of recorder on the market. The "Dey" Time Register, in addition to recording the times of the arrival and departure of each employee, produces at the end of the week a wages sheet, which the Wages Clerk can treat as the basis of his record, totalling on it the hours indicated and then pricing the total hours out at the wages rate. The general appearance and *modus operandi* of the "Dey" may be seen from the illustration above, and Form No. 13 (showing a "Dey" wages sheet) is annexed.

Although cards may be used with it for cost keeping, referred to elsewhere, so far as time recording is concerned, it is complete in itself. When the pointer is pushed into the hole opposite the employee's number on the big dial surrounding the clock, it prints the exact hour and minute opposite his proper consecutive number

THE "GLEDHILL-BROOK" TYPE

on the time-sheet, no matter in what order the employees register, a bell ringing to indicate that the operation has been completed and that the register is ready for the next man. The use of keys or tallies for each employee is, therefore, unnecessary.

Some types of time recorder are operated by keys, thus differing from the "Dey" by registering the employees' arrival in chronological order. This is useful where it is principally desired to keep the late comers' names all together and know the lost time of each, all the others being booked full time, the absentees being noted by their keys remaining on the "out" keyboard. This machine does not need frequent re-filling as the records are made on a continuous roll of paper tape, and the capacity of the Recorder is unlimited, an increase of staff involving only additional recording keys. On the other hand, these records cannot be used as a wages sheet, but must be transferred by clerical labour.

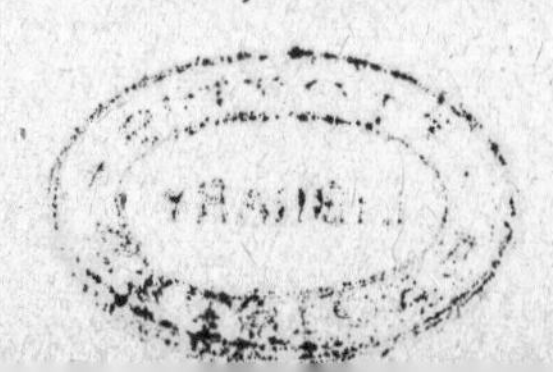

Recorders of the "Gledhill-Brook" type register the time for one person on one card for one week. The cards can be ruled and printed to suit any type of business and so as to give ordinary time, overtime, etc. (see Form No. 14). No disputes can arise with workmen, each being his own time-keeper and seeing the printed record of his time on his own card. The cards are kept on an "in" and "out" board which can be kept locked when not in use. The machine is so set that it is not possible to record time in the wrong space.

A very important adaptation of the Automatic Time Recording Clock System is in connection with costing; but, as this is in itself a very wide subject, it is deemed advisable not to refer to it at length here, but to reserve it for its special chapter.

Modern practice has taken advantage of mechanical "listers" and "tabulators" for assistance in preparing pay rolls from the time sheets or clock cards. These are like typewriters to which have been added means of rapidly moving the carriage to the several columns, while adding registers automatically take care both of cross additions (and subtractions) and of the totals of each column.

In many large Works, one or other of the various systems of piece-work payment is in operation, but the Trade Unions in certain districts object to the method, and full inquiries as to local conditions should be made before commencing it, if it is desired to employ Union men.

The principal aim of the piece-work system, or any system of bonus payment, is to encourage workmen to use their brains and their skill to the utmost, and its advocates believe that this is a result which is attained, when the value of such work is to the direct benefit of the workmen themselves as well as to the firm for which they work. There are several different methods, one of the principal being that in which the Works Manager, who from his experience is able to calculate very closely what should be the cost of labour in connection with a certain operation or piece of manufacture, prepares an estimate of what it should cost. He then adds to this cost an amount sufficient to allow the workmen engaged upon it to realize a minimum profit of a quarter over and above their day-work time.

The work to be done and the price to be paid for it are then written on a contract form, on which the workmen agree not only

Name .... No. ....

	Hours	Rate	£	s.	d.
Wages for week of					
O.T.					
Extras					
Lost					
Signature of person authorizing payment		£			

....

DAY		IN	OUT	IN	OUT	Lost T.	O.T.	Total
S	AM							
	PM							
S	AM							
	PM							
M	AM							
	PM							
T	AM							
	PM							
W	AM							
	PM							
T	AM							
	PM							
F	AM							
	PM				*			
* Week commences here.					Totals			
				Net O.T. or Lost T.				

Received ....

(*Form No.* 14)

EARLHAM MANUFACTURING CO., LTD.

No.........*200*........

Cont............*670*............ ....*Jan*.........*8th*........*19*....

Workmen's Numbers.

15,	*17.*
19,	*27.*

WE, the undersigned, agree to execute the work named to the complete satisfaction of the Firm and the Works Manager at the prices stated below—

Quantity	Description	Price Each	Extension		
2	*Cars Built complete, all Moulds and Roofs, etc.*	*£15–0–0 each*	*30*	–	–
	Paid on a/c P.W.		*22*	*10*	*7*
	Balance		*£7*	*9*	*5*

Signatures of Men.
....................*G. Jones*............................
....................*H. W. Bley*.........................
....................*J. D. Henderson*................
....................*K. Wardle*..........................

Firm's Signature—
............*Earlham Manufacturing Co.,*.......................
................*A. H. Blake,*.......................................
.........................*Manager*.......................................

Works Manager's Signature—
...........................*A. C. Wilson*..

(*Form No.* 15)

Name J. Jones No. 15 Date Jany 18/34

Contract No.	Thursday N.	Friday	Saturday	Monday	Tuesday	Wednesday	Thursday	TOTAL
670	2	7¾	4		3	2	7	25¾
625		2½	2				2¾	7¼
651				5		2		7
689				4¾	4½	5½		14¾
	J.K.	J.K.	J.K.	J.K.	J.K.	J.K.	J.K.	
TOTALS	2	10¼	6	9¾	7½	9½	9¾	54¾

J. Keenan,
Foreman.

(*Form No.* 16)

to do the work to the satisfaction of the Works Manager, but also to stand by the price named in the contract. Form No. 15 is a customary form of contract.

The contract having been submitted to the men and the price agreed, it is signed by them and afterwards by the management. Whilst the work concerned is in progress, each of the men has a card similar to Form No. 16.

On this card is filled the number of the contract on which time has been worked, and the number of hours so worked, the foreman of the particular shop or department checking the entry each day and initialing it. At the end of the week the cards are sent to the office, where the hours are booked against the respective contracts and the workmen are, until a contract is finished, paid what is called "On a/c Piece Work," that is to say, the time actually worked, at whatever the ordinary day-work rate is for the particular class of work being performed. On the completion of a contract, the money drawn as "On a/c Piece Work" by the men engaged on it is added up, the total deducted from the agreed contract price, and the balance divided between the workmen.

Under this system, the workmen know that, if the job is not satisfactorily executed, the firm has the right to call upon them to do it over again, which will be, of course, at their own cost, and on the other hand they have every incentive to do the work in the most expeditious and satisfactory manner, as work done in this way will increase the amount of wages they have to draw.

CHAPTER XII

Stores—Records of Stores inwards and outwards—Systems of control and connection thereof with Financial Accounts—Distinction between Stores and Stock

THE Stores Department of every undertaking, no matter what its size, is one which should be run on very exact and definite lines, as any possibility of leakage should be prevented so far as rules and forms are capable of preventing it.

In the Chart in Chapter IV (page 32), showing the division of responsibility amongst the various sub-departments, it will be noted that the Storekeeper is answerable direct to the Manager, whereas the Purchasing Clerk is on the staff of the Accountant. The two officials should be brought into contact with each other as little as possible. The former should have nothing to do with the placing of orders for materials, and the latter should have nothing to do with the certifying of the arrival or of the quality of the materials he orders.

It is impossible to lay down any definite lines for the arrangement of Stores, as this necessarily varies with every type of business. A general rule, however, may be laid down that Stores should not be stinted in space. Each separate type of article should have a definite place assigned to it, instead of bundles of B goods being thrown on top of barrels of A goods, both being shut off from view by sacks of C goods. If orderliness is desirable in an office, it is still more desirable in a Stores, and the best Storekeeper will be found to be the most orderly. Apart from the waste of time involved, unless a place is provided for it, in rummaging round for an article which is not frequently required, it is more liable to become damaged, and more liable to be allowed to run out of stock.

A useful plan to adopt is to have a Stores Reference Number assigned to each article, a supply of which should be in hand, and for this number to be prominently displayed on the shelves, or other part of the Stores Department, kept for it. When the reserve of that article requires replenishing, the Storekeeper makes an entry in his Stores Order Book, giving the quantity of the article required with its Reference Number. These Reference numbers are often part of an elaborate "code" which enables the initiated to know

STORES ORDER BOOK

Date.	Article required.	Stores Reference No.	Quantity.	Works Warrant No. (if any).	Authorized.	Contractor's Name.	Office Order No.	Remarks.	Storekeeper's Date of Receipt of Goods.
19 . . Nov. 1	Engine Oil, best quality	75	2 Brls	Stores.	(Initials of Manager or his Assistant.)		(This No. should be inserted by Orders Clerk.)		
	00 Copper Wire	52	200 ft.	3182				To be passed by Works Manager.	

(*Form No.* 17)

No.....*2000*.... ....*19*........

Messrs. ....

Stores Order Book Fo.	Please Supply to

Ordered for ....

(Signature)...

Manager.

EARLHAM MANUFAC

TOXTETH WORKS,

ORDER

No.........*2000*............ ....

Messrs. ....

Please Supply to

To be sent *via*

Carriage

(Signature) ....

The Earlham Manufacturing Co. do liable for any work or articles supplied Printed Form, duly signed.

NOTE. This Order is to be retained by whom it is sent, and the Invoice and the Accountant IMMEDIATELY AFTER OF THE ORDER; a Delivery Note, to be sent with every delivery.

(Form

TURING CO.
Bow, E.11

................19........

....

Manager.

not hold themselves
unless ordered on a

the Tradesman to
Account returned to
THE EXECUTION
quoting Order No.,

No. 18)

**** The Particulars and Price of the Goods or Works are to be inserted, and the Invoice or Account returned when the Order is executed.*

INVOICE

....*19*........ No..........*2000*........

THE EARLHAM MANUFACTURING CO.
Toxteth Works, Bow, E.11

Drs. To.......................................*of*..

Date	Articles Supplied or Work Done		£	s.	d.

Ordered for.................................... Total £

Certified ....
Accountant.

To be paid..
Manager.

the class, or even the description, of the goods by a glance at the number.

The general form in use for a Stores Order Book is shown in Form No. 17.

This Stores Order Book is to be sent in daily to the Manager, who will either personally or by deputy authorize the ordering of the goods, and the book will then be passed on to the Accountant's Department, where the Orders Clerk will make out the order, subsequently returning the book to the Storekeeper. It is evident that loose forms can, at option, take the place of a ruled book.

In some Factories, the Storekeeper inserts on his order the name of the supplier from whom the goods are to be obtained, but this may be thought to be wrong in principle, as the source of supply should be beyond his control, if not unknown to him.

It will be the duty of the purchasing officer to make himself aware of the current prices of all goods and of the best sources from which supplies may be obtained. Where there is a regular consumption of particular goods, many firms make a practice of making annual contracts, for which tenders are invited either by advertisement or by inquiry. It is usual for such inquiries to give rough particulars as to the probable requirements during the period for which tenders are invited, and, wherever possible, standard samples of the exact description and quality of the goods required should be prepared for inspection. The form of tender should be very explicit in insisting upon all goods supplied being up to the standard sample, and it is quite possible for power to be retained to order elsewhere, and to charge the contractor for any excess payments involved, in connection with any endeavour to substitute goods of inferior quality. It is imperative that all contract goods should be examined immediately on delivery and compared with the standard sample, or otherwise examined as to quality.

When ordering goods not obtained under contract, the source of supply should be settled either by obtaining special quotations from selected firms or in accordance with general instructions issued by the Manager.

All orders should be issued from an official numbered Order Book, with counterfoils or carbon copies, and no goods—except small sundries which may be bought locally in emergencies, through petty cash—should be obtained without the issue of such official order.

A form of order is given merely as a suggestion on pages 148 and 149 (Form No. 18); it will be noticed that this includes a form of invoice to be used by the supplier. It is probable that such a scheme is possible only for large undertakings in a position to dictate to the supplier; but, where practicable, this arrangement has the advantage of standardizing the documents on the firm's invoice files and, incidentally, of making quite certain that the proper reference number is quoted on all invoices.

No delivery of goods should be accepted by the Storekeeper unless accompanied by a delivery note, stating name of supplier, the nature of the article, the quantity sent and the order number. The Storekeeper then carefully checks the quantity and examines the quality of the goods delivered, provided he is able to judge of the latter. In cases where he is not able to do this, and in such cases as have been marked on his Stores Order as requiring the inspection of the Works Manager or other official, he arranges for an inspection and then fills up an entry in his Stores Received Book.

STORES RECEIVED BOOK

Date................

Received from.................... Address..................

per............

Cases ...... Barrels ...... Boxes ...... Sacks...........

Stores Order No.	Office Order No.	Quantity.	Goods.	Weight.			Checked by.	Inspected by.	Rejected and Cause.	Stores Ledger Folio.

(*Form No.* 19)

This book has duplicate pages, the one written on being flimsy paper perforated at the binding edge, and the second a carbon copy of the first on ordinary paper. The flimsy copy is torn off and sent attached to the contractor's delivery note to the Orders Clerk. All rejected goods should be entered in a Stores Rejected Book so as to ensure the receipt of a proper credit note from the contractor.

The Purchasing Clerk files the Delivery Note and Stores Received voucher pending receipt of the invoice, which he is thus able to certify subsequently without sending on to the Storekeeper; the latter has thus no necessity to know the prices being paid for the various grades of goods. In many businesses of a large size, it is deemed advisable to keep in the general office a book called the

STORES REJECTED BOOK.

Stores Order No.	Contractor.	Goods.	Weight.			Cause of Rejection.	Returned per.	Credit Note received.

(*Form No.* 20)

"Purchases Book" in which all such stores delivered are entered, the Orders Clerk marking off each item with the date on which he has certified the corresponding invoice for payment. This book not merely minimizes the risk of goods being twice paid for, but is useful for reference at balancing times to see what invoices, if any, are outstanding for goods which have been delivered into Stores, and the value of which has been included in the stock-taking figures.

This book should not be one requiring much clerical work, as it is, of course, in one sense, duplicate work. The following will be found sufficient for most purposes—

PURCHASES BOOK

Order No.	Date.	Firm.	Goods.	Weight or Quantity.	Date. delivered.	Stores Voucher No.	Invoice certified.	Initials.

(*Form No.* 21)

STORES LEDGER

TROLLEY WHEELS

AVAILABLE Maximum........*150*........
Minimum........*100* ....

ORDERED			REQUIRED		
Date	Order No.	Quantity	Warrant No.	Quantity	Available Quantity
	Stock in hand				*150*

RECEIPTS								
Date	Invoice No.	Order No.	Quantity	Total rec'd	Price	Cost		
						£	s.	d.
	*				*		*	

ISSUES								
Date	Warrant No.	Quantity	Total del'd	Price	Cost			In Stock
					£	s.	d.	
				*		*		

* *These headings appear only when the Storekeeper is allowed to see the Invoices, and so ascertains the Prices.*

(*Form No.* 22)

Another plan which is preferred by some Managers is for the invoice to be sent direct to the office, there compared with the counterfoil order and checked as to price, then certified as to receipt by the Storekeeper (and, where necessary, as to quality by the Works Manager or other official), and finally paid by the Cashier—less the proper discount—on the final certificate of the Accountant. This method can be practised with more facility if suppliers are required to send invoices in duplicate (or triplicate) so that separate copies can be certified by the parties mentioned, the copies being finally assembled into complete sets before payment is made.

To return to the Storekeeper's work in connection with stores inwards, it will be his duty, after making his entry in the Stores Received Book and forwarding copy to the office, to post this entry into the Stores Ledger. In the specimen heading for this book on Form No. 22, the columns headed "Required" are provided for utilization in such cases as the following—

The Storekeeper has 150 trolley wheels in Stores, this being the maximum number which he should have available at all times: he receives a Stores Warrant from the Works Manager for the issue of 50 of these for use in connection with works in progress, and another Stores Warrant from the office for five to be used as samples. He enters these two warrants, finds that they reduce his available stores to 95, which is below the minimum, and he thereupon issues a Stores Order for a further supply.

The Works Manager, or Foreman entrusted with the charge of certain operations of the manufacturing work, requisitions on Stores for the supplies which he requires by means of a Stores Warrant

STORES ISSUE BOOK

Date.	Article.	No.	Quantity.	Supplied to	Job No.	Purpose.	Stores Ledger Folio.

(*Form No.* 23)

Stores Warrant No. .... (This number will be inserted by the Storekeeper.)

Date ....

To the Storekeeper,—

Please supply bearer with the following—

Article	No.	Weight			Job No.	Purpose

(Signed) .... Works Manager.
Foreman.

Received the above.

....

(*Form No.* 24)

in some such form as No. 24, the book being in triplicate, two copies on paper of different colour being sent to the Storekeeper.

After supplying these goods, the Storekeeper will enter the Warrant in his Stores Ledger, and send the duplicate copy (blue), initialed as having been issued, to the Costs Clerk.

In some cases, Managers prefer that the Stores Ledger should be kept in the office. In this case it will probably be found better to retain the price column shown in the suggested form, and the Storekeeper should be furnished with a Stores Issue Book (No. 23), in which to record goods delivered by him in response to Stores Warrants. On the whole, the best plan (as a rule) is for the Storekeeper to keep a Stores Ledger in *quantities* only, and for the regular ledger (in quantities *and values*) to be kept in the Cost Office. These records may well take the form of Card Ledgers.

It will be observed that the term " Stores " has been used throughout to describe goods which are provided either for consumption by the firm itself, or for issue to the Works Department for use in the manufacture of the finished goods which the firm sells. When the Works have turned out the finished article, this is then styled " Stock," to differentiate between it and the raw materials or parts which have been designated " Stores." Similarly, it is customary to refer to the place in which " Stock " is kept as the Warehouse. It is hardly necessary to go *seriatim* into the books kept in the Warehouse, as they are practically duplicates of the Storekeeper's books. On the completion by the Works of the articles referred to in a certain Job Order No. for replenishment of Stock, the Works Manager will send to the Warehouse the articles, obtaining the Warehouseman's receipt, and sending at the same time to the Costs Clerk a Stock Output Note as shown on page 157.

The Costs Clerk will—from the information he has compiled as to the wages, materials, etc., allocated to the Job Number for this work—insert in the Costs Rate column the figure arrived at, and work out the " Amount " column, then send the note on to the Warehouseman, who will now have the complete information for entry in his Stock Ledger. This Ledger and the Stock Warrant on which he will issue finished goods from Stock to the Packing Department will be similar to the Stores Ledger and the Stores Warrant of the Storekeeper, except that the Stock Warrant (Form No. 26) must contain proper particulars filled in by the Sales

STOCK OUTPUT NOTE No.—

No. ....

Sent to Warehouse 1st December, 19..				Sent to Warehouse 1st December, 19..				Stock Received. Book Folio....	
Article.	No.	Weight.	Job No.	Article.	No.	Weight.	Job No.	Costs Rate.	Amount.

Taken to Warehouse by .... Received .... Warehouseman.

(*Form No.* 25)

Department as to consignee, method of dispatch, etc., and the Warehouseman must send to the Accountant's Department a Stock Issue Note so that the machinery already described in Chapter VII for raising a charge against the customer may be set in motion.

STOCK WARRANT

Please forward Stock as follows to ....

Per ....

Article.	No.	Weight.	Customer's Order No.	Sales Order No.	Stock Ledger Folio.

(Signed) .... Date ....

(*Form No.* 26)

CHAPTER XIII

Cost Accounts—Their nature and importance—General neglect of the subject—Fallacious and imperfect results generally

THERE is no part of office organization which is so significant of the vast change from the methods of the past to the methods of to-day as the system known as Cost Accounts. Even a very few decades ago, such a term had little or no meaning in the mind of the average Manufacturer or Manager, and businesses may still be found in all parts of the country where the words will be known, but will convey only a very hazy notion of what is meant by such a system when operated by an efficient Manager or Accountant.

The term " Cost Accounts " is applied to a system which enables a Manager to tell what it has cost him to carry out every contract he has undertaken; what it has cost him to produce and sell every article or piece of machinery which his Factory or Works has turned out. It will be seen from the wording of the last sentence that while this system aims primarily at providing information as to the direct expenditure in production in the Works, which is an expenditure known as " Prime Cost," and which is, of course, highly necessary and useful information, yet it is also capable of attempting to allocate to the various units of production the "overhead" or "fixed" costs which are not directly incurred in connection with production.

The importance of an efficient system of Cost Accounts cannot be magnified in the eyes of an experienced Manager conducting a manufacturing business. His commercial books may be kept on the most modern and accurate principles but—unless he is able to know the exact Prime Cost of each of his manufacturing operations, and the "Overhead" (sometimes called "Oncost" or "Burden") which each of those operations should bear in order to cover his miscellaneous expenses in the shape of upkeep of machinery and buildings, rent, rates, office and management, selling and forwarding costs—the foundations of his business are built on shifting sand. He cannot possibly fix his quotations and tenders upon knowledge of what is the lowest figure which will recoup his actual outlay under all headings, and all his estimates are, therefore, more or less leaps in the dark. Similarly, from the point of view of internal efficiency and economy, unless he can ascertain the precise cost of each component article he is manufacturing, he does not know whether it would not pay him better to buy some of them in the open market, and he is not aware to which particular shop or department of his Works special attention must be paid in order to reduce an unduly heavy cost which may be caused by improper appliances, waste of stores, inefficient labour, careless supervision, lack of knowledge of the best material, uneconomical purchase of parts or general ineptitude of management.

In the light of these remarks it is easy to see that a Cost Account System is of vital importance; but the Manager must, on the other hand, guard himself against any system which is not thoroughly reliable, inclusive, and accurate, or which, by its very intricacy, involves so much clerical work that its own cost adds appreciably to the expenditure, and is not clear enough to permit of its methods and information being readily apprehended by his Principal. It is quite possible for a badly thought-out or imperfectly executed scheme of Costing to produce such fallacious results as to cause the most serious complications. Every care should, therefore, be exercised to adopt a Cost System which is applicable to the precise requirements of the individual business, simple and economical in its operation, trustworthy and clear in its results.

It will readily be understood that each particular type of business will have important modifications to make in any general Cost Account System, and it will probably be sufficient to give in this Chapter a short description of a simple method which can be adapted to individual requirements.

At the very commencement it is necessary to decide what, for the particular business, is the natural "unit of production" of which the cost is to be ascertained. It may be, for a contractor, the contract or job; or, for a brewer, the barrel brewed; or, for a tramway, the passenger-mile; or, for a manufacturer who manufactures for stock, the "production order." The obvious limits of such a book as this compel us to confine our exposition to undertakings of the jobbing or "production order" type.

So far as Prime Cost is concerned, it will be necessary to be able to allocate to each "Job" (or "Sub-Job") or "Production Order" the labour, materials, and direct expenses (i.e. expenses more directly attached to the job than general overhead expenses) chargeable in connection with it. There can be little doubt that a card or loose leaf system used with an automatic time recorder is incomparably the best for a Costing System, and the system now being described is upon this basis.

Prior to an order being given to the Works Manager—whether such order be for work covered by a contract or for work in connection with some article to be placed into Stock, it is understood that an estimate of cost has been prepared, as described in the Chapter on Estimates, etc. A complete list of materials required is prepared at the same time and handed with the Production Order to the Works Manager, a copy being sent to the Costing Clerk. The form of a Production Order varies very much, some bearing only the name of the articles to be manufactured, others giving the fullest possible particulars connected with the order and blanks for notes on all its processes of manufacture. The Production Order having been received, the Works Manager will requisition the Storekeeper for the materials, as described in the chapter on Stores, and then assign the "Job" to one of his foreman and a gang of men. Each man, in addition to his daily time card for wages purposes (coloured red, see Form 14 in Chapter XI) is furnished with a white card, bearing on its face his name and number with the date and the Job Order No., and on its back particulars of the work he is to carry out. (See Forms 27, 28, and 29.) These forms are alternatives according to the particular system of wages-contract in force. Each man, on entering the Works in the morning, takes his red time card from his number pocket on the "Out" rack next to the automatic clock, registers it in the clock and places the card into the proper number on the "In" rack on the other side of the clock. He then is handed his white Job Card duly filled up by the foreman, which card he takes to the clock, registers the time he begins upon the work and places the card under his own number on the "In" rack for white cards, and proceeds with his job. When he has finished it, or is leaving for the day, he takes his Job Card from the "In" rack, registers it in the clock and places it in the "Out" white card rack and, in the case of that operation concluding his day's work, also registers his red wages card and places it on the proper "Out" rack.

It is the duty of the Costing Clerk, the first thing each morning, to collect the white cards of the preceding day, endorse the total number of hours worked on each, and calculate the wages, endorsing this figure also, and (after comparing the total hours worked by the one employee on his different white Job Cards with the total hours for the day registered on his red Wages Card) place the white cards in the Cost rack under their respective Works Production Order Numbers. Any time shown on the red Wages Cards as having been spent in the Works without being accounted for on any white Job Card has to be charged against "Overhead Lost Time Account," and the attention of the Works Manager should be called to any glaring cases, this being a fruitful source of unnecessary expenditure, and being—when it occurs in a flourishing and busy concern—a direct reflection upon the foreman, who should so arrange the work that he has a new Job Card ready for each man as he completes the one upon which he is working. It is a useful and additional check upon the accuracy of the weekly wages account that its total can be compared with the total shown by the Job Cards *plus* "Lost Time Account" and indirect labour. If the whole time of a foreman is spent in supervising the work under one Job Number, he should register a white Job Card for himself, which will be treated by the Costing Clerk in the same manner as the men's cards; otherwise the salary of the foreman is treated as falling into Overhead.

The Costs Clerk then proceeds to price out the blue Materials Issue Cards he has received from the Storekeeper (Form No. 24, Chapter XII) and places them in his Costs rack under the proper Works Production Numbers.

The Costing Clerk has now got his labour and materials in connection with each Works Production Order and, on the completion of each, he adds to it its own direct chargeable expenses. These may be travelling expenses, use of machine tools as shown on the Job Cards, royalties payable on some portion of the work, or other expenses he may be advised of from the office. The total thus obtained is the Prime Cost of the Works Production Order.

Now comes the more difficult question of Overhead. This includes all indirect charges and expenses both in the office (implying administration, advertising, and selling under the general term "office") and in the Works, and these are more satisfactorily dealt with separately.

In connection with both, if the business is quite new, these items

BONUS JOB CARD.

Tally No..................

	Hrs.	Rate	£	s.	d.
Time allowed ...					
Time taken					
Time saved					
Premium...........					
Time delayed ...					
Machine Hours					
TOTAL COST					

DAY		Begun	Stopp'd	Restart	Finish	Total
T	AM					
	PM					
F	AM					
	PM					
S	AM					
	PM					
SUN	AM					
	PM					
M	AM					
	PM					
T	AM					
	PM					
W	AM					
	PM					

Works Order No. TOTAL Hrs.

....

Date ....

(*Form No. 27*)

THIS SIDE OUT.

No.

Name ....

Machine Tool No. ....

Adjusting Altering Annealing Assembling Assisting Baking Balancing Banding Bending Bolting Boring Building Burnishing Bushing Checking Cleaning Closing Connecting Counting Cutting Disconnecting Dismantling Drawing Dressing Drifting Drilling Electro-plating Ending Erecting Examining Facing Filing Filling-in Finishing	Fitting Fixing Flanging Forging Forming Gearing Greasing Grinding Guttering Heating Insulating Jointing Keying Keyseating Lacquering Levelling Lighting Loading Machining Making Marking-off Milling Notching Numbering Oiling Opening Packing Painting Papering	Placing Planing Polishing Preparing Punching Repairing Refitting Rewinding Rivetting Rubbing down Running Screwing Setting Shaping Slotting Spacing Splitting Stamping Straightening Studding Sweating Taping Tapping Tempering Testing Tinning Turning Unloading Unpacking Varnishing Wedging Welding Winding

PARTS

....

....

....

Form No. 28 (back of No. 27)

JOB CARD.

No............ Job Order No............

Time allowed..............	Wages @......	......	......	......
Time taken................				
Premium 50%..............	Bonus......	......	......	......
Total Time	Total Wages			

DAY		IN	OUT	IN	OUT	Total
T	AM					
	PM					
F	AM					
	PM					
S	AM					
	PM					
SUN	AM					
	PM					
M	AM					
	PM					
T	AM					
	PM					
W	AM					
	PM					

Name..

Week ending..

Foreman's Initials..................................

(*Form No.* 29)

No.

Commenced..............
Finished..............
Cost..............

THIS SIDE OUT.

Operation	No.	Parts
ASSEMBLING		
BORING		
BRAZING		
BUFFING		
CENTERING		
CUTTING		
DRILLING		
ERECTING		
FACING		
FILING		
FORGING		
GRINDING		
INSERTING		
LOADING		
MARKING OFF		
MILLING		
PAINTING		
PATTERN MAKING		
PLANING		
PLATING		
POLISHING		
PUNCHING		
REAMING		
REPAIRING		
RIVETTING		
SCRAPING		
SCREWING		
SHAPING		
SLOTTING		
TAPPING		
TESTING		
TURNING		
UNLOADING		

Form No. 29 (*back*)

will perforce have to be estimated. At the conclusion of a chosen definite period, a total must be made of the Works General Expenses, which will include such items as salary of the Works Manager and (subject as above stated) wages of his foremen, wages for indirect labour in connection with the repair and upkeep of machinery, wages of timekeepers, engineers, stokers, crane drivers, rent and rates of Works, etc. It need hardly be said that allowance must be made for any conditions of abnormality of output during the period chosen for this computation. "Works Overhead" is allocated to jobs by taking the percentage the total so ascertained bears to the total of Direct Wages of the same period, or to the total amount of Direct Wages and Materials, or by dividing it by the number of hours included in Direct Wages. Each of these three methods has supporters, those who select Direct Wages in preference to Direct Wages and Materials holding that the differences in the prices of materials should have no bearing on the apportionment of Works Overhead, which should be levied on the wages alone as being much more relatively important and less subject to fluctuations. Those who prefer the number of hours represented by Direct Wages as the basis do so because the cheaper unskilled labour represents the larger share of the wages and requires a greater expenditure of supervision and other unproductive labour. In the majority of businesses, the percentage basis which will be found most useful, and certainly most easy to work, will be that represented by the Works General Expenses to the Direct Wages. Accordingly, in the cost accounts, each job is usually loaded for works overhead with the determined percentage of the direct wages expended on that particular job. No uniform system can, however, work equitably in all circumstances, and every case must be considered on its own merits. As a general remark it may be said that greater accuracy can be obtained if the business be departmentalized and each department be treated separately.

The Office General Expenses of all descriptions are then taken out for the same period and "Office Overhead" obtained, either by taking the percentage of that total upon the Total Works Cost, as found by adding Prime Cost and Works Overhead, or by taking its percentage upon Prime Cost.

Costing Systems can be carried out so as to show the minutest details of all operations, but the foregoing will probably be sufficiently explanatory for a book of this description, and the Manager must not forget the warning in the earlier part of the Chapter against embarking upon a system so elaborate as to obscure instant appreciation of the facts, to provide which is the chief aim of any system. Finally, and by way of a last word of caution, it may be added that no system which cannot produce *prompt* results can be regarded as satisfactory. What is wanted here is NEWS—not ancient history. Over elaboration which delays the ascertainment of results thus defeats its own ends. It is particularly true, in connection with costing, that mechanical appliances which perform calculating, tabulating, and listing work and which obviate human error and fatigue are an invaluable aid in obtaining speedy and accurate results.

CHAPTER XIV

Departmental and Branch Accounts—Foreign Branches—Foreign Currencies —Departmental and Branch Returns—Tabulation of Results—Employment of Curves and Diagrams

In a business of any magnitude it is nowadays considered essential to know not only what profit has been made, but the method of obtaining it and the exact sources from which it has come. An up-to-date Manager must have his profit divided as far as possible into Departments, and know which Departments are making good profits and which the reverse. There are two methods of obtaining this information, viz. (1) by means of thoroughgoing Cost Accounts described in Chapter XIII, and (2) by an adaptation of the bookkeeping such as will be described in this chapter, designed to produce what are known as Departmental Accounts. Both, of course, can be combined. In businesses where the latter method is adopted, the sales will in the first instance be ascertained for each Department, either by means of analysis columns added to the Sales Journal which will, therefore, appear in the following form—

SALES JOURNAL

Date.	Description.	Folio.	Details.	Total.	Dept. A.	Dept. B.	Dept. C.	Dept. D.

(*Form No.* 30)

or by means of a special book into which an ordinary Sales Journal is dissected or through the medium of the sorting and aggregation (on an adding machine) of carbon copies of invoices.

Similar means may be adopted on the purchasing side and if there is a Purchases Book it will have additional columns to allow for further dissection of the purchases into various Departments as well as for nominal accounts only—thus, in addition to the ordinary columns for indirect expenses, the raw material and similar purchases may be provided with special columns to show, say—

Dept. A.—" Raw Material," " Carriage," " Direct Expenses," " Advertising."

Dept. B.—" Raw Material," " Carriage," " Direct Expenses."

Dept. C.—" Raw Material," " Carriage," " Direct Expenses," " Advertising."

Dept. D (a trading Department only).—" Goods," " Direct Expenses."

By this means, all direct expenses passing through the purchase records can be ascertained. Other direct expenses are Wages (which are ascertained by separate pay rolls for each Department or by columns for analysis or by mechanical tabulation) and items coming direct from the Cash Book, such as travelling expenses which, where belonging to a special Department, are posted direct to the special Departmental Account in the Ledger and, in other cases (e.g. a traveller representing all Departments), will be posted to a Travelling Expenses Account and treated as an indirect expense. Where Raw Materials of the same kind are used in more than one Department, they are posted to a General Account in the Ledger, and the exact amount used by each Department is ascertained from the Stores Issued Book, the amounts being then transferred from the General Account to the Raw Materials Account of the Departments concerned.

An additional set of records will have to be kept where goods are frequently transferred from one Department to another, to deal with such transfers, and the totals of the goods in question will each month-end be debited to the various Departments taking the goods and credited to those passing them over. For this purpose cost prices will be used. The ruling on page 170 will meet the requirements of the case.

Alternatively, typed forms may be made to serve the same purpose. In any event the Purchases Account of the transferor department must be credited and that of the transferee department debited, at cost prices in each case.

Where the transfers are comparatively few in number, they may be dealt with as " Purchases Returns " by the transferring department and as "Purchases" by the receiving department. Cross entries in this case thus take the place of a separate book.

From the particulars given above, the gross profit on each Department may be ascertained, and many business men remain satisfied with this knowledge. Others, however, prefer to analyse the indirect expenses also, and (to do this) split all expenses of this nature over the various Departments in an agreed ratio.

The principal headings of indirect charges are *Rent, Rates, and Taxes,* which are charged over the various Departments

Goods transferred from Department "A," January, 19...

Date.	Dept.	Particulars of Goods.	Price.	Details.	Total.	B. Dept.	C. Dept.	D. Dept.

(*Form No.* 31)

in proportion to the cubic space or the square area occupied by each Department; *Motive Power,* which is usually based on the requirements of each section; *Office and Travelling Salaries and Expenses,* which are charged proportionately to the turnover of each Department; *Motor Expenses,* which are charged proportionately to the use made of motors by each Department; *Management Expenses,* charged proportionately to the turnover; *Interest,* charged according to the capital invested in each; *Depreciation,* according to the machinery, etc., used by each department.

The above is a common method of calculating the indirect expenses, though they may be arbitrarily varied to suit particular cases; for instance, one Department may do its turnover in comparatively small amounts, and the clerical work involved may take up at least one half of the time of the office staff, although in receipts the turnover may amount to only one-sixth of the whole.

The capital employed by each department may be ascertained as follows: Add together the average Stock held, the average amount of book debts outstanding, and the plant and machinery required: deduct the amount of liabilities.

The nature of the Returns to be demanded from Branch establishments will depend entirely upon the character of the work done locally.

Branches may be classified for this purpose into—

(1*a*) Branches with power to sell for cash only.
(1*b*) " " " " or on credit.
(2*a*) " for manufacturing only.
(2*b*) " " " with power of purchase.
(3*a*) " worked as entirely distinct businesses, save for Management and Finance.
(3*b*) Branches worked as entirely distinct businesses, save for Management.
(4) Foreign Branches, involving all or any of the above.

In the case of the first of these, the Branch in question is worked best on the "Multiple Shop" system. Goods sent to it will be charged out at the ordinary selling price. A special Cash Book will be allowed to the Branch Manager, from which to make his necessary Disbursements, which will be kept on the "Imprest" system as described in Chapter XV. The only item allowed to be "received" in this book will be the weekly cheque from the Head Office to cover his disbursements for the previous week. All cash received by him for sales will be entered in a separate account, and the total cash must be sent to the Head Office in the manner and at the time directed. Stock must be taken periodically, and the amount of the Branch Stock, as at last stocktaking, plus the goods since charged out to it (at selling price) and less the cash remitted, should be the Stock in hand, at selling price. In practice there will certainly be a small difference (to be written off) but experience will enable the management to recognize the percentage beyond which these shortages should not go.

The records kept at the Head Office would consist of two personal accounts with the branch, one dealing with the Branch Cash (for outgoings) and the other debiting it with the goods at selling price, as in the case of an ordinary customer, the credit being the cash returned. If credit sales are allowed, the balance will consist partly of stock and partly of book debts, and credit must also be given for discount and allowances (if any). At the time of taking out a Balance Sheet, however, it must be remembered that these balances are not ordinary book debts, but include stock at selling price and a reserve must, therefore, be made to reduce this figure to cost price.

Where the Branch has power to sell on credit and receive payment of its own accounts, to the system dealt with at the Branch (as above) must be added a Sales Day Book and Ledger, and the keeping of these books will be on the same principle as may be used at the Head Office. To the Return of the Cash Receipts and Imprest Cash Payments must be added, in many cases, a list of credit sales, and, in all cases, a list of the outstanding balances as extracted from the Sales Ledger. The Branch Balancing Statement in these circumstances will appear as follows—

19..	£ s. d.	19..	£ s. d.
Jan. 1.—To stock at date	- - -	Mch. 31.—By cash sent to H.O. ..	- - -
,, ,, — ,, Book debts at date ..	- - -	,, ,, — ,, Discount and allowances per list . ..	- - -
Mch 31.— ,, Goods received during quarter ..	- - -	,, ,, — ,, Stock at date.. ..	- - -
		,, ,, — ,, Book debts at date ..	- - -
	- - -		- - -

(*Form No.* 32)

It is evident that in cases where selling prices cannot definitely be fixed in advance (as in the case of perishable goods) it is not practicable to charge the local manager at selling prices. Hence the system described above must be modified to the extent of charging the goods at cost, stock also being taken at cost. In such circumstances the Branch Statement illustrated in Form No. 32 will reveal an excess of credits equal to the Branch gross profit for the period.

Yet again, it may be thought undesirable to reveal the real amount of the gross profit to the local manager. If so, it is not difficult to charge the goods at cost plus a percentage known only to Head Office. Hence the profit disclosed by the Branch Statement will be short of the truth to the extent of this secret loading.

Branches which are used for manufacturing purposes, but have not power to purchase, will usually be worked simply as a Department, and may be treated as such throughout

Where the Manufacturing Branch has power to purchase, but such purchases are paid for by the Head Office, a special Branch Goods Received Book should be kept at the Branch, and invoices received should be marked off therein as passed and then—after having a rubber stamp impressed upon them and being duly initialed by the responsible parties—be forwarded to Head Office. The rubber stamp will be a special one for the Branch and ought to contain the following particulars—

STRATFORD BRANCH

Goods recd. ....
Recd. Book fo. ....
Price checked ....
Manager (Branch) ....
Calculation checked ....
Manager (General) ....

(*Form No.* 33)

The cash would be kept as before, and the Returns would be rendered periodically according to the class of trade; these would consist of (1) Summary of Cash Payments, (2) Summary of Purchases (i.e. "invoices forwarded herewith"), (3) Particulars of Output and goods sent to the Head Office, or direct to customers, if so instructed, (4) Particulars of stock on hand (whenever taken), (5) List of goods received, or expenses incurred, for which no invoice has yet arrived.

The entries in the books at the Head Office might consist of a personal Cash Account with the Branch Manager, as previously described, and a special Purchase Book, the totals of which could be taken out for statistical purposes to set against the output in order to compare the cost with similar work done at the Head Office.

Where the Branch is worked as a separate business save for finance and management, assuming that all accounts are received and paid at the Head Office, the Branch must forward to the

Head Office—in addition to the cash statement—particulars of all purchases as above, and particulars of all sales, forwarding the cash for any small cash sale which may occur. The method of dealing with sales varies in different businesses, but perhaps the method most economical of time is to instruct the Branch to issue all invoices for goods sold by means of typewritten forms with two carbon duplicates. In this way they obtain, in addition to the original which is sent to the customer, two copies of each invoice outward, one of which they retain for reference and the other is forwarded to the Head Office with a summary of the sales. Allowances, if claimed at the Branch and passed by it, should be dealt with by means of a credit note which is issued to the customers in the same way as if it were a sale, and one copy should be forwarded to the Head Office with the monthly summary.

In the Head Office, the totals of these sales, purchase expenses, and allowances will be dealt with in a separate series of impersonal accounts, which will show the profit or loss made at the Branch. If there are several Branches but some of the customers are the same people, very frequently one personal account only is opened for each, to which account the sales from all Branches are posted. On the other hand, if it is desired to keep the accounts distinct it is usually better to do so by means of two columns on the debit side of the ledger, if there are two Branches only, rather than by having separate ledger accounts, as, if there are two (or more) accounts for the same customers, a customer who is not considered "safe" may get a larger credit than he would otherwise be allowed.

In the last type, viz. where the Branches, except for being under one General Manager, are separate concerns, and have full power to pay and receive accounts, the usual course is to give the Branch a full set of books and a local clerical staff. The books will be kept at the Branch where a Profit and Loss Account and Balance Sheet will be prepared, in the usual way, the only difference between a Branch of this nature and an ordinary business being that a "Remittance Account"—and, if necessary, a "Goods Account"—will be opened with the Head Office to record the transactions between the two in cash and goods respectively, and there will also be a Head Office Account to which the balances of the "Remittance Account," "Goods Account," and "Profit and Loss Account" will all be transferred.

The Returns to be sent to the Head Office will comprise such monthly Returns as to Sales, Purchases, Cash, etc., as may be required to be submitted to the Board—or the Proprietor, as the case may be—and at the year end a detailed Profit and Loss Account and Balance Sheet, to be incorporated with the Head Office Accounts.

At the Head Office, the Branch Remittance Account and the Goods Account will be transferred to the Branch Account; their own Profit and Loss Account will be prepared in the ordinary way, and they will enter in their ledger *in detail* a Branch Profit and Loss Account, carrying the profit to the debit of the Branch Account. These two Profit and Loss Accounts will then be combined, if the business is of the same class; and a combined Balance Sheet will be prepared from the Head Office and Branch Balance Sheets by adding together the Stock, Book Debts, etc., and striking out the Head Office Account from the Branch Balance Sheet and the Branch Account from the Head Office Balance Sheet. This will not affect the aggregate balance, as the debit which exists in the Head Office books as the investment in the Branch should agree exactly with the credit in the Branch books for the Head Office Account. If they do not agree and the entries are correct, the difference will arise from some cash or goods in transit which have been charged by the one side and not yet credited by the other as received, and this amount will go to increase the cash or stock respectively. A Reconciliation Account—similar to that employed to check a bank pass book—should be prepared in all such cases.

Where a Foreign Branch is owned, the same procedure as the last described will almost certainly be adopted, subject to the following notes: The question of foreign exchange will arise; the Branch Accounts will almost certainly require adjustment for cash or goods in transit; and quite possibly fixed assets will be recorded in the Head Office books only. The reason for this latter point is that fixed assets must appear at cost price (less depreciation), and it complicates the books unnecessarily if a different rate of exchange has to be adopted for this class of item from all the other Branch figures, while to ascertain cost in that case involves calculating the rate of exchange at the rate ruling when these assets were purchased or erected. The best method is to transfer, each year, the assets so purchased by the Branch to the Head Office

Account in the Branch books, and in the Head Office make corresponding entries—debiting the Branch asset concerned and crediting Branch Account.

The question of Exchange will affect the keeping of the Remittance Account and the method of dealing with the final accounts. The former must be kept with two money columns on each side, showing not only the amount remitted but also the exact figure which each remittance has realized in the other money denomination. The methods of dealing with the final accounts differ, but perhaps the simplest is the one below described, viz.—

Take the Branch (Currency) Trial Balance and,

(*a*) Convert fixed assets (if any) at rate ruling at time of purchase.

(*b*) Convert depreciation of these assets at the same rate.

(*c*) Convert current assets and liabilities at rate current at end of period.

(*d*) State remittances at actually realized figures.

(*e*) Convert expenses and income at an average rate.

(*f*) Insert any consequent sterling difference into the sterling Trial Balance as "difference on exchange." If a debit this should be written off; if a credit it is usually held as a reserve against future adverse fluctuations of exchange.

The most substantial advantage which will accrue to the Manager from a satisfactory system of book-keeping is perhaps the promptness and ease with which all kinds of useful information can be obtained; and one of the most convenient forms for this purpose is undoubtedly the tabular statistical statement. These statements will vary according to the class and size of the business, but should include a statement of all overdue accounts, a summary of the book debts and liabilities, bank balance, estimate of stock (if possible), and statements of the turnovers, purchases, wages and expenses (with the percentages that these latter bear to the turnover), together with comparisons with the previous year, or years, in tabular form.

The statement of overdue accounts should show the name of the debtor, amount, date contracted, date due, amount paid on account (if any), and remarks as to the cause of the delay (if known), e.g. claim on account of defective work, inferior quality, delivery, or other *bona fide* dispute.

The statements of other book debts and the liabilities may safely be taken from the balances of the Sales and Purchases Ledgers Adjustment Accounts, as described in Chapter XVIII, if that system is in use; these are submitted to the Manager with the cash and bank balances to show the amounts which are payable by the concern during the current month and the funds in hand, or likely to be available, to meet such payments. Bills Receivable in hand (if any) should also appear in this statement as, if funds are insufficient, they can always be discounted.

If from the Stock Book an estimate of the Stock in hand can be given, this is also desirable, and will be useful—in fact, necessary—to ascertain the estimated cost as detailed below.

The production will be set out in tabular form showing details as under. It must be clearly understood that in this statement either quantities must be used (as distinct from money values) or the "sales" figures must be reduced to cost.

STATEMENT OF SALES, 19..

	19..	19..	19..
Sales to Aug. 31st			
,, for Sept.			
Total sales to Sept. 30th.			
Add estimated Stock of manufactured goods at date.			
Deduct Stock at Jan. 1st.			
Production to date.			
Sales for Sept.			
Add estimated stock at Sept. 30th			
Deduct estimated Stock at Aug. 31st			
Production for Sept.			

(*Form No* 34)

The Purchases and Expenses will require more detail and probably a subsidiary statement for accrued items and for estimate of Stock. A good form is shown on page 178.

The foregoing statement shows the consumption and expenses for the month, and a sheet ruled in a similar manner would show the consumption for the nine months ending Sept. 30th.

These figures will be carried to another statement, the form of which is self-explanatory.

MONTH ENDING SEPTEMBER, 19..

Nature of Charge	Purchases per Invoice Book	Payments per Cash Book	Accrued to date	Estimated Stock at Aug. 31	Total Debit	Deduct		Net Debit being consumption or charge
						Estimated Stock at Sept. 30	Items accrued at Aug. 31	
Raw Material								
Wages, etc.								

(*Form No.* 35)

The estimated net profit in this statement is the excess of production at selling prices over total consumption and if Cost Accounts are kept the figure of estimated profits can be satisfactorily compared with the amount ascertained from the Cost records. This should correspond closely with the ascertained profits at the year end, as disclosed by the Profit and Loss Account.

Nature of Charge.	Consumption for month Sept. 19..	Percentage on production for month.	Similar columns for 19.. and if desired for 19..	Consumption for 9 months ended Sept. 19..	Percentage on production for period.	Similar columns for 19.. and 19..
Raw Material						
Wages, etc.						
Estimated Net Profit						

(*Form No.* 36)

Some firms also submit an analysis of Cash Receipts and Payments, but if a good system exists with regard to these, and statements similar to the above are submitted, this is scarcely necessary and conveys comparatively little information in an ordinary business concern.

Statements in tabular form should be prepared for each Branch and Department from these Returns, and a summary comparing those engaged in similar work should also be submitted.

Another way of conveying the information is by means of diagrams and curves, which are much more graphic, and much less bewildering to the eye and the brain than returns of figures in many columns. Take, for example, the curve showing the sales per quarter by three selling branches of a firm.

CURVE SHOWING BRANCH SALES

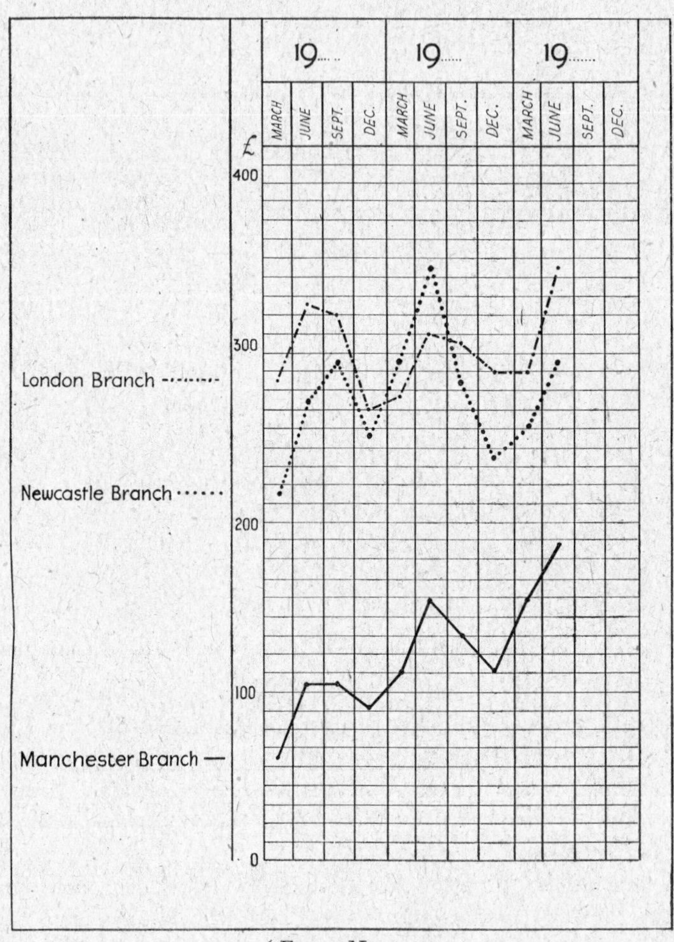

(*Form No.* 37)

The following diagram shows the value of the Stock of a certain article of manufacture in the Warehouse at the beginning of each quarter and the value of the sales made during that quarter—

DIAGRAM SHOWING QUARTERLY STOCK AND SALES

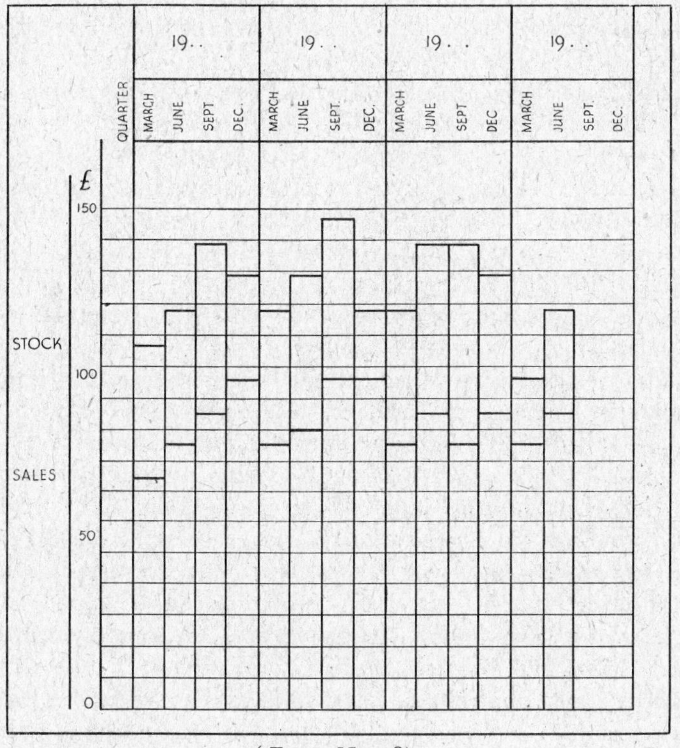

(*Form No.* 38)

It is, however, of the utmost importance that such diagrams as the above should invariably be prepared *on the same scale,* or their appearance will be entirely misleading.

CHAPTER XV

Finance—Banking Accounts—Loans, Overdrafts, Mortgages, Debentures, Bills of Exchange, etc.

THE question of Finance is perhaps the most important one which arises in the modern business world. According to the official returns, " insufficiency of capital " is one of the most frequent causes of failure, but experience and judicious management can often mitigate the inconvenience arising from the insufficiency.

With a view to paying a good rate of interest or dividend on the money invested, the Manager should see that there is no unnecessary money in the concern, but there must be sufficient to provide working capital after the full equipment of the business. This working capital should consist of enough money to provide and hold an adequate stock, a reasonable amount of book debts, and a margin in the bank to ensure a prompt settlement of creditors' claims, with something over to enable the Manager to take advantage of a specially good offer owing to a sudden drop in the market, etc. It is only by close supervision of all these points that success can be looked for in these days of keen competition. Without the adequate provision for stock and book debts, orders will go past the concern to others who can give prompter delivery or longer credit; and, without the other two requirements named, it is impossible to obtain those favourable terms for the purchasing of goods which are essential to cheap production. On the other hand, if more capital is used than is absolutely necessary as stated above, the rate of the return will suffer and the business appear to be less remunerative or less well managed than it really is.

To work this important section satisfactorily, the Manager must have a good system, and the cordial and efficient co-operation of his Cashier and his Accountant.

The " good system " will show itself in the method of dealing with book debts and cash, and the arrangements with the bank. To take these in the order given, the system of book debts should be based on the assumption that all sales are promptly charged out, and all the postings made daily from all the subsidiary records which lead up to the personal ledgers. The terms of credit (if they vary) should appear at the head of each ledger account, and once a month at least the Accountant should submit to the Manager a list of all overdue book debts. To ensure this, in many trades a book or loose sheet is ruled to show the statements as delivered, with the allowances and the dates of payment of the account. If used, this record would be purely statistical, and might be put in the following form—

ACCOUNTS DUE JANUARY 1ST

Ledger Folio.	Name.	Amount.	Allowances.	Cash and Discount.	Date paid.	Remarks.
		£ s. d.	£ s. d.	£ s. d.		
3	A	17 10 6	—	17 10 6	Jan. 4th	
19	B	104 3 2	4 0 0	100 3 2	,, 11th	
25	C	91 16 10	—	91 16 10	Mch. 15th	Statement and letter sent Feb. 2nd. Strong letter Mch. 11th

(*Form No.* 39)

By the adoption of this system or of an alternative method, to ensure that accounts overdue are not neglected, the amounts owing to the concern can be kept at a minimum, which is very necessary in order to prevent waste of interest and loss by way of bad debts.

With regard to the system adopted for cash, the receipts should be given only on the firm's official forms from counterfoil (or carbon duplicate) receipt books with all receipts numbered consecutively. Immediately upon the receipt of the money, it should be entered into the Cash Book and, if it does not balance the statement enclosed with the remittance, the Cashier should compare it with the ledger account to see whether the difference is accounted for by some return or other credit, not to hand at the time the statement was sent, and, in the alternative, send a receipt on account only. Each day, the *total* amount received should be banked entire, and no portion of it retained to pay small accounts, even though in cash.

All trade payments, after being passed by the Accountant's Department, should be made by the Cashier by means of "crossed" cheques payable to order, and marked "not negotiable." The only cheque drawn "uncrossed" should be the weekly one for the exact amount of wages and petty cash required.

The petty cash should be under the control of a responsible person who should hold an advance of a sum sufficient to bear all expenses under this head for an agreed period, depending upon the amount of expenditure involved. Each week he must produce his book to a stated official—the Manager, Accountant, Cashier, or Staff Auditor, as the case may be—who should examine it with the vouchers and certify the amount spent. This amount should then be repaid (against surrender of the relative vouchers) to petty cash out of the next wages cheque, or by a special cheque, thus bringing the cash balance once more to its original amount. The petty cash payments should be set out by means of analysis columns under various headings, and the amount expended posted direct from the main Cash Book to the nominal accounts involved.

PETTY CASH BOOK

Amount received	Date	Items.	Total.	Carriage	Station-ery.	Postage and Tel-egrams.	General Expen-ses.	Sun-dries.
£ s. d.	19..		£ s. d.	£ s. d.	£ s. d.	£ s. d.	£ s. d.	£ s. d.
10 0 0	Jan. 1.	To Cash						
	" "	By Cable, India ..	12 6			12 6		
	" "	" Tram fare R. G. to Bank ..	2				2	
	" 2-8.	" Sundries ..	6 4 1	3 2 0	1 6 0	1 10 0	6 1	
	" 8.	" Balance ..	3 3 3					Balance 3 3 3
10 0 0			10 0 0	3 2 0	1 6 0	2 2 6	6 3	3 3 3
3 3 3	Jan. 9.	To Balance.						
6 16 9	" "	" Cash.						

(*Form No* 40)

The petty Cashier should never be allowed to *receive* small miscellaneous sums. His only receipts should be the proceeds of cheques re-imbursing the exact amount of his payments.

It cannot be too often impressed upon anyone in charge of whatever system may be adopted that, in no circumstances, should the Cashier be allowed to post to the Ledgers, which latter should be under the direct and sole control of the Accountant. Furthermore, he should never be the *first* person to handle receipts, and should not be allowed to acknowledge them direct. Breach of this rule opens the door to peculation of incoming cash, the matter being covered up by the making of false entries under another heading to the credit of the account of the payer.

The banking arrangements, which next require consideration, will depend largely upon the position and turnover of the firm, the district in which the works are situated, and the bank's own internal arrangements.

With regard to the ordinary current accounts, the bank may treat the receipts as being received when the cash and cheques are paid in, in which case they usually arrange that though, as a matter of book-keeping, they give credit on that day it is only for book-keeping purposes, and on the understanding that, in the case of country cheques, etc., no responsibility is accepted until they are actually collected; that is to say, the bank acts as collecting agent, and, in case of non-collection on account of dishonour, etc., the amount will be debited again to the customer. This is, of course, only fair and right; but it is also good law. This method saves a good deal of trouble to the bank's customers in checking the account. On the other hand, the bank may elect to give credit for the cheques only as and when collected. In every case the payments will be debited against the account when the cheques are presented, and will be entered either in the name of the payee or by the number of the cheque. A "Pass Book"[1] will be issued by the bank which will set out particulars of the cheques paid on behalf of the customer, distinguishing each by its name or number on the one side, and on the other the daily totals of the amounts paid in as appearing on the paying-in slips. Most banks issue a "Paying-in Slip Book," bound with counterfoils to be initialed by the bank teller, and, when this is obtainable, it is, of course, preferable to the use of a loose slip for each entry.

The Pass Book itself will appear headed either "The Blankshire Banking Co., Ltd., in account with the Earlham Manufacturing Co.," in which case moneys paid into the bank will appear on the debit side, and cheques issued and cash withdrawn will appear on the credit side; or with the heading "The Earlham Manufacturing Co. in account with the Blankshire Banking Co., Ltd.," in which case the entries in it will appear on the reverse sides.

This Pass Book should be left frequently at the bank to be written

[1] Where the bank's ledgers are posted by machine the "pass book" takes the form of loose sheets embodying a copy of the account.

up, and, on its return, should be compared carefully with the Cash Book and a reconciliation account prepared in the usual way.

The bank charges for services take various forms with different banks. Some accounts, usually in the case of small ones, are worked on the basis of a minimum balance being kept in the bank, and the bank then makes no charge, looking for its return to the profit it makes on the use of the money held. Others are charged a fixed commission on the turnover of, say, 2s. 6d. for every £100 withdrawn. In other cases, a fixed charge of, say, £50 a year is made. In the two latter cases, the bank may (as an exceptional arrangement) credit the customer with some interest on the money which it holds. This fixed charge is, of course, in addition to the bank's out-of-pockets, or discount on bills negotiated, if any.

With regard to loans from the bank, the practice again varies with the account and with the bank engaged. In some cases—in fact, in some parts of the provinces the practice is almost invariable—if a loan is required, the customer is allowed to overdraw his Current Account up to the agreed amount, whilst in others the bank grants the loan on a separate account and credits the Current Account with the amount, the loan, of course, carrying interest at an agreed rate, and the Current Account being dealt with as before. By this latter method, of course, the bank has the advantage of receiving interest on the *full* amount of the loan during the whole period it is in existence—the interest (if any) allowed on the balance of Current Account being usually much smaller.

In the case of a limited company, the bank, except where a well-known and strong company is concerned, invariably requires security, which may take the form of a personal guarantee by the Directors or an issue to the bank of debentures.

The usual method of calculating interest by the bank is on the formula that the number of pounds multiplied by the number of days and the product divided by 7300[1] will equal the interest (at 5 per cent) in pounds; but, in endeavouring to check this figure, it must be remembered that while, in the Pass Book, the bank has probably entered the receipts on the day they accepted them, they will (properly) allow interest only from the day on which the proceeds were *collected*. The following figures will show how this

[1] The correct divisor is in all cases to be found by multiplying the number of days in the year by 100 and dividing by the rate per cent.

interest may be checked, assuming that the dates entered are the correct ones from the interest point of view (interest 5 per cent)—

Date.	Money withdrawn.	Money deposited.	Days standing.	Balance.	Products.
19..	£ s. d.	£ s. d.		£	
June 20	100 0 0	—	3	100	300 (i.e. 100 × 3)
,, 23	—	50 0 0	1	50	50
,, 24	250 0 0	100 0 0	6	200	1,200
,, 30	—	Balance. 200 0 0	—	—	
	£350 0 0	£350 0 0			1,550

£1,550 ÷ 7,300 = £0 4s. 2d. interest.

The interest charged would be arranged with the bank and would probably be on the lines of 1 or 1½ per cent above bank rate, with a minimum of 5 per cent. As a loan or overdraft is usually repayable on demand, it constitutes a very unsatisfactory—because unstable —method of raising working capital, except for temporary or seasonal purposes.

It is now necessary to speak of other ways of raising money through the bank. The commonest regular method open to all is by means of a mortgage.

A mortgage applies to land and interests in land only, and differs from pawn or pledge in the following particulars: A pledge is the legal property of the debtor, but is in the possession of the creditor until his claim is duly satisfied. A mortgage,[1] on the other hand, legally conveys property to the creditor in consideration of his loan, but such property remains in possession of the debtor so long as the covenants which he has undertaken in the deed are fulfilled. The debtor (known as the mortgagor) usually covenants to pay interest on the advance, which is acknowledged by the deed, at an agreed rate on stated days, to insure the property from fire risks, to discharge the chief rent (if any) and all rates and taxes, and to repay the principal when required to do so on such

[1] Mortgages effected since the Law of Property Act, 1925, came into operation are subject to the provisions of that Act, and now operate by giving the mortgagee a long leasehold interest.

notice as he may have stipulated for. The creditor (known as the mortgagee) on the other hand, agrees to re-convey the property to the debtor, or his nominee, on payment of his principal (after the stipulated notice) together with his interest. It must be remembered that, in addition to the deed, certain statutory rights accrue to the creditor; for instance if the debtor fails to pay the interest, or breaks any other covenant of the deed, the mortgagee has power to appoint a Receiver of the property, who will pay all moneys received therefrom to the mortgagee until his claims are satisfied. The relation which subsists between the mortgagor and the mortgagee is that of debtor and creditor, and, if the property mortgaged is not sufficient to satisfy the creditor's claim, he may sue the debtor for the balance. Entailing, as it does, the legal conveyance of land, the expense of a mortgage for a comparatively short time is a very serious addition to the charge of interest, and the practice has, therefore, arisen to make what is known as an equitable mortgage. This form of mortgage consists simply in depositing the deeds of the property with the mortgagee, together with an undertaking to execute a legal mortgage of the property either on default or on request. No bank will, however, accept such a security without the deeds being examined by a solicitor, and without a survey of the property, but the costs involved are not necessarily heavy. Where the advance of money may be required for some length of time, the bank rate of interest (which would be payable in connection with an equitable mortgage) may easily be higher than the ordinary rate of interest on money advanced on mortgage. If the bank had to enforce their rights against the security, they would possibly arrange to sell the property and obtain a conveyance from the debtor direct to the purchaser.

Banks will usually lend money on reputable stock exchange securities. The relative share certificates accompanied by a form of transfer into the names of nominees of the bank, must be handed to the bank. The bank will be careful to maintain a safe margin between the amount of the loan and the current value of the investment. Life policies (within the surrender value) form another favourite security. The policy must usually be assigned formally to the bank (or its nominee) and notice of the assignment must be given to head office of the assurance company concerned.

Another means available to raise money—in this case, however, for a limited liability company only—is by the issue of debentures. Debentures are the securities for loans granted by creditors to the company in the terms set out under the Bond or Trust Deed acknowledging the debt. They may be for loans by a single individual or by a number of separate individuals to the company, or they may be part of a series covered by one trust deed, in which case they are usually known as debenture stock. In the former case, they are generally covered by bonds issued by the company, setting out the number of such bonds, and that they rank *pari passu* in case of deficiency of assets, if they are charged upon the assets of the company.

As regards the charge which debenture holders may have upon the assets, this depends entirely upon the rights given by the document creating the debenture; that is to say, a debenture holder, as such, has no secured claim upon the assets of the Company, although the modern practice is to give the holders a floating charge over the whole of the assets. A floating charge covers the whole body of assets as they may exist at the moment when the security is enforced; hence the charge may very well extend to assets not in existence at the time when the debentures were issued. When the debentures give a floating charge only, if the charge is given by a trust deed for the benefit of all who subscribe to a particular issue of the stock, the trustees named in the deed are quasi mortgagees and, on a breach of a covenant, can appoint a receiver by writing under their hands; but their position is not so strong as that of a mortgagee, for, until the receiver is actually appointed, the company (or its Directors) may sell, mortgage, or charge any of the assets specifically to others, and these sales or specific charges entered into before a receiver may have been appointed, i.e. before the floating charge has "crystallized" take precedence over the floating charge given by the trust deed. Where no trust deed exists, the document constituting the debenture usually gives power to the holder to appoint a Receiver by writing under his hand, or alternatively he may apply to the High Court (Chancery Division) to make the appointment. A receiver enforces the charge by taking possession of the assets which it covers. He often has power to carry on the business. In either case the Receiver applies the money he receives or realizes to repaying their loans to the debenture holders. If debentures are not already created, and if further money is required, it is well for the Manager to remember that an issue of debentures not giving a charge on the company's assets would probably not be taken up by the public, whilst an issue giving such a charge requires registration at Somerset House, and, except in the case of a very strong company, would probably affect its credit adversely.

Another subject which must engage the attention of the Manager is the question of Bills of Exchange, and to what extent the firm is going to employ them. A Bill of Exchange is defined by the Bills of Exchange Act of 1882 to be "an unconditional order in writing given by one person to another, signed by the person giving it, requiring the person to whom it is addressed to pay on demand or at a fixed or determinable future date, a sum certain in money to, or to the order of, a specified person or to bearer."

The usual form is given in Form No. 41. From the point of view of the Earlham Company this is a "Bill Payable," but from Smith's point of view it is a "Bill Receivable."

On the Earlham Manufacturing Company undertaking to pay this on the specified date, they would signify the same by writing *across* the bill the word "Accepted," and would probably add the name of their bankers from whom it could be collected, e.g. "Payable at the Blankshire Bank, London," and their signature (for and on behalf of The Earlham Manufacturing Company, Limited, Albert Jones, Secretary). John Smith would then send it through his own bank to be collected on its due date,

No. 73. £134 6s. 2d. 16 Prior's Court,
London, E.C.2
Jan. 4th, 19..

Three months after date pay to my order the sum of One hundred and thirty-four pounds six shillings and two pence for value received.

JNO. SMITH.

The Earlham Manufacturing Co., Limited,
Bow, E.11

(*Form No.* 41)

viz. April 7th, three days (known as "days of grace") being invariably added according to English law, save on bills payable "on demand," or bills drawn "without grace."

If John Smith is a wealthy man, he will probably keep the bill in hand until, say, the 4th of April, when he will pay it into his bank for collection; if, on the other hand, his means are limited, he will probably "discount" the bill with the bank, i.e. he will arrange with the latter to advance him at once the amount of the bill, less a charge which is in the nature of interest. He will "endorse" the bill by writing his name on the back and will hand it over to the bank. As a matter of fact the discount rate is more severe than interest rate, as will be seen from the following example: For a bill of £100 due one year hence at 5 per cent discount, the holder would receive £95, whilst £95 for one year with interest at 5 per cent would amount to £99 15s. only, the difference being due to the fact that discount is calculated on the *total* amount and then deducted from that figure to ascertain the amount payable, whilst interest is calculated only upon the actual cash advanced. It may be added that banks willingly discount bills whereon good names appear, this being a prominent part of their business, because in the event of dishonour they have recourse against all parties to the bills and because the regular and foreseeable recurrence of due dates enables the banks to maintain the maximum liquidity of their funds.

A Bill of Exchange must be stamped before it is drawn, with a twopenny stamp if payable on demand, or within three days thereof; but otherwise on an *ad valorem* scale which (for an Inland bill) is as follows—

	Not exceeding £10	2d.	Impressed Stamps[1]
Exceeding £10	" " £25	3d.	
" £25	" " £50	6d.	
" £50	" " £75	9d.	
" £75	" " £100	1s.	

and 1s. for every additional £100 or part of £100.

Foreign bills payable in the United Kingdom are liable to an equal duty, paid by adhesive stamps affixed before the bill is negotiated here.

[1] The twopenny duty on bills at sight, on demand, on presentation, or within three days after date or sight, may be denoted by either an adhesive or impressed stamp.

BILLS RECEIVABLE BOOK

Date received	From whom received	Drawer	Acceptor	Where Payable	Date of Bill	Term	Date due	Amount	Interest	Fo.	Credit to Customer	Remarks	Date disposed of	How disposed of	Fo.	Amount
								£ s. d.	£ s. d.		£ s. d.					£ s. d.

(*Form No.* 42)

By the Finance Act, 1899, the duty on a Bill of Exchange drawn and expressed to be payable outside the United Kingdom when actually paid or endorsed or in any way negotiated in the United Kingdom shall, where the amount for which the bill is drawn exceeds £50, be reduced so as to be—

Where the amount exceeds £50 and does not exceed £100 .... 6d.
Exceeding £100, for every £100, also for a fractional part of £100.................................. 6d.
With certain exemptions.

Bills of Exchange, when entered into by parties of unimpeachable financial integrity, present certain advantages to both parties which may be summarized as follows. The *debtor* (i.e. the party liable on the bill) is enabled to bridge the time gap between purchase of his raw material and final sale of his finished goods, for he may so arrange matters that his bills become payable at about the same time as he reasonably expects to receive the proceeds of ultimate sale. On the other hand, it must be remembered that the consequences of dishonour of a bill are, commercially, very serious indeed, and liability should not be undertaken unless the most careful financial arrangements have been made. To the *creditor* (i.e. the holder of the bill) the advantages are even more apparent. He knows exactly when he may expect payment, and may make his arrangements accordingly. He may realize immediate cash, by discounting his bill, while still extending to his creditor the benefits of credit and, finally, if it should be necessary to enforce payment by action at law, production of the bill proves the debt, no defence being available which calls in question (apart from fraud) the details of the original transaction.

As aids to *foreign* trade bills are an indispensable adjunct to the banking system. Obviously, parties in widely distant parts of the world cannot be expected to possess the mutual confidence which would enable them to send to one another goods without money, or money without goods. If, however, the exporter attaches to the relative Bill of Lading and insurance policy a draft (i.e. an unaccepted bill of exchange) he can usually arrange for the bill to be at once discounted by his banker, on terms that it is to be sent (as a "documentary bill") to the foreign agent of the banker and not to be released by that agent until payment (in a satisfactory arranged form) has been made by the foreign importer.

Where the company prefer to keep their own bills until maturity, each bill must be entered in a special book worked on the same method as a Cash Book, and care must be taken that the bills are sent to the bank in ample time for collection. (See Form No. 42.)

In case a bill is dishonoured, the liability of the parties to the bill is in the following order—

(*a*) Acceptor, (*b*) Drawer, (*c*) Successive endorsees in order of endorsement, and each party is liable to indemnify any person who is liable only after him, if such person is called upon to pay it; but, of course, may, in his turn, claim the amount from anyone liable before him. It is important that the holder of a bill should notify all parties liable immediately upon dishonour, as otherwise they may escape liability. The usual practice is, where the person from whom the bill was received is a man of substance, simply to recover the amount from him (after dishonour by the acceptor) and leave him to secure his own position from his predecessors (if any). In the case of the bill illustrated the Company is both drawee and acceptor, while John Smith is the drawer.

Foreign bills are governed by similar rules, save that the days of grace vary in different countries, and the law of the country of payment decides the due date, also that the bill is frequently discounted or negotiated before it is accepted, in which case, if the drawee fails to accept it, the bill is said to be dishonoured by non-acceptance and the drawer is not liable upon it although all other liabilities remain the same. In some cases where a foreign bill is already stamped according to the laws of its country of issue, half the above charges only are necessary, and these are affixed by adhesive stamps.

It should be clearly understood that the holder of a bill is not in any sense a *secured* creditor, particularly in case of bankruptcy. His debt is proved and certain but has no preference.

Promissory notes are comparatively little used in business. They are subject to practically the same laws as Bills of Exchange, except that the stamp even for notes payable on demand is always on an *ad valorem* scale.

The usual form is—

> 2s. Stamp
>
> Bow, E.11
>
> £134 6s. 2d. Jan. 6th, 19..
>
> Three months after date We promise to pay Mr John Smith or order the sum of One hundred and thirty-four pounds six shillings and two pence value received.
>
> For and on behalf of
>
> Mr. John Smith, Earlham Manufacturing Co., Ltd.
>
> 16 Priors Court, E.C.2. A. H. BLAKE,
>
> Manager.

(*Form No.* 43)

CHAPTER XVI

Financial Books—Principles underlying the selection of suitable Systems of Accounts—Connection of Financial with Statistical Books—Mechanical aids, including Ledger Posting and Punched Card machines—Double Account System—Income Tax

In framing an Accounting System to meet the requirements of any particular business or undertaking, too much regard cannot be paid to the fundamental principles which govern and control the science of accountancy.

No system can be adequate or thorough which fails to recognize these principles, and it becomes only a matter of time and opportunity for such a system to be rendered ineffective, if not altogether abandoned.

It is, therefore, imperative, in considering this branch of the subject, to emphasize the following rules, which may be taken as a guide in securing a system which will be at once expedient and reliable—

(1) There should be a daily banking of all moneys received.

(2) The Cashier should not keep any book other than his own Office Cash Book or Cash Inwards Book.

(3) Consecutively numbered Receipt Check Books should be kept, and an acknowledgment given therefrom for all amounts received.

(4) A periodical internal Audit should be conducted to ensure that all moneys received are duly brought into account.

(5) No goods should be issued from stock or stores without being first entered up.

(6) As many independent persons as possible should be concerned in all transactions involving the receipt or issue of goods.

(7) The services of a duly qualified Auditor should be secured, and his advice should be sought as to the efficiency of the accounting system in operation, and on the points at which it is necessary for an internal examination to have control.

It will be obvious that, in many cases, the foregoing principles will be differently adapted in practice to meet the requirements of different classes of accounts, but a careful consideration of them should lead to the selection of the most suitable system and should obviate many of the irregularities and complications which might otherwise result.

Cases have been known in which a Cashier has been entrusted with the keeping of the Debtors' Ledger. A system which permits such an anomaly as this clearly invites irregularity, and there can be little wonder if an official should go astray in the execution of his duty when the means of delinquency are so easy and obvious.

Many private firms are disposed to trust their staff to such an extent as to make no provision for the professional audit of their accounts. Whilst it is, of course, eminently desirable that officials should have proper confidence reposed in them, it is wholly inadvisable for this to be carried to the extent of foregoing, as unnecessary, a periodical examination of the transactions for which they are responsible. The Principal or the Manager who has failed to institute some adequate means of audit, as a protection to his firm and a deterrent to his employees, is himself largely to blame for any irregularities or fraudulent mistakes which may arise.

The great majority of the transactions arising in any trade, business, or undertaking consist in (*a*) Receipt and Payment of Cash, (*b*) Purchase and Sale of Goods; and, although there may be various channels required, through which transactions are passed, yet the simple facts stated above cannot be too clearly kept in view, for they really constitute the Alpha and the Omega of the life of the business concerned.

By the English system of book-keeping, as opposed to the Continental system, the process of journalizing is greatly diminished without in any degree interfering with the principle of double entry. Various subsidiary books are employed which replace, to a great extent, the work of the Journal as the book of original entry. In these subsidiary books, transactions of a similar nature are collated, and, by this method, the work of posting is considerably lessened.

In practical working, the most important books of account are

(1) Cash Book, (2) Purchases Book for recording Credit Purchases, (3) Sales Book for recording Credit Sales, (4) Journal (or Journals) for recording transactions which cannot be dealt with otherwise, and (5) Ledger.

With regard to the Cash Book, it must be remembered that—unless the monthly totals are posted to the Ledger, as described later on—this is not a book of first entry merely, but really a part of the Ledger itself, from which it is kept distinct merely for the sake of convenience. Where all cash and remittances received are not deposited intact in the bank the most expedient form of Cash Book is one which combines all cash transactions, whether made by cheque drawn on the firm's bankers or by cash from the office, and which also includes a column on both sides of the account for recording the operation of discount. These discount columns constitute, in effect, a Discount Journal, which by being kept in conjunction with the Cash Book proper obviates the necessity of posting the individual items to the Discount Account in the Ledger. The several columns will be totalled monthly and the totals carried to the particular account in the Nominal Ledger. The form of Cash Book which is required is shown in Form No. 44.

Unless, however, it is desired that the Cash Book shall not show the bank balance, it is quite unnecessary to post the monthly totals of its "Cash" and "Bank" columns to a Ledger Account as the balances may be carried forward from month to month in the Cash Book.

It should be added that modern practice follows the salutary rule of paying all remittances into the bank and making all payments (except Petty Cash) by cheque. In such a case the "Cash" column of Form No. 44 will be unnecessary.

There are many different methods of recording transactions relating to the Purchase and Sale of Goods on credit. The following essentials must, however, be noted in adopting a satisfactory and reliable book for this purpose. The book must record—

(*a*) Date of Purchase or Sale.

(*b*) Name of Vendor or Purchaser.

(*c*) Quantity, description, and cost of the goods bought or sold. It is frequently found that goods have been insufficiently described when the original entry has been madé, with the certain result that the classification in the Stock Ledger is either misleading or

Dr. **COLUMNAR CASH BOOK** *Cr.*

Date	Receipt No.	Corresponding Credit	Ledger Folio	Discount £	s.	d.	Cash £	s.	d.	Bank £	s.	d.
19				£	s.	d.	£	s.	d.	£	s.	d.
Jan. 1		To Goods sold .					30	0	0			
1		,, Bank . .	C				20	0	0			
8	2.	,, J. Jones .		1	2	6				45	0	0
12	3	,, B. White .			17	0				34	0	0
15		,, Goods sold .					65	0	0			
15		,, Cash . .	C							30	0	0
25	4	,, Stone & Co. .		1	2	0				44	0	0
29		,, Bank . .	C				25	0	0			
31		,, Goods sold .					54	0	0			
		Totals carried to Nominal Ledger		£3	1	6	£194	0	0	£153	0	0

Date	Voucher No.	Corresponding Debit	Ledger Folio	Discount £	s.	d.	Cash £	s.	d.	Bank £	s.	d.
19				£	s.	d.	£	s.	d.	£	s.	d.
Jan. 1	1	By Brown & Co.		2	10	0	22	0	0			
1		,, Cash . .	C							20	0	0
1	2	,, Long Trading Co. . .		5	0	0				100	0	0
1		,, Wages . .					20	10	0			
6	3	,, Poplar Boro' Council (Rates) .					5	12	0			
15		,, Bank . .	C				30	0	0			
15		,, Wages . .					18	15	0			
15		,, Self (Drawing A/c) . .					10	0	0			
25		,, Goods purchased .			6	6				12	10	0
29	4	,, Lees & Co. .			3	0	6	0	0			
29	5	,, J. Black (Rent) .								5	10	0
29		,, Cash . .	C							25	0	0
29		,, Wages . .					17	10	0			
31		,, Carriage .					12	0	0			
				£7	19	6	£142	7	0	£163	0	0

(*Form No.* 44)

inaccurate. This should be avoided, as much subsequent inquiry will be saved by a careful description in the book of original entry.

It is highly desirable that the results of the trading in each Department of a business shall be separately ascertained. For

TABULAR SALES BOOK

Ledger Folio	Press Book Folio	January, 19	Rate	Total			Bricks			Coal			Lime		
				£	s.	d.	£	s.	d.	£	s.	d.	£	s.	d.
		—3—													
		J. Jones													
		10,000 Bricks .	25s.	12	10	0	12	10	0						
		5 tons Lime .	20s.	5	0	0							5	0	0
		—6—													
		Stone & Co.													
		10 tons Nuts .	12s.	6	0	0				6	0	0			
		5,000 Bricks .	30s.	7	10	0	7	10	0						
		—20—													
		B. White													
		10 tons Lime .	22s.	11	0	0							11	0	0
		15,000 Bricks .	21s.	15	15	0	15	15	0						
		5 tons Best Coal .	25s.	11	5	0				11	5	0			
		—26—													
		Builders Supply Co.													
		20,000 Bricks .	30s.	30	0	0	30	0	0						
		Total .		99	0	0									
		Bricks A/c *Cr.*					65	15	0						
		Coal A/c *Cr.*								17	5	0			
		Lime A/c *Cr.*											16	0	0

(*Form No.* 45)

this purpose, it is advisable to keep both the Purchases and the Sales Books on an analytical method. Form No. 45 shows a convenient form of Analysed Sales Book.

In practice, the Journal need be used only for recording transactions which are outside the scope of other books, such as Interest, Depreciation, Bad and Doubtful Debts, Bills (if no Bill Books are kept), as well as for recording all opening and closing entries. The details of the various subsidiary books are sometimes journalized, although this is by no means necessary, save to facilitate sectional balancing of the Ledgers.

In the English system of book-keeping, the Ledger is by far the most important book. As is well known, it includes, in a classified form, a record of every financial transaction which has taken place in the business or undertaking concerned. It is not necessary for the purposes of this book to explain in any detail the method whereby the several Ledger Accounts are linked together, but it should always be borne in mind that this book is for *postings* only from the various books of original entry, and that no items should be included therein which have not been first recorded either in the Cash Book or in one or other of the books of first entry.

In large counting-houses, it is necessary to keep Sectional Ledgers, in order to avoid the employment of a book too large and inconvenient to be easily handled, and also in order to effect a fair distribution of the posting work. By employing different ledgers in this way, or by employing the Card or Loose-Leaf Ledger system, the posting can easily be proceeded with concurrently by numerous different book-keepers.

The reader will already have been prepared, from statements made earlier in this book, for the knowledge that in modern countinghouses the originating documents (if going outwards) and records of original entry are prepared, analysed, and totalled by mechanical means. It must now be stated that it is a commonplace of modern practice that these original records should be posted to Ledger Accounts through the medium of machines. To enter into a fully detailed explanation of the working of these appliances would be outside the scope of this work, but it may be said that the general appearance of the common type of ledger-posting machine is not greatly unlike that of a typewriter with which the characteristics of an adding machine have been combined. If we take the process of posting to the Personal Accounts of a Sold Ledger as typical of general procedure we may say that these Personal Accounts appear on specially ruled cards or loose leaves. There are the usual columns for date, reference, and particulars and these are followed by four financial columns, respectively for debit, credit, balance, and "pick-up." Usually, the first operation in posting a batch of carbon copies of selling invoices is to make a list of the amounts on an ordinary listing adding machine, arriving at what is technically called the "predetermined total." Each card to be posted is then injected into the machine and the existing balance shown thereon is set up into the machine. The correct taking up of this quantity (which will ultimately appear in the "pick-up" column) is obviously a matter of supreme importance, for if the machine is, as it were, given the wrong initial information the ultimate balance which it produces must correspondingly be wrong. Consequently, in practice, there are several devices of procedure, too detailed to be dealt with here, designed to ensure the correctness of this initial step. The amount to be posted is then set up into the machine which, on depression of a motor bar which actuates the electric power, automatically prints the amount into the debit or credit column and in the balance column the resulting balance on the account, credits being shown in distinctive type. Usually, throughout the day's run, there is retained in the machine a document called a "journal sheet" or "proof sheet" on which a carbon copy of every successive entry is kept line by line so that, if considered necessary, the day's postings can be called back with the originating documents. Not only does the machine compute the balance produced on each successive account but it also accumulates a total of the day's postings, whether debit or credit, which can be compared with the "predetermined total" mentioned above and which, in turn, can be posted into the Control Account which is kept as one of the ordinary accounts in the Card Ledger. Under some systems the opening balances and closing balances are also separately totalled by the automatic operation of the machine, and the difference between these is obviously the net amount posted into the Ledger during the day.

After the sales have so been posted to the debit of Personal Accounts it is obviously possible to post their dissection to the credit of the various Departmental Sales Accounts, and the total of these entries should evidently correspond with the total already posted to the debit of customers. Under some systems, as notably in the case of the Elliot Fisher machines, two cards, respectively for the debit and the credit involved in each transaction, are in the machine at the same time and one continuous operation effects the posting of the two cards, the equality of debit and credit being assured, entry by entry, by the fact that the machine "clears" itself in respect of each transaction and it is impossible to proceed unless this effect has been reached.

The ledger cards under a machine system are different in appearance from the accounts in a hand-written Ledger in that all transactions follow one another line by line in strictly chronological order, whereas in the hand-written Ledger all debits are on one side and all credits are opposite and contiguous on the other. The consequence is that, although in a machine Ledger it is possible to be confident that the balance last appearing in the balance column is arithmetically correct, nevertheless it is not always easy to see exactly how it is made up. The inference to be drawn from this statement is that it is necessary to work mechanical systems on a very strictly prescribed routine and queries which occur, particularly in regard to discount and returns, must be instantly investigated and dealt with. Otherwise the arithmetical correctness of the Ledger will be, in fact, misleading, and the accountant relying on it will be living in a veritable fool's paradise.

Perhaps the ultimate development of machinery as applied to accounting is to be seen in the punched card system. Very briefly indeed, the system consists in the allocation of a card, about the size of an ordinary cheque, to each transaction. The card is divided perpendicularly into as many "fields" or divisions as may be required to represent all the aspects of accounting significance attached to the transaction. Within the fields numerical quantities can be indicated by the positioning of punched holes. The necessary mechanism falls into three sections. First, there are punches capable of punching the holes with rapidity and certainty. Next, there is an ingenious sorting mechanism which, in any desired field, can arrange the cards in strict numerical order. Finally, a "tabulator" can take the cards thus arranged and translate the information therein contained back into plain language conveyed by typewritten characters on continuous rolls or separate statement forms. Further, the tabulator will accumulate and display both sub-totals and grand totals. It is thus evident that if we have a series of cards representing, say, sales to customers, we can by sorting them in the "customer's number" field tabulate the equivalent of Ledger Accounts for those customers. Then by resorting the cards in the "class of goods" field we can tabulate the equivalent of a series of Sales Accounts. There is then nothing to prevent a resorting and retabulation of the same cards according to the traveller who booked the order, or according to the geographical location of the customer, or indeed according to any other incident of accounting interest in connection with the sales.

A Manufacturing Account to some extent combines the functions of a Goods Account and a Profit and Loss Account. In arriving at the Manufacturing Profits, only such charges should be debited to the account as are included in the Cost Accounts, so that both may show the same result—the factory profit on the articles manufactured.

In establishments containing several departments, it is desirable to keep separate Trading (or Manufacturing) Accounts, for the purpose of ascertaining what profits are severally realized. Each separate account should be debited with a fair proportion of establishment charges, whenever it is practicable so to apportion them upon a reasonable basis, but not otherwise.

It is of advantage to divide the Profit and Loss Account into two sections, the first of which will show the Establishment and General Charges and the Gross Profit brought from the Trading Account. The other section of the Account will show the credit balance brought down from the first section together with any income derived from dividends, rents, etc., and on the debtor side will be included all losses which are independent of the actual trading of the business, namely, salaries of partners, interest, etc., as well as the division of Net Profit.

Limited companies should deal with the allocation of divisible profits in a special section; indeed, in most large undertakings, it is necessary to open an Appropriation Account for the purpose of showing the application of the Net Profit. This account would be credited with the Net Profit brought down from the Profit and Loss Account, together with any unappropriated profit from a previous period, while on the other side would be shown the dividends paid out to shareholders and the provision made for Reserve. It must be borne in mind that the Appropriation Account should be credited only with the net profit actually available for division *after all proper charges have been duly provided for.*

The Double Account System is almost exclusively adopted where capital has been contributed for purposes of a "public utility," and applies to companies authorized to construct or acquire railways, tramways, or gas, electric light, and water undertakings, etc. The system is statutorily imposed, e.g. on companies governed by the Railway Companies (Accounts and Returns) Act, 1911, and the Gas Regulation Act, 1920.

Under the Double Account System, the cost of all capital assets is exhibited in one Capital Account, being there set against the cash received for shares, stock, and debentures, and the balance is taken to the General Balance Sheet. It must also be remembered that the Capital Expenditure is always stated at its original cost, no adjustment of Capital Assets being (as a rule) allowed.

The principal object sought by the Double Account System appears to be that the amount of capital raised for any specific purpose should be shown in direct connection with the application of such capital in the acquisition of permanent or fixed assets. The chief objection to the system lies in the fact that the cost of replacement of worn-out assets is made against Revenue as and when such replacement actually occurs, thus often making such charges very uneven, but if an *estimated* amount is charged annually against Revenue to provide a reserve for replacement or renewals the necessary expenditure may be equitably spread over the full period commensurate with the life of the various assets. By merely charging Revenue with the actual cost of replacement or renewal from time to time, the net profits—particularly in the early years of the undertaking—are liable to be occasionally over-stated, and can only by a pure coincidence represent the true net profits earned, in the commercial sense.

The statement of profits for the purpose of Income Tax assessment is a question which must be included in any work dealing with office management and accounts. The importance of being able to prepare an adequate statement for submission to the Inspector of Taxes cannot be too highly appreciated, as it must be borne in mind that where such a statement is not rendered to the Inland Revenue authorities, they have power to make such an assessment as appears appropriate—a practice which is often not to the financial advantage of the trader. The various rules applicable (which are subject to very considerable complication) are set forth in the Income Tax Act, 1918, and subsequent annual Finance Acts.

Of the five schedules under which Income Tax is assessed, Schedule " D " relates to Income derived from Trading and Manufacturing. It is under this Schedule, therefore, that the Statement of Profits above referred to is prepared. This tax is in most cases now assessed on the profit for the financial year preceding the year of assessment, so that if the year of assessment is, say, that ending on the 5th April, 1940, and the books have been balanced at the 31st December in each year, the accounts which will be required for the purposes of the assessment for the fiscal year 1939–40 will be those relating to the year 1938. The Statement of Profits which has to be rendered under Schedule " D " is prepared from the Trading and Profit and Loss Accounts ; but a considerable modification of these accounts is necessary in consequence of amounts having been charged therein which, for the purpose of Income Tax assessment, are not allowed to be deducted from Gross Profit, and *vice versa*. It is, therefore, very desirable that the nature of the deductions allowed should be clearly understood in preparing the Statement of Profit.

No deduction is allowed in respect of (*a*) expenses not "wholly and exclusively laid out or expended for the purposes of the trade" ; in a particular case damages paid by an innkeeper for injuries to a guest were excluded under this far-reaching provision ; (*b*) maintenance of the taxpayer or his family ; (*c*) losses not connected with or arising out of the trade ; (*d*) capital expenditure ; (*e*) any "annual payment" such as interest or dividend, the reason being that the payer is entitled by statute to recoup himself of tax by deducting the current standard rate when making the relative payment.

On the other hand, deductions are allowed in respect of—

(1) Repair of premises occupied for trading purposes and for the supply or repair of implements, utensils, or articles employed in the trade.

(2) Specific Bad Debts ; also specific Doubtful Debts, according to their estimated value.

(3) Rent (or net annual value, if higher) of Trade premises.

(4) Rent (or net annual value, if higher) of any dwelling-house used partly for the purpose of business, such sum not to exceed two-thirds of the rent or value as the case may be.

(5) Rates, Taxes (except Income Tax), and Insurance (fire, burglary, or guarantee).

(6) Loss of stock by fire (not covered by insurance).

(7) Bank interest and charges.

STATEMENT OF PROFITS FOR ASSESSMENT TO INCOME TAX FOR THE FISCAL YEAR 1939–40

Dr. | *Cr.*

	Year ended 31st December, 1938				Year ended 31st December, 1938		
	£	*s.*	*d.*		£	*s.*	*d.*
To Rent and Local Rates	150	0	0	By Gross Profit from Trading Account	4,500	0	0
,, Charitable Subscriptions	10	0	0				
,, Income Tax	600	0	0				
,, Depreciation of Plant and Machinery	400	0	0				
,, Interest on Mortgage	30	0	0				
,, Partners' Salaries	600	0	0				
,, Interest on Capital	400	0	0				
,, Balance carried down	2,310	0	0				
	£4,500	0	0		£4,500	0	0
To Assessment under Schedule A on Works owned and occupied by the Firm	100	0	0	By Balance brought down	2,310	0	0
,, Balance being Profit assessable to Income Tax subject to allowance for Wear and Tear of Plant and Machinery	4,250	0	0	,, Deductions as per contra not allowed for Income Tax Assessment—			
				Charitable Subscriptions	10	0	0
				Income Tax	600	0	0
				Depreciation	400	0	0
				Interest on Mortgage	30	0	0
				Partners' Salaries	600	0	0
				Interest on Capital	400	0	0
	£4,350	0	0		£4,350	0	0

(*Form No.* 46)

(8) Profit derived from casual transactions not amounting to the carrying on of a trade or business.

(9) Profits already taxed at their source.

In addition to the deductions above mentioned, it is customary for the Commissioners to make allowance for wear and tear of plant and machinery. The rate of allowance is technically within the discretion of local bodies of Commissioners but, in practice, rates have been agreed with the authorities at Somerset House and these are of general application. The allowance is deducted from the assessable profits, but does not affect the profits themselves. As soon as the amount so allowed totals up to a sum equal to the original cost of the asset all allowance for wear and tear ceases; but in the meantime it is cumulative, in the sense that if the assessable profits are nil the allowances for that year may be carried forward and charged against subsequent years' assessable profits, and if the allowance exceeds the assessable profits in any year the excess may similarly be carried forward.

Form No. 46 is a convenient form in which the Statement of Profits may be prepared, and is one usually accepted by the Income Tax Authorities.

In all cases where a loss is revealed, the assessment for the following fiscal year will, of course, be *nil*; but there are, broadly speaking, three other forms of relief, viz.—(*a*) the assessment *for the year itself* may be reduced, under Section 34 of the Income Tax Act, 1918, to the extent of any actual loss sustained during the fiscal year. (*b*) If two distinct businesses owned by the same taxpayer show the one a loss and the other a profit in the same year, the loss may be set off against the profit. The authority for this concession is Rule 13 of Schedule D. (*c*) Any balance of loss not used in *either* of these ways may be carried forward and set off against any assessable profits of the business in the next six years of assessment, but a new owner cannot take any benefit.

The assessable profits of companies, together with interest, rents, and other annual payments, rank as "investment" income; but the profits of partners, and the remuneration of employees, directors, etc., are "earned income." A limited partner's share of profits is "investment income." The distinction is of importance, for "earned" income, up to a maximum of £1500, is subject to an abatement of one-fifth in taxation.

Under the Finance Act, 1937, a National Defence Contribution is levied at the rate of 5 per cent on the profits of companies and 4 per cent on the profits of individuals and firms. The tax is levied according to accounting (not Government fiscal) periods and the methods of computation follow Income Tax principles except that "annual payments" (see (*e*) on p. 206) need not be disallowed. The war of 1939 has also brought forth an Excess Profits Tax but that is too technical to be within the scope of this book.

CHAPTER XVII

Stocktaking—By whom undertaken—Responsibility for Quantities, Values and Calculations—Allowances for movement of Stock in lengthy jobs—Effect of errors on results—Continuous stocktaking

STOCKTAKING is probably the most important part of the work which goes to make the books the record of the business. On its accuracy depends the correctness of the Profit and Loss Account and Balance Sheet. It will also directly involve the accuracy of the figures relating to the production by the Works, by means of the valuation put on the Stock of finished goods, the amount of raw materials used, and, in businesses where repairs are done on the premises, the charges for material used for repairs, and even some of the indirect expenses in many businesses where the stock of stationery and advertising material is taken into account. This latter class of Stock should always be taken into account where such expenditure is considerable, so as to ascertain the actual amount of goods *used* each year instead of amount of money spent. In many businesses, also, a considerable amount of packing material is kept in stock, and should be taken into account so as to reduce the cost of packing for the year to its proper amount.

Not only will an error on stocktaking affect the amount of profit believed to be earned and the figures of materials and expenses (and, consequently, the percentages of the same as shown above), but it will also have an effect on future years, as, if there is keen competition in the trade carried on, the percentages on which the costing of the estimates for future years is based may very likely be altered and consequent loss caused by too low a figure being taken.

The question of stocktaking involves also a heavier responsibility on the Manager, because, while in other directions he is usually under the direction of the Board or the Proprietors, and the actions of both himself and his Board are open to the criticism of the Auditor, in this matter the Directors and Auditors can only lay down the principle upon which Stock shall be taken and check the arithmetical accuracy of the figures which the Manager lays before them. The Auditor almost invariably (and particularly since the decision given in the Law Courts in the case of *The Kingston Cotton*

Mills Company, Ltd.), states in his report that the Stock is taken and certified by the Manager (unless that fact is stated in the Balance Sheet itself) and accepts a certificate from him as to its accuracy. It must further be remembered that, if a Limited Company declares a dividend which has not been earned out of profits (which might occur through an over-valuation of Stock), the parties responsible for such over-statement would be liable, and might, under certain circumstances, be called upon to repay such sums wrongfully distributed.

Enough has been said to show the importance of Stocktaking, both to the concern and to the Manager, and it now remains to be seen how best to deal with the matter to ensure as far as possible that no unfortunate mistake shall arise.

Where the business is not of the largest dimensions, it is usual to defer the actual taking of an inventory until the close of the financial period, but, where the size of the undertaking warrants the setting up of the necessary organization, stocktaking can be "continuous." We shall speak first of the first-named process deferring our remarks about "continuous" stocktaking till the end of the chapter.

It must be remembered that a complete stocktaking crowded into one brief period of two or three days must necessarily entail a certain amount of dislocation of the ordinary business, and, to minimize this, all arrangements should be made before the date fixed for taking the Stock. The departments should be carefully gone over, and a responsible man put in charge of each and provided with as many reliable assistants as may be required, or as may be practicable.

If a certain material or section of the goods is not likely to be required for a few days prior to the Stocktaking, this might even be counted and marked as to quantity a few days previously; but, in this case, great care must be taken to mark distinctly on the docket any goods removed, if it should be found necessary to touch this Stock before the day itself arrives.

If the manufactured Stock is boxed, or otherwise packed in separate parcels before delivery (and is, in the meantime, in that form), these boxes or parcels should be examined to see that they all contain the supposed quantity, and, if accurate, should be initialed by the man counting them. If they do not show the full quantity, the number or weight contained should be distinctly marked on the box, and, as before, if it is necessary to disturb any of them to complete an order, etc., the number must be crossed off immediately, so that no error can arise.

In any event, immediately before the Stock is actually taken down, all goods of the same kind should be put together as far as possible, and, if the staff is sufficient to take down the Stock all in one day, very little difficulty should arise. Everything must be counted, or weighed, as the case may be, and then Stock should be taken, starting at one end of the room, or Works, and going straight forward to ensure that nothing is missed, setting out the article in sufficient detail to avoid mistakes, and giving the exact quantity in Stock. If practicable, the Stock should be taken down on sheets with spaces left to show the price per unit and the calculation of amount in Stock; otherwise the sheets will have to be re-copied in the office on to sheets (or into a book) with these columns. It is desirable also to have an extra money column for details. The necessity for this re-copying should be avoided in all possible cases, as it is a fruitful source of error. In general, it is a great convenience to use Loose-Leaf Stock books, as these can readily be kept separate as long as necessary, and afterwards readily bound together.

By this process, the quantities of Finished Goods, Raw Materials, Repairs, Packing, etc., will all appear under suitable headings, and it only remains to take the work in progress. The character of this will vary according to the business. In the case of an Engineering, Contracting, or similar business, the Cost Book of the jobs in hand will be taken as the criterion. In other concerns, the quantity of the goods in progress will have to be ascertained and dealt with, either according to the Cost Book, if it has arrived exactly at a position which can be valued as being the termination of a particular process, or else it must be valued on its merits by the head of the department and the Manager in consultation.

So far, no difficulty should have arisen, but, if it is impossible to take down all the Stock in one day or whilst the Works are stopped, new complications are immediately presented. In that case, everything must be taken down as far as possible, and, when the Works recommence the ordinary routine once more, if Stock is still incomplete, a special staff must be told off to finish it. The work in progress must always be taken on the day in question, as on such work, wages and materials continue to be expended, and, if the Stocktaking day (or days) pass without this Stock being completed, the final account will inevitably be wrong. Other items, however, may be accurately completed at a later date, provided due care is exercised.

Any raw materials which may have already been taken into Stock may be safely given out for use on work in progress, or the latter may be removed on completion to Finished Goods which have already been taken into Stock without fear of error. But, if any raw material which has not yet been taken into Stock is required for work in progress, a careful note must be taken of the same, and the quantity so removed added to the Stock in hand of the material in question. Similarly, if any class of goods which has already been recorded requires for any reason to be removed to another part of the Works where Stock is not yet taken, a note must be made, and the amount so removed and its value deducted from the goods already put down on the sheets. Work in progress must be similarly dealt with when necessary.

The best way to prevent error is to make one man responsible for all this, and to require *everyone* to report to this official any goods which he may have to remove, at the same time filling in a note stating, "class of goods, quantity, when taken, from where taken, and to where." The official in question, if he is not already aware of the facts, must then immediately find out whether this will affect the Stock (and, if so, in what manner), and make forthwith a note as to the effect; and he should personally see to the necessary adjustments before the quantities of the Stock sheets are completed as correct and sent to the office.

It will be necessary to go over the various classes of goods to be taken into Stock with the Accountant, and to make sure that such items are legitimate and proper entries. For instance, in some businesses, loose tools are taken into Stock and in others they are not. The reason for this is that, in the first case, the tools are considered as changing too rapidly to be safely treated as fixed assets, and, instead of capitalizing the original cost in the first instance and then writing off a depreciation and charging all renewals to repairs, all purchases—whether they are additional tools or only renewals—are debited to "Loose Tools Account." The tools in hand are then taken as "Stock," and entered in Loose Tools Account as an asset, and the difference between the total debit and the present value, ascertained as above, is written off as Depreciation, or cost of Loose Tools. The same point occurs in Packing. In many trades, the necessary packages are capitalized in the first instance, and renewals and depreciation charged against Revenue, while, in other cases, these articles are debited to Packing Account, and their value included with the packing stock at the year end. The Accountant will also be able to inform the Manager whether or not any such class of goods was taken into Stock at all in the previous year. Many concerns, for instance, do not put any value for Stocktaking purposes upon their stationery, fuel, samples, etc., while others are in the habit of doing so, and, if such items have been omitted in previous years, they must not be taken into account for the current year, as this would have the effect of reducing the proper charge for the year involved. For instance, suppose that the order forms, stationery, etc., amounted at December 31st to £55, but had not previously been taken into Stock, then to include this amount in this year's stock without taking into account the value of stationery on hand at January 1st, but since used, would have the effect of reducing the sum expended by £55. If, for purposes of accuracy, it is desired to include the figure, an adjusting entry would have to be made in the old account by the Accountant. An exception to this might arise under the following circumstances, as in the case of a concern with the necessary storing accommodation buying, in anticipation of a coal strike, a very large quantity of fuel. Such excess might properly be dealt with as Stock on hand, even though coal had not been included previously in the Stock.

When all quantities have been entered upon the sheets, these are taken into the office for completion. The first thing required is to ascertain the prices, which are best filled in under the personal supervision of the Manager or the Accountant.

Finished Goods should be valued at cost, unless in the meantime the market price has become the lower of the two. Cost will be ascertained from the Cost Book, or other similar source. The exceptions to this rule are—

(1) In the case of certain trades where maturing is usual or necessary—for example, timber, wines, etc.—Stock increases in value with age, and, indeed, must necessarily be kept a certain time before being used; in these and

similar cases, interest is generally added to the original cost;

(2) Where the goods are already sold under a contract, even though the price has fallen in the meantime, they are usually taken at the cost figure;

(3) Certain trades manufacturing a standard article, the price of which varies according to the market, will frequently take the market price, less a percentage.

Work in progress will be valued, as before stated, by the Manager and the head of the department on similar lines to the Finished Goods, and based as far as possible on cost.

In both these cases, it is usual for engineers' contractors, etc., to ascertain the cost by taking from the Cost Book wages and material, and adding thereto a percentage for indirect expenses and a further percentage for the office charges, etc. In most other businesses, the cost of wages and materials only is taken, without any addition for the indirect charges. The Manager, however, will follow the basis of previous Stocktakings, or, in the case of a first Stocktaking, the instructions of the Board or the Proprietor, who will probably decide the principle in consultation with the Auditor, the Accountant, and the Manager.

Raw materials will be priced at cost, after comparison with the current purchasable price, which is often taken if it is lower. It is also desirable to value these at a lower price, if they are not worth so much to the firm as at the time when they were bought. For example, a newer invention may make certain materials which have been in stock some time almost obsolete for the purpose for which they were originally purchased, and yet not have affected the market price, because they may keep at their old value in other trades. It is right to add that many modern accountants criticize the view expressed in this paragraph and take no notice of a mere fall in current price of raw materials if it may reasonably be expected that the finished article will be sold at a profit.

Loose tools and packages—if necessary to be dealt with as Stock (as to which see above)—must be re-valued each time, as it would be a manifest absurdity to enter at cost price a tool which may have been in use for months and may be nearly worn out. Some firms enter unused tools, etc., in stores at cost, and take a percentage up to 50 per cent or more (according to the residue of value, if any) from those tools which are in use in the Works.

Other classes of Stock will be priced at cost or market price, whichever is lower, excepting where, in any particular case, it is considered advisable for any reason to write off a special discount.

In estimating these prices, it must be remembered that many trades allow a trade discount off the goods they supply, and, if this exists, it must be marked distinctly on the sheets in red ink and the net amount only entered. It is for this purpose that a second money column is desirable on the Stock sheets, so that those classes of goods liable to a trade discount may be entered in the inner column and the discount deducted from the total, only the net figure being extended.

The quantity and prices all being entered, the next step is for the Office Staff to calculate the value of the Stock on hand by the extension of the figures. This is purely routine work if the prices are entered clearly and distinctly, and similar clearness of entry must apply to the unit of purchase, as this, if not properly entered, may easily lead to an error. For instance, many classes of goods are bought (as in the dyeing and kindred trades) by the bag, and, if the Stock appears, as it probably will, at so many pounds avoirdupois, an error may arise with a careless clerk or even with one who, though fairly careful, has little or no practical knowledge—unless the *unit* of purchase is given as well as the price. Similar examples of this occur in purchases by the kilogram, dozen, etc., where the same unit is not invariably used in the Works. All the sheets must be calculated, therefore, with great care, and be checked by a second clerk, each signing every sheet for which he may be responsible. This class of work lends itself admirably to the use of calculating machines of suitable types.

A summary of the Stocktaking will be prepared for the use of the Accountant, dividing the Stock under the various headings of Finished Goods, Raw Materials, etc.; and, if Departmental Accounts are kept, these divisions must be separated further into Finished Goods, Department A; Finished Goods, Department B; etc.

The sole duty now remaining to be executed is to compare the Stock in hand, as actually taken, with the Stock as appearing in the Stores Ledger described in Chapter XII. Each item must be

entered in that book under its appropriate heading, and the account ruled off as if it were an ordinary Ledger Account. The difference between the two sides will represent the difference between the Stock on paper (as ascertained by adding the opening stock and all purchases, in the case of raw materials, and deducting from that total all the Stock given out, for the purpose of manufacture or otherwise) and the actual Stock in hand, as ascertained by counting or weighing the commodity in question. This difference should be entered in each case in red ink to show it clearly, and the account will then be ruled off and the Stock in hand will be brought down for the purpose of showing the amount actually in hand with which to commence the new year.

A full list of the variations should be given to the Manager, setting out in detail which articles are over and which are short, with any explanation opposite each variation. The items which are over must be investigated carefully, to acertain, if it is still possible to do so, the actual Stock on hand for fear of a wrong designation. The invoices for the receipt of such goods should be examined to see that none have escaped from the stores records, and the records of stores issued must also be carefully checked to see that the full quantity handed out has been accounted for and is duly charged against the proper accounts. Far more usually, however, the stores will be *short*, and will require checking in the same way. Small leakages will frequently occur, and can hardly be guarded against in the ordinary course of events. Take, for example, a chemical which is bought by the quarter, the hundredweight, or even the ton. This will be served out, as required, probably by the pound, possibly even by the ounce, and a certain leakage will occur here, as the full weight will be necessary in each such issue and it is impossible to weigh to a featherweight. There will thus be a loss arising from the necessity of turning the scale in the numerous weighings. Other classes of goods will possibly suffer loss by evaporation or breakage, though, in this latter case, the broken articles should exist as a voucher for the loss, and they should be thrown away only if there is no residue of value, periodically, and after inspection by the Staff Auditor or some other appointed official. In this case, the destruction should take place in his presence, after he has counted and certified the quantity, to prevent the same breakages being produced again at a later time to account for whole articles which have been lost or stolen.

The cases of legitimate depreciation in this manner will, however, be known to the experienced Manager, who will know what is a reasonable percentage of loss, and, if this is not exceeded, he will pass such difference without comment. If, however, a large discrepancy exists, he must go carefully into the matter: have that portion of Stock checked more frequently, and, if the deficiency of the Stock continues, or if it is general over several distinct classes of goods, the only explanation is either that the Storekeeper is incompetent or is guilty of peculation, or that outside theft is going on. Watch should be kept to see that it is not the latter, the length and nature of the guard depending upon the circumstances of the case, and, if that does not reveal the cause of the shortness of goods, the only alternative is to obtain a new Storekeeper.

The Stocktaking having been fully completed and the summary prepared, the Manager will usually be required to give the Auditor a certificate to cover the entire Stock, probably in a form similar to the following—

"I hereby certify that the Stock of the above-named Company has been taken under my directions, that the quantities are correct to the best of my knowledge and belief, that the prices do not exceed cost price or market price, whichever may in each case be lower, and that the stock so taken amounts to £......., as set out in the schedule hereto annexed.

(Signed) A—— B——,
Manager."

In some concerns, the Stock is re-copied into a book if it is not already in that form. It is, however, better to have the Stock made up in the first instance on specially designed sheets, to enable as many as possible to work at the calculations and additions, and then to bind up the sheets in proper binders similar to (but not usually so substantial as) those employed for Loose Leaf Ledgers.

Many firms keep the sheets simply loose in their original form; but it is safer and better to secure them against loss by the simple means suggested above.

We now deal specially with those cases mentioned earlier in this chapter where "continuous" stocktaking is practised. The great and obvious drawback of the "once a year" plan is that the errors and discrepancies discovered are usually past beyond recall and the utmost that can be done is to ensure, as far as possible, that they do not recur. "Continuous" stocktaking is designed to provide a never-ceasing, systematic watch on the movements of stores and a continuous review of the efficiency of their custody and record. A corps of expert stocktakers is appointed and to them is assigned the specialized duty of passing continually round the stores for the purpose of testing *recorded* quantities against *actual* quantities. Needless to say this itinerary must be very carefully planned and supervised with a view to seeing that every part of the stores is in fact covered a given number of times in the year. If the itinerary be varied from time to time, the moral strength of check they exercise is obviously greater. As each item is covered, they render their report setting forth the shortages and excesses discovered, and *immediate* inquiry is set on foot with a view either to rectifying the error or to bringing the Stores Ledger (under proper authority) into agreement with the actual state of the inventory.

Where such a plan is in force, the end of the financial year has fewer terrors, for the accountant usually feels justified in accepting the balances on the Stores Ledger as the equivalent of a detailed inventory, subject perhaps to a special examination of large items which have not recently been brought under scrutiny in the ordinary way. Needless to repeat, however, the whole idea stands or falls on the *systematic* nature of the plan which underlies it and on the conscientious and independent enforcement of the instructions given to the stocktakers.

CHAPTER XVIII

Balancing Books and Audit—Proper Time for Balancing—Provision for Depreciation and Bad Debts—Reserves and Secret Reserves—Staff Audit and Professional Audit distinguished—Safeguards against Fraud

THE first point for consideration in connection with the Balance Sheet is when it should be prepared. The majority of businesses attempt to prepare a formal Balance Sheet only once a year, and if the trade of any particular firm is at all a "season trade," or if, at any time of the year, their Stock is comparatively low and trade quiet, that period is generally selected for this important piece of work. If, on the other hand, Stock is not subject to any special fluctuations varying with the seasons, it is usual to fix the period for stock-taking at the end of one of the quarters, March 31st, June 30th, September 30th, or December 31st.

If the Ledgers have been posted by any form of ledger-posting machine, it is more than probable that the scheme is such that at every point of time throughout the year they are in a state of balance, and that the fact is testified by the existence of "Control" Accounts summarizing into single figures the entries appearing in each Ledger. This will certainly be true of the Personal Ledgers. In such cases all that will be necessary in place of the preliminary steps to be described below, will be to extract (probably on an adding machine) a schedule of the open balances, agreeing them in total, and Ledger by Ledger, with the "Control" Accounts.

Where a mechanical system is either absent or incomplete, it will be necessary to prepare a Trial Balance for the technical purpose of "balancing the books." The Ledger Accounts are all added, and the balance of each account is placed upon a sheet containing columns for Ledger Folio, Name of Account, and two money columns to represent the debit and credit balances respectively. If these two columns agree with each other in total, the Balance Sheet proper may be proceeded with, but if, on the other hand, they differ—which is, perhaps, the more usual—it is first necessary to discover the cause of difference.

The principle upon which they should balance is, of course, the theory of double-entry book-keeping, that every debit has entailed a corresponding credit, and, if the Accountant is unable to balance the two totals in any other way, the only course is again to check all additions and postings, and the extraction of the balances. A considerable amount of this work may be saved if it is possible to localize the error to a particular section of the books by any of the methods available for that purpose. Of these methods, the most usual in England is that known as "Self-balancing" Ledgers, which takes advantage of the provision of "Control" or "Adjustment" Accounts (the two terms are interchangeable) and which is worked in the following manner: Suppose that it is desired to balance the Sales Ledger entirely separately from the general books. A statement will be prepared from the particulars furnished by the books and records of first entry showing, in total, the entries, debit and credit, which go to make that Ledger. The debit entries will consist of—

(*a*) The opening debit balances at the previous balancing period, say January 1st of the year under review:
(*b*) All the sales which have been posted to it during the period:
(*c*) Any postings made to it from the credit side of the Cash Book, which would include (1) payments made to the customers to meet any over-payment or allowance made to them subsequent to the payment of their account; (2) any cheques or bills receivable discounted which had been given by them to the firm and had been returned dishonoured, etc.:
(*d*) Any other debit postings which appeared in the Ledger in question, which should be obtained by carefully analysing the debit postings of the Journal:
(*e*) Any credit balance which may exist through over-payment or allowance at the end of the period.

The credit entries would consist of—

(1) All cash receipts and discount allowed to customers, which would be entered on the debit side of the Cash Book and be posted thence to the credit side of this Ledger:
(2) Any returns, allowances, or overcharges made in respect of the sales:
(3) The amount of Bills Receivable (if any), as per the Bills Receivable Book:
(4) Any transfer to other Ledgers or other credit postings, such

as bad debts written off, etc., which would be obtained by an analysis of the credit postings of the Journal:

(5) The closing debit balance (i.e. the total of debtors) as extracted from the Ledgers on the list of balances.

If these two sides, as prepared above, then balance, the error in the Trial Balance will certainly not be in the Sales Ledger.

The statement will then appear in the following form—

SALES LEDGER ADJUSTMENT ACCOUNT

19..		£	s.	d.	19..		£	s.	d.
Jan. 1	To Balance at date	4715	6	8	Dec. 31	By Cash & Discount	34081	11	11
Dec. 31	" Sales for year	37801	3	2	" "	" Bills receivable	2046	4	1
" "	" Cheques returned, etc.	37	10	4	" "	" Returns and allowances	317	6	4
" "	" Sundries per Journal	429	1	3	" "	" Sundries per Journal	1422	2	3
" "	" Credit balances at date		7	4	" "	" Balance at date (debit)	5116	4	2
		£42983	8	9			£42983	8	9

(*Form No.* 47)

If the business is of sufficient size to justify the subdivision of the Sales Ledger into more books than one, each of these may, by a suitable arrangement of the subsidiary books, be balanced with equal ease separately. The most common subdivision of a Ledger in these circumstances is an alphabetical one, and, if three Sales Ledgers were required, they might be respectively called the "A-G Sales Ledger," the "H-O Sales Ledger," and the "P-Z Sales Ledger." They are also subdivided in other ways, some according to the class of trade, if two or more entirely distinct departments are worked by the same company, each with its own set of customers, and some according to geographical subdivision, such as London, Provinces, Scotch, Irish, European, etc.

In the first case, to balance the "A-G Ledger" separately, the following alterations would be necessary in the forms of the subsidiary books—

The Sales Book would, in addition to the ordinary ruling, have three money columns added for the purpose of analysis, headed respectively "A-G Ledger," "H-O Ledger," and "P-Z Ledger;" or, alternatively, a separate Sales Book would be provided for each ledger, and the total of the special column for each ledger (or the total of the special Day Book, as the case may be) would be carried into that Ledger's Adjustment Account. Another method

—greatly to be preferred in many cases, as being more flexible—is to employ a suitable scheme whereby carbon copies of originating documents are sorted into groups according to the section of the Ledger affected, the groups being then added by machine.

Cash items from the credit side would be entered in an analysis column which would be used for all the Sales Ledgers, as these would be few in number and, by means of this column, easily ascertained.

The Journal would be in the ordinary form, and would require to be analysed for the entries in question, or a Special Transfer Journal may be used if the entries are sufficiently numerous.

The opening and closing balances, debit and credit, would, of course, be obtained from the lists extracted.

The figures appearing on the credit side of the statement would be obtained by a similar arrangement for returns to that adopted for the sales. The Bills Receivable and the Journal would require to be analysed, and the Cash Book items would be obtained either by the employment of separate subsidiary Sales Ledger Cash Books, or by a special ruling of the Cash Book, of which the debit side would appear as follows—

CASH BOOK (SPECIAL RULING FOR ANALYSIS)

Date.	Item.	Posting folio.	Disct.	Cash.	Bank.	Total.	Analysis.			
							A-G.	H-O.	P-Z.	Other Ledgers.

(*Form No.* 48)

By a similar arrangement (subject to the modifications mentioned) for the purchases, and for the credit side of the Cash Book, the Purchases Ledger (or Ledgers) may be balanced separately, or at least the error in the general accounts may be traced to a specific ledger.

In the absence of automatic mechanical arrangements this system of sectional balancing should be regularly applied monthly, in order to discover mistakes at an early date, and to avoid a congestion of work at Stocktaking.

Where it is thus in use continuously, and not merely to find or to localize an error at stocktaking, very frequently, in order to complete the double entry, the figures involved appear in the Journal and are posted to a Sales Ledger Adjustment Account in the "Nominal Ledger" on one side, and to a "Nominal Ledger Adjustment Account" on the other side in the Sales Ledger, the entries being—

		£ s. d.	£ s. d.
Dec. 31.	Sales Ledger Adjustment Account (in the Nominal Ledger) Dr.	£37,801 3 2	
	To Nominal Ledger Adjustment Account (in Sales Ledger) being sales for year per Sales Book..		£37,801 3 2

If this method be adopted, each Ledger should, on the extraction of the balances, show an agreement of the two sides as if it were the only book of the system.

Although, however, this last-named piece of book-keeping is not infrequently adopted in practice, in order to make each separate Ledger self-balancing, it may perhaps be argued that it is unscientific, and that it renders a clear understanding of the principles involved difficult. The whole basis of the theory of self-balancing Ledgers is that, in each separate Ledger, all those transactions which are recorded *at all* are recorded *by double entry*; but that those transactions which would not be recorded by double entry in that Ledger, if it were not kept upon self-balancing lines, are posted to the Adjustment Account in that Ledger and, therefore, naturally in as summarized a form as possible. This can easily be arranged if each separate Ledger is provided with its own books of first entry, or its own columns in those books. Thus, in the Sold Ledger, postings of Sales would be made in detail to the debit of the Personal Accounts from the Sales Day Book, and in totals to the credit of the Nominal Ledger Adjustment Account therein: in the General Ledger, these same Sales would be recorded in monthly totals through the Journal, to the debit of Sold Ledger Adjustment Account, and to the credit of Sales Account. In this way, each Adjustment Account is built up independently, forming somewhat of a check upon each other, and they may frequently be utilized with advantage in that way.

The Continental method of localizing the error is by means of a special extraction of the balances with four columns, showing total postings to debit and credit in addition to the balances—

TRIAL BALANCE (CONTINENTAL SYSTEM)

Fo.	Name.	Debit Postings.	Credit Postings.	Debit Balance.	Credit Balance.
1	A &c.	1,000	950	50	

(*Form No.* 49)

The system in use in those countries involves the passing of all items (or at any rate totals of all like items) through the Journal, and the total postings in such a case should, therefore, agree with the total of the Journal in addition to their mutual agreement. In England, by means of adding the total of the Sales, Purchases and Journal entries, together with the cash totals less the cash balances entered at the periodical balances of the Cash Book, the figure for the total postings should be produced, provided that there are no direct transfers from one ledger account to another. In practice, however, this system is not as largely used in England as it might be. It possesses the material advantage of disclosing direct transfers, which should always be regarded as irregular entries.

When the Trial Balance is finally agreed, the next step in the preparation of the Balance Sheet is to enter into the books the necessary closing figures for Stock, Reserves, and Depreciation.

The figure for the Stock will be taken from the Stock Book, which sets out the actual materials, etc., in hand, as already described in Chapter XVII.

The amount to be set aside for Provisions will require to be carefully ascertained under the respective headings involved. The first of these is, in respect of Book Debts, for any Bad Debts which may have occurred during the previous year, or debts which, owing to the financial standing of the debtor, are not expected to realize their full amount. Where, in a case of insolvency, a final dividend has been paid, the balance of the account should already have been written off to "Bad Debts Account"; but, where a final dividend has not yet been paid, it is the more usual practice to provide a round sum which should approximately cover the estimated loss and leave the personal account open until such dividend has been received.

In some cases, a provision against loss by way of Bad and Doubtful Debts is built up by charging against Revenue each year a small percentage upon the *Sales* for the period. Assuming that a percentage can be hit upon which will coincide with the average actually experienced over a lengthy period of time, this is perhaps the fairest way of apportioning the loss year by year; but it would be unwise, merely because this system were adopted, to allow the Provision for Bad Debts to amount at any time to *less* than the estimated loss that is likely to be sustained, as gauged by an inspection of the Sold Ledger balances.

In undertakings where a certain amount of Bad Debts must be expected in the ordinary course of business, it is desirable to take special steps to supervise the collection of accounts, in order to keep these losses as low as possible. With this object in view, a Doubtful Debts Ledger is sometimes employed, to which all overdue accounts are transferred—thus bringing them under the attention of a special clerk whose duty it is to attend to overdue accounts (if necessary, by providing the solicitor with the necessary facts to enable him to take proceedings), to attend meetings of insolvent customers, and deal generally with all questions arising in this department. If all doubtful accounts are collected together into one Ledger, the work of this clerk is greatly simplified, and can be more efficiently performed. Moreover, it becomes a far simpler matter to arrive at a reliable estimate of the Provision necessary to cover expected losses. When Card or Loose-Leaf Ledgers are employed, the bodily transfer of accounts from one ledger to another would be a simple process physically, but might, in practice, lead to confusion. Distinctively coloured tabs can, however, be attached to the cards, or sheets, dealing with the overdue accounts of customers, and by the aid of these tabs the doubtful accounts can be readily referred to at any time, either in detail or collectively. In the event of payment being received, the tab can be removed, and the account then resumes its normal place in the book-keeping system.

The next provision on book debts is made to cover any returns, claims or allowances received, or admitted, only after the books relating to the year under review were closed. A full and sufficient estimate for all items of this nature will, of course, be required.

The treatment of Cash Discount varies according to the trade. Where a fixed rate of discount is allowed on all accounts, the usual method is simply to deduct that percentage from the net debtors, that is, after deduction, from the total figure, of the provision made for Bad Debts, Returns, and Allowances, as discount, of course, will not be allowed on these. Where, however, the practice of the trade gives different terms to different customers, or classes of customers, the list of debtors as extracted from the ledger will require to be marked with the discount each is entitled to claim, and the actual figure to be provided will be ascertained from this total. To enable this to be done readily, the lists of debtors should be extracted in columnar form.

The treatment of the Personal Credit balances will be similar, so far as the Discounts and Allowances are concerned, though, of course, no question of bad debts arises on this side of the Balance Sheet. Some traders lean to the side of prudence by ignoring discounts on creditors' accounts. When speaking of Discount for these purposes only the ordinary Cash Discount is, of course, referred to—that is to say, the 2½ per cent, 3 per cent, 5 per cent, etc., allowed for the prompt payment of cash. The trade discount which is allowed in many trades off a standard Price List must in every case be deducted from the sales and purchases at the time they are entered in the Day books, only the net figure being entered in the final column and posted to the Ledger, which, therefore, shows only the net figure, subject to cash discount, if any.

The Nominal Accounts must then be carefully scrutinized, and if any items have been paid in advance, the due proportion for the period not yet expired will form a carry forward for the benefit of the period under review. Items of this nature will include Rates, which are usually levied and are payable at the commencement of the period to which they relate; Telephone Rent, and Insurances of all kinds, which are invariably charged for each year in advance; Rent, which is occasionally (but not usually) paid in advance; and, sometimes, Commission, where the person entitled to it is well known to the firm and is allowed to receive what is due to him, or a part of it, on handing in the order and when the sale has not, as yet, gone through the books.

All Nominal Accounts of every nature must then be carefully examined for any items which are accruing due but not yet payable. Rates, sometimes, and Rent, usually, will come under this heading, and a charge must be made against the period to cover any portion not yet charged. "Wages" is almost invariably the subject of a provision for the odd days elapsing from the date at which wages were last made up to the day of balancing, and the actual amount payable for the work done between those two dates or else a proportionate part of the next week's wages will be taken as a liability. Frequently, where the accounts are closed promptly, the Railway Carriage account for the last month is not received in time to be incorporated, and a fair figure must be provided under this heading. Many small tradesmen send in accounts only once each quarter, and care must be taken to see that these items are included. If they are not already in the books, it will be necessary to ascertain or estimate the amount, and provide accordingly. In fact, strict inquiry must be made in *all* directions to ensure that every item which is properly chargeable against the accounts is duly debited to them, either through the Purchase Book or Journal in the ordinary way, or by way of Provision. At this stage, it will also be convenient to see, by means of comparison between the Goods Received Book and the Purchase Book, that invoices have been duly received and charged through for all goods which have been taken into stock.

The method of entering these Provisions in the books is to debit the nominal account involved (Rent, Wages, Carriage, etc.) and to credit a "Suspense Account" for all items which have accrued but are not yet charged out. The total of these amounts will increase the liabilities in the Balance Sheet, and also increase the debit to Profit and Loss Account under the headings of their respective Nominal Accounts. Items paid in advance will be treated on exactly the same principle, but on the opposite sides of the accounts, that is, Suspense Account will be debited, and Rates, Insurance, etc., credited with the relative amounts, and the total will appear as an asset in the Balance Sheet and will go to reduce the charge under these several headings in Profit and Loss Account. With regard to the provision for Discounts and Allowances, the figures in question are deducted from the amounts of Debtors and Creditors in the Balance Sheet, instead of appearing as a liability and asset respectively. Sometimes Suspense Account is eliminated, and the respective items are then carried down as balances on the Nominal Accounts to which they relate.

The question of Depreciation next arises and is usually dealt with by one of four methods—

(*a*) To write an agreed percentage off the original cost of the Asset each year ;

(*b*) To add to the Asset any item spent upon it other than ordinary repairs and renewals during the year, and to write off the agreed percentage, bringing down the balance to the next year's account, and in following years to add expenditure, as before, and write the agreed percentage off the account as it then stands. (This is known as depreciation written off the diminishing value) ;

(*c*) To raise what is commonly called a " Sinking Fund " by debiting Profit and Loss Account, and setting aside and investing outside the business each year a sum which with interest reinvested will, at the expected date of the expiration of the Asset, amount to its original cost ;

(*d*) To deal with Depreciation on the Annuity System, by charging the Asset and crediting Revenue with interest on the balance of the account, and writing off each year a sufficient (equal) amount to reduce the Asset to the required figure at the end of a desired period.

There is also the method of re-valuing the Assets periodically and charging the loss on re-valuation to Revenue as Depreciation ; but owing to the expense and also to the question of market fluctuations, which a valuer would take into account for purposes of his valuation (but which do not, of course, affect the loss by " wear and tear " of the machinery), this method is scarcely ever adopted except for animals or Assets of the nature of loose tools, etc.

The necessity for Depreciation must be obvious, in that any article consumed in the process of manufacture must be treated as part of the cost of the articles manufactured during its working life. This applies no more to articles consumed or worn out in a few months, or hours, than to articles whose working life extends over a considerable period of time; but, whereas in the former case the cost of the article is at once treated as a charge against Revenue, and, therefore, correctly dealt with in the accounts of the current period, in the latter case it would be unfair to charge Revenue with the whole of the cost of Assets which at the end of the current financial period possess a residual value, frequently representing a very large percentage of that original cost. Such expenditure is therefore "capitalized"; but it should be borne in mind that it can only be capitalized temporarily, and that eventually it will require to be renewed, in which event (if not before) a charge *must* fall upon Revenue. The object of providing for Depreciation is to avoid the expense of heavy renewals falling against the profits of any one period; it aims at equitably apportioning original cost over the whole of the period during which the Asset has been utilised. The problem of Depreciation may be looked at from yet another point of view, which perhaps will tend to make its necessity as a Revenue charge even clearer. Any Asset which, in the ordinary course of events, is subject to Depreciation might be hired; and, were it to be hired, the cost of the hire would obviously be a Revenue charge. If, however, the Asset is purchased, instead of being hired, what is saved is not the whole of the cost of hire, but the profit that would otherwise have been made by the person from whom the Asset was so hired—that is to say, the difference between the cost of hire and the expenses incurred by that person. By acquiring Assets for itself, instead of hiring for all purposes, the business is virtually opening up a new department, the income of which represents the amount hitherto paid for hire (thus making this item drop out upon both sides of the Revenue Account), while the expenses that will remain to be met will be the expenses formerly incurred by the person letting out Assets for hire.

No true Cost Accounts can possibly be prepared which omit to make proper charges for Depreciation, and for this—if for no other—reason it is necessary that Depreciation should also be dealt with in the Financial Accounts, so that the results shown by both may be consistent.

From the Balance-Sheet point of view, also, it is obvious that unless provision is made for the loss of utility arising from wear and tear, from the lapse of time, or from obsolescence, the effective value of the Asset will be overstated, and the financial stability of the undertaking accordingly exaggerated.

The method of providing for Depreciation and the rate of provision should, in the first instance, be decided by the practical and the financial authorities of the concern in consultation, and will depend upon the nature of the Asset, its probable " life " and its residue of value after it has ceased to be of use to the Company.

The first method is frequently adopted for Buildings, Patents, and Short Leases, where the additions and repairs are few in comparison with the cost of the Asset, and the residue of value is either small or even nothing. The second method is more frequently used for fixed Assets other than these, e.g. Leases and Loose Tools, and would include Engines, Boilers, Plant, Machinery, Fittings, Fixtures, Shafting, etc. This class of Asset is liable to continual addition and repairs, and, in deciding which of these two methods to adopt, it is well to remember that the second method falls more heavily upon the earlier years, when repairs will be fewer and smaller, and also that this method invariably leaves a residue of value.

The table given below shows the difference arising from the depreciation of an asset valued at £100 at the rate of 7½ per cent under the first method and 10 per cent under the second—

	Depreciation at 7½ % on original cost.		Depreciation at 10 % on diminishing value.	
	Depreciation for year.	Balance standing at end of year.	Depreciation for year.	Balance standing at end of year.
1st year	7 10 0	92 10 0	10 0 0	90 0 0
2nd	7 10 0	85 0 0	9 0 0	81 0 0
3rd	7 10 0	77 10 0	8 2 0	72 18 0
4th	7 10 0	70 0 0	7 5 10	65 12 2
5th	7 10 0	62 10 0	6 11 2	59 1 0
6th	7 10 0	55 0 0	5 18 1	53 2 11
7th	7 10 0	47 10 0	5 6 3	47 16 8
8th	7 10 0	40 0 0	4 15 8	43 1 0
9th	7 10 0	32 10 0	4 6 1	38 14 11
10th	7 10 0	25 0 0	3 17 6	34 17 5

From this table it will be seen that, after the third year, 10 per cent on the diminishing value is less severe than 7½ per cent on the original amount, and that to reduce an Asset to the same amount in 10 years, 10 per cent on diminishing value is equal to $6\frac{1}{2}$ per cent on the original cost.

The third or Sinking Fund method is used generally in the case of longer leases, and should be applied not only to the lease itself but to any buildings, fixtures, plant, etc., which will pass to the freeholder at the termination of the lease and which will not be worn out before the lease expires. Interest will be added to the balance outstanding annually, and the Sinking Fund should be sufficient to extinguish the Assets at the termination of the lease. It must be remembered that, on the occurrence of that event, the freeholder has generally a claim for dilapidations, which may be provided for either by an addition to the amount charged annually to Sinking Fund, or by treating the lease as expiring 12 or 18 months before the actual date. The amount so transferred annually to the Sinking Fund should be invested outside the business in first-class securities, to provide a sufficient sum, without disturbing the working capital of the business, when the lease or other Asset requires renewal. The amount written off under the other methods may, of course, be treated in this way and, indeed, should be so treated, if a large sum is likely to be required at one time.

The Annuity Method causes heavier book charges to fall upon Revenue in later years, because, although the direct charge for Depreciation is constant, the amount credited to Revenue (as representing Interest upon the diminishing value of the Asset from year to year) is naturally a constantly diminishing quantity, so that, upon balance, the net charge against Revenue steadily increases. This has been thought by some to be an objection, and from one point of view it may be so regarded, inasmuch as it is certainly prudent to get a substantial amount written off an Asset while it is new, and therefore presumably at its highest stage of working efficiency. At the same time, the Annuity system is valuable in the case of quite long-lived Assets, or of Assets of considerable value where no Sinking Fund is provided for their renewal, as it equitably apportions the charge over the several years of the Assets' life without ignoring the factor of interest, which, under the circumstances named, may easily assume a considerable importance. Thus, in the case of a Lease, it is notorious that the Depreciation of a 99 years' Lease during the first ten years is practically *nil*, but that, with each succeeding year after (say) the first thirty, the annual Depreciation becomes greater. Any valuer will confirm this statement, which must, indeed, be obvious to anyone who takes the trouble to consider the effect of compound interest over an extended period. With regard to especially valuable, but short-lived, Assets, the Annuity System is occasionally useful, as affording some assistance towards the solution of a question of considerable practical importance, namely, as to which is really the more economical—a well-constructed article costing a considerable sum, but having a long working life: or a less substantially constructed article of a shorter working life, but considerably less costly. Such a question as this cannot be accurately solved if the important subject of interest is altogether ignored.

It is, as a rule, desirable that the actual calculation of annual Depreciation charges should be left to the Professional Auditors, the principles having first been settled by the Directors, the Manager, the Accountant, and the Auditors in consultation.

According to the legal decisions given in various cases brought before the Courts in Company matters, there is no necessity to depreciate Goodwill in the books of a business. It is not usual to charge depreciation against Freehold Land, nor, indeed, is there any necessity legally to provide for it, even in the case of a lease, where the Company is formed solely to work that lease. In this latter case, however, the omission of Depreciation is very doubtful finance, and it is only fair to the shareholders to let them know that their dividends (so called) really include part of their capital, as, on the expiration of the lease, their property or most of it will have expired or become valueless. The reader must remember that any provisions in the Articles of Association relating to Depreciation must be strictly observed.

The actual rates charged under these various schemes will depend, as stated before, on the prospect of the probable existence of the Asset and the chance of its obsolescence, and, in estimating this in the case of machinery, the likelihood of running at high pressure or excessive speed must be taken into account.

With regard to Loose Tools and Horses, as mentioned, a re-valuation is frequently adopted, but, if this is found to be impracticable, a liberal rate of depreciation should be allowed, and a re-valuation of both of these Assets should take place, say, once in five years, the amount appearing in the books being readjusted.

In all the above remarks, it is assumed that all repairs are charged against Revenue for the year in which the expense was incurred.

The usual method of dealing with Depreciation is to debit the Profit and Loss Account and credit the Asset in question with the amount to be written off.

Under the Companies Act, 1929, every balance sheet must *inter alia*—

(*a*) Distinguish between fixed and floating assets, and state how the values of the former are arrived at;

(*b*) Show the value placed upon goodwill as a separate item, if possible;

(*c*) State what liabilities (if any) are secured;

(*d*) Show shares in, and loans to, subsidiary companies as separate items;

(*e*) Show (in a separate statement signed by the directors) how the profits or losses of subsidiary companies have been dealt with;

(*f*) Mention (in the same statement) any qualifications there may be in the auditors' reports upon the balance sheets of subsidiary companies;

(*g*) Give particulars of loans to, and the remuneration of, directors, etc., including any derived from subsidiary companies.

A subsidiary company is defined (Sect. 127) as one in which the company holds more than 50 per cent of the issued share capital or voting power, or one in which the company has power directly or indirectly to appoint the majority of the directors.

In a Limited Company, when the Profit and Loss Account has been completed, a suggestion is very frequently made, if the year has been successful, to raise a Secret Reserve Fund: that is, profits are not fully and truly disclosed to the shareholders, but a smaller figure is stated as being the profit for the year, and the so-called Secret Reserve remains in the business in the shape of undisclosed or deliberately undervalued Assets, or overvalued Liabilities. The professed reason for this is to put the business on a sounder financial basis, as it is considered human nature on the part of the shareholders to wish to obtain as much as possible out of the Company, and the practice is so well known in the case of banks and other financial institutions as not to require any defence at the present time. The usual method employed by Companies of this description is to undervalue (or, in some cases, even omit) the premises and fixtures they own, to value investments at a price much below market price, or to make an over-estimate for possible bad debts. Trading concerns often include profit balances under an omnibus caption such as "Sundry creditors and credit balances."

With regard to Trading or Manufacturing concerns, the practice of building up undisclosed reserves is not universal, and is open to certain objections, of which the most important are perhaps (1) that if, in a series of good years, a large Secret Reserve has been built up, it is possible, by gradually reducing this item, to conceal for a long time faulty management which may actually be running the business at a loss, whilst an apparent profit may still be shown owing to the manipulation of this figure; (2) that the possibility of paying dividends may suddenly cease when the Secret Reserve has been exhausted; and (3) that shareholders may be induced to sell their shares at an artificially low price.

The simplest methods of raising a Secret Reserve in a Manufacturing Company are (1) by over-depreciating machinery and other fixed assets; (2) by setting aside a larger sum than is necessary to meet Bad Debts; and (3) by undervaluing the Stock. The first of these methods is the least objectionable from the point of view of the ease or otherwise of "juggling" with the figures, whilst the third is the most objectionable from that standpoint. Upon the whole, perhaps the fairest way, subject to a small reasonable Secret Reserve for contingencies, is to provide by the Articles of Association "That no higher rate of dividend shall be paid than is recommended by the Directors," and to trust them to build up a (disclosed) Reserve Fund sufficient to put the Company on a sound and satisfactory financial basis.

Having now ascertained and entered in the books all items affecting the Profit and Loss Account, the next step is to close the Ledger Accounts properly. Where a mechanical system is not in operation the Personal Accounts will be closed by entering as a balance the difference between the two sides, then adding and ruling off each side of the Ledger and bringing down the balance on its proper side, viz. the opposite side to that on which it was previously entered. The Real Accounts (that is, those representing property, such as Machinery, Plant, etc.) will be closed in the same way, and the balances brought down. The Nominal Accounts which represent only cost, expenses, and profits will be closed by transferring the balances to the Profit and Loss Account and ruling them off.

The Depreciation written off the fixed Assets will also appear in the Profit and Loss Account, and the figure of Stock will appear in the Trading or Manufacturing Account as described in the previous chapter.

The accounts still remaining in the Ledgers will then be grouped under convenient headings and entered, together with the balance of the Profit and Loss Account, in the Balance Sheet.

All that now remains is for the statements which have been prepared to be laid before the Directors or the Proprietors, in as full and complete a form as possible, calculated to show them at a glance the actual position of the concern financially, and the results of the past year's trading, profits, and expenses.

As before mentioned, the " Profit and Loss Account " is usually divided into what are generally called the Trading Account and the Profit and Loss Account proper. A difference of opinion exists as to how the expenses should be divided in these two accounts, one set of authorities holding the view that *all* expenses of manufacturing should go into the first section. Following this view, as apparently the more theoretically correct, on the credit side of the Trading Account would appear Sales *less* the opening Stock of Manufactured Goods *plus* the closing Stock of Manufactured Goods. This is the best way of stating Sales, as it gives the production of the Works as the basis for percentages. On the debit side of the Trading Account will appear Wages, Raw Material, Coal and Motive Power, Carriage Inwards, Salary of Works Manager, Rent, Rates and Insurance of Works (as distinguished from Warehouse and Office), Depreciation, Repairs, etc. Under this system, the second section, or Profit and Loss Account in its more limited application, should contain on the credit side the balance of gross profit as brought down from the previous statement, Cash Discount receivable, Interest, Rents Receivable (if any), and other sources of profit. The debit side should consist of all expenses not included in the previous section, including all costs of warehousing, and selling, clerical and financial charges, Directors' Fees, Manager's salary, etc.

The other set of authorities include in their first section only such costs of manufacture as vary directly with the production, which would, of course, exclude Works Salaries, Rent and Rates, Repairs and Depreciation, on the ground that these are fixed charges and more useful percentages may be obtained without these items. The excluded figures are treated in the second section under this system. This plan is useful for a small concern, where no Cost Accounts are kept, but appears unsuitable for ordinary manufacturing businesses.

Where more than one Department exists, separate Trading Accounts may be prepared for each, the balance of each appearing to the credit of the Profit and Loss Account, and the debits appearing as before.

The form for submission to the Directors will then appear as shown in Form No. 50.

TRADING ACCOUNT

Dr. FOR THE YEAR ENDING DECEMBER 31ST, 19.. *Cr.*

		£	£			£	£
19 Dec. 31	To Materials		11,875	19 Dec. 31	By Sales	26,500	
	,, Wages		4,500		Less Returns	940	
	,, Coal and Motive Power		650			25,560	
	,, Rates and Taxes (Works)		150		Less Stock at Jan. 1st, 19..	8,750	
	,, Repairs		203			16,810	
	,, Depreciation:						
	Machinery	688			Add Stock at Dec. 31st, 19..	8,175	
	Loose Tools	65					
	Buildings (Works)	140					24,985
			893				
	,, Balance being Gross Profit		6,714				
			£24,985				£24,985

PROFIT AND LOSS ACCOUNT

Dr. FOR THE YEAR ENDING DECEMBER 31ST, 19.. *Cr.*

		£			£
19 Dec. 31	To Salaries	1,130	19 Dec. 31	By Balance, Gross Profit brought down	6,714
	,, Discount allowed	663	,, ,,	,, Discount received	298
	,, Rates and Taxes (Office and Warehouse)	130			
	,, Office Expenses, Stationery, etc.	205			
	,, Travelling Expenses	270			
	,, General Expenses	195			
	,, Bad Debts	425			
	,, Directors and Auditors	670			
	,, Debenture Interest	400			
	,, Depreciation of Buildings, Office and Furniture	60			
	,, Depreciation of Fixtures	30			
	,, Balance, being net profit for the year	2,834			
		£7,012			£7,012

(*Form No.* 50)

It will be noticed that the Stock in the Trading Account and the Stock in the Balance Sheet do not agree. The difference arises as explained in the previous chapter, because the former figure is the stock of manufactured goods only and the latter the entire stock in hand—including, in addition to Raw Material, Stores, Stationery (if valued), necessary stock of repairing materials, etc.

It will also be noticed in the Balance Sheet (Form No. 51) that the Assets are set out in full detail for the purpose of submitting it to the Board of Directors. The Shareholders, however, usually receive a very much abbreviated statement, as the falling into the hands of a trade competitor of such particulars as these might prove very prejudicial to the Company. In the case of a public Limited Company, it is not possible to prevent the published accounts from becoming public property.

Columns may well be provided to show the ratio, by percentage,

Balance Sheet, Dec. 31st, 19..

Liabilities.	£	£	*Assets.*	£	£
Capital, 35,000 shares of £1 each		35,000	Land and Buildings per last Account	17,500	
Debentures		10,000	*Less* Depreciation of Buildings	200	17,300
Creditors:			Machinery and Plant per last Account	13,115	
Trade Account	2,070		Additions during year	635	
Less Reserve for Discounts	52			13,750	
	2,018		*Less* Depreciation at 5%	688	13,062
Add reserve for items accruing	60	2,078	Loose Tools per last account	440	
Profit and Loss Acct., Balance per last account	753		Additions during year	60	
Add profit for year	2,834	3,587		500	
			Less Depreciation at 12½%	63	437
			Fixtures per last account	600	
			Less Depreciation at 5 %	30	570
			Stock as taken and valued by Mr. Blank		9,047
			Sundry Debtors	3,400	
			Less Provision for Bad Debts	185	
				3,215	
			Less Provision for Discount at 2½ %	80	
				3,135	3,135
			District Banking Co., Ltd.		7,114
		£50,665			£50,665

(*Form No.* 51)

which the various items bear to the net production of the period. Columns are also sometimes added to show the figures and percentages for the previous period.

The Statement of this Company as rendered to its shareholders might very possibly contain only such particulars as appear in Form No. 52.

The accounts being now finally completed and approved by the Board are ready for the Auditors, although, in practice, these officials will possibly have done already a considerable portion of their work for the year.

In the case of Limited Companies, the employment of Auditors was first made compulsory by the Act of 1900, although, long

BALANCE SHEET, DEC. 31ST, 19..

Liabilities.	£	£	*Assets.*	£
Nominal Capital, 50,000 shares of £1 each		£50,000	Land and Buildings at cost *less* depreciation	17,300
Capital Issued and Called up 35,000 shares of £1 each		35,000	Machinery and Plant at cost *less* depreciation	13,062
First Mortgage Debentures 4 % Redeemable 19..		10,000	Loose Tools at cost *less* depreciation	437
Sundry Creditors		2.078	Fixtures at cost *less* depreciation	570
Profit and Loss Account, per last Account	753		Stock	9,047
Add profit for year	2,834		Sundry Debtors	3,135
		3,587	District Banking Co., Ltd.	7,114
		£50,665		£50,665

PROFIT AND LOSS ACCOUNT

FOR THE YEAR ENDING DEC. 31ST, 19..

Dr.		£		*Cr.*	£
19.. Dec. 31	To Depreciation	983	19.. Dec. 31	By Balance forward	753
	,, Debenture Interest	400	19.. Dec. 31	,, Net Balance for Year as per Detailed Profit and Loss Account	6,002
	,, Directors' Fees	590			
	,, Auditors' Fees	70			
	,, Bad Debts	425			
	,, Income Tax	700			
	,, Balance available for distribution	3,587			
		£6,755			£6,755

PROPOSED APPROPRIATION OF PROFIT.

	£
Dividend of 5% per annum, free of tax	1,750
Transfer to form a Reserve Fund . .	1,000
Balance carried forward	837
	£3,587

(*Form No.* 52)

before that date, most Companies were in the habit of having their accounts audited, and the position of the Auditors was almost as strongly defined in the Articles of Association of the Companies registered prior to 1901 as it is in the Act referred to. Auditors have at law (*vide* Companies Act, 1929) a right of access to the books of the Company at all reasonable times. They are appointed by the Company, in general meeting, to act until the next general meeting, and are eligible for re-election, which, as a matter of fact, is almost universally accorded. If it is desired to propose for election by a general meeting as Auditor some person other than the retiring Auditor, due notice must be given to the Company not less than fourteen days before the general meeting is held. The retiring Auditor also receives this notice and is entitled to attend the meeting and to make any statement he thinks fit.

The Profit and Loss Account and Balance Sheet should (strictly speaking) be completed and a copy handed to the Auditors prior to their entering upon their final examination of the accounts. All accounts should be duly ruled off and everything entered in ink, and the Manager should ascertain whether they propose to come and check the cash in hand on the last day of the year. If not, the Manager should instruct the Cashier to pay all the money he may have into the bank as a proof that it is actually available in cash, which fact can then be verified by the Auditor even if he does not arrive at the Works for some days. It should be seen that all vouchers are arranged in numerical order to correspond with the books; that a full statement of the provisions and adjustments to be made is ready and drawn up in such a manner as to enable the Auditor readily to check it; that the Stock sheets are completed and signed by all responsible for the sections or subsidiary parts thereof; that the Bank Pass Book is entered up and reconciled with the Cash Book, and, in fact, that anything he may require is ready to hand if and when he should ask for it.

The Manager must, on the other hand, distinguish carefully between the staff and the professional audits. The former is directed and controlled by himself, probably on lines defined by himself, with the advice of the professional Auditor, and irregularities which may be discovered from time to time will be reported to and must be rectified by him, whereas the professional Auditor is appointed by the Shareholders and has an entirely distinct authority, and, further, is as much entitled to information, even from the Manager himself, as the Staff Auditors are to explanations from the Cashier. The professional Auditor is the only safeguard and check which the Shareholders have upon the Directors and Manager, and he serves them directly in a critical capacity in the same way as the Directors do in an executive capacity.

From this, the Manager must not in any way assume that the interests of an Auditor and his own clash, for the Auditor is almost invariably an officer whose desire will be to work cordially with the executive, and who will probably be an experienced and useful ally, especially in everything connected with figures, and their important bearing on modern business in the direction of the Costing, Statistical, and Financial Departments.

It will be noticed that the latter part of this chapter refers almost entirely to a business conducted as a Limited Company. It has been presented in this form because, except in connection with the small items of the published accounts and the method of appointment of the Auditor, the lines indicated will apply equally to a privately owned undertaking, save that a sole proprietor has naturally the right to settle everything on his own plan and on his undivided responsibility, and may dispense with, or reduce the scope of, the audit if he should think fit.

CHAPTER XIX

Company Work and Returns—Special Procedure in connection with Joint Stock Companies—Issue of Capital—Statutory Returns, etc.

NEEDLESS to say, the first point to be considered in connection with a Limited Company is its construction and formation.

A Company, as it exists at present, is almost invariably one formed under the Companies Acts, which are now embodied in the Companies Act, 1929, and is limited by shares. This chapter will, therefore, be exclusively devoted to Companies of this class, but the reader is reminded that it is possible for a Company to be limited "by guarantee," that is to say the members pay in no capital but incur an obligation to pay in each a stated amount in the event of a winding-up.

Once a Company has been formed (by registration of the proper documents at the official Companies Registry) it acquires in the eye of the law a (fictitious) personality entirely distinct from the (natural) personality of the individuals composing it. In the technical phrase it is "an entity" with a separate existence. Once the individual members have aggregated their several contributions, by taking up shares, the Company's capital becomes its own as a permanent fixed fund which can not be returned to the members short of liquidation or order of the Court.

Companies may be divided for the present purpose into two classes—Public Companies and Private Companies. The former class covers most of the larger Companies and many of the smaller and may be defined as that type of Company which issues a prospectus to the general public inviting them to become shareholders and, therefore, part proprietors of the concern. The latter class consists of those Companies which are formed by private individuals and their relatives, immediate friends or confidential servants, in order to obtain the advantages of incorporation. Private Companies must incorporate in their Articles of Association clauses prohibiting any invitation to the public to subscribe for their shares or debentures, providing a restriction on the transfer of their shares, and limiting the number of members (exclusive of employees and former employees) to fifty.

The advantages which the transformation of an individually owned business into a private Limited Company offer are many, of which—apart altogether from the very important one of limiting the owner's or any partner's personal liabilities, which matter is dealt with below—the following may be enumerated—

(*a*) The right to sue or be sued in the Corporate name;

(*b*) Continuity of existence and non-withdrawal of capital;

(*c*) Simple division of profits where many parties are interested, and an easier adjustment thereof;

(*d*) Safeguards to a certain extent against certain frauds, or against mismanagement by partners.

The simplicity of point (*a*) is obvious to all, but the other points may require a little explanation.

Point (*b*) implies that a man who has once paid his money into the concern cannot withdraw it; if he desires to do so, he may sell his shares to a new holder (subject to any restrictions in the Articles of Association), but he cannot withdraw the money from the operations of the business. In the case of partnerships, for instance, the death of a partner *ipso facto* dissolves a firm, except in cases where, by the Articles of Partnership, the continuing partners may carry on the business; but, even then, the deceased partner's share must usually be paid out in a comparatively short time, and this may easily hamper a business severely for years.

Point (*c*) enables a firm desiring to increase the share of a junior partner to do so by the simple expedient of transferring to him a few shares, or exchanging some of his preference shares for ordinary shares held by other partners, or by allotting to him additional shares for cash. It also enables a proprietor to leave or give his daughters shares in the business, the sons continuing to manage it as before, whilst a partnership under such arrangements would almost certainly lead to friction and the business would probably fall entirely into the hands of the sons.

Point (*d*) gives safeguards in the following directions—the powers of the Directors may be limited by the Articles of Association, and, since these are registered with the Registrar and are open to the inspection of all, everyone is presumed to be aware of their terms; so that, if a Director exceeded his power, an outsider could not, in the ordinary cases, make the Company liable. On the other hand, in a partnership, even if one partner's powers were limited by the deed of partnership, any other partner seeking to protect the firm from an action caused through this partner exceeding his power would have to prove that the third party was aware of this limitation, if the act which caused the trouble was within the apparent scope of the partnership business.

Having decided to turn a business into a Limited Company, the first step is to draw up the necessary forms and documents to enable the Registrar to grant a Certificate of Incorporation. Of course, in no circumstances should the registration of a Company be attempted without proper legal and other expert advice, but the general procedure may perhaps be outlined here with advantage. The first of these documents is the Memorandum of Association, which usually contains five clauses, viz.—

(1) The name of the Company ;

(2) Statement as to the part of the United Kingdom in which the registered office is to be situated (England or Scotland) ;

(3) The objects of the Company ;

(4) A statement that the liability of the members is limited ;

(5) Particulars of the capital, stating the total amount, the number of shares, amount of each share and generally the different classes of shares into which the capital is to be subdivided.

With regard to Clause 1, the name of the Company : this must be submitted to the Registrar of Companies for his approval, which is usually given if no Company already registered has appropriated the title, or one so similar as to lead to possible confusion, except where the company in existence is in the course of being dissolved and signifies its consent in such manner as the Registrar requires. Apart from special permission of the Board of Trade, such words as "Royal" or "Imperial" must be avoided.

Clause 2 calls for no comment.

Clause 3 is of supreme importance, as no act can be done or business transacted by the Company which is not provided for in this clause. Its drafting should, of course, be left in the solicitor's hands, as in the event of the Company's powers being exceeded, any act purporting to be done so in excess of the powers is, in the eye of the law, void and of no effect, being said to be *ultra vires*.

Clause 4 bestows on the Company and its members the protection of limited liability. A sole trader, or a firm of partners, may be liable for business debts even to the full extent of any private property but where a person takes up shares in a Company and pays in the full amount of those shares in accordance with his contract he is freed from all further liability. It must be understood that the Company's own property may be distrained on if it should neglect to pay its debts but the Company's creditors have, in ordinary circumstances, no rights against the property of individual members.

Clause 5, dealing with the capital, must also be carefully prepared, but is covered by the description of the rights of the different classes of shareholders referred to later in this chapter.

The next point for consideration is whether or not to have special Articles of Association. This document, when one is drawn up, is bound up with the Memorandum of Association. On this latter document, the Certificate of Incorporation is granted, and it also settles the constitution of the Company, and is both a practical and legal necessity to every Company. But special Articles (which regulate all internal and some external questions of management, etc.) are optional, because a *pro forma* set of Articles (known as " Table A ") is appended to the Companies Act, 1929, which comprises the Regulations of every Company, excepting in so far as they are varied or excluded by the special Articles (if any) of that particular Company.

In practice most large Companies find it convenient to have "special" Articles of Association, but small Companies may save expense by adopting "Table A" in part.

A private company cannot adopt "Table A" completely on account of the restrictions imposed by Section 26.

The Memorandum of Association must then be signed by seven[1] subscribers, who undertake to subscribe for the number of shares set opposite their names, which number shall be not less than one share each, and no Certificate of Incorporation will be granted to any Company which has not the prescribed minimum number of members, nor must the number of the shareholders at any time fall below the statutory number, otherwise the members aware of it lose their right to limited liability, after the business has been so carried on for a period of six months, and the Company may be

[1] Two are sufficient in the case of a " private " company.

wound up. The Articles of Association also are signed by the same subscribers, and these documents, together with the written consents of the persons willing to serve as Directors and together with the fees payable (which vary with the amount of the capital) must be deposited at Bush House. A statutory declaration by a solicitor, director or secretary that all requirements have been complied with must also be produced.

It is also usual to send, with these papers, a notice of the Registered Office of the Company which, in this case, must consist of the full postal address, although 28 days from date of incorporation is allowed for filing, and it may here be noted that any change of such Registered Office must be filed within 28 days of the change, together with a five shilling fee, to the Registrar of Companies.

On these documents, when in order, the Certificate of Incorporation will be granted, and the Company may (in the case of a private Company) start trading at once.

By the Companies Act, 1929, a prospectus (which is a document inviting the public to subscribe for shares or debentures) must contain, *inter alia*, the following particulars—

The contents of the Memorandum, with the names, etc., of the signatories;

Names and addresses of Directors, and particulars of their qualification and remuneration, as set out in the Articles;

Minimum subscription on which the Directors may proceed to allotment, and the amount payable on application and allotment of each share; and in the case of a second or subsequent offer of shares, particulars of each previous allotment made within two years;

Amount of Shares and Debentures issued or agreed to be issued for other than cash consideration within the two preceding years;

Names and addresses of Vendors and amount payable as purchase money (goodwill being stated separately);

Particulars of the interest of every Director or proposed Director in the sale of any property which it is proposed to acquire;

Remuneration of the Promoter;

Voting rights of different classes of shares;

Statement of underwriting commission authorized;

Estimates of Preliminary Expenses;
Details of all material contracts; and
Names and Addresses of Auditors (if any).

A report by the Company's Auditors setting out *separately* the profits for each of the three financial years (if any) immediately preceding the issue of the prospectus; this report must mention the rates of dividend (if any) paid in each of the three years.

If a business is to be purchased out of the proceeds of the issue, a report by accountants named in the prospectus (not necessarily the Auditors) as to the profits made by that business in the three financial years preceding the issue.

The prospectus will be prepared by the solicitor, and approved by the Promoter and Directors, and must, before its public issue, be sent to the Registrar of Companies. When no prospectus is issued by a Public Company, or where one is issued but the company does not proceed to allotment, a statement in lieu thereof in the prescribed form must be filed with the Registrar of Companies at least three days before any allotment of shares or debentures.

Unless and until the minimum subscription has been allotted to various applicants, and a deposit of at least 5 per cent has been received thereon, a Public Company cannot commence business or exercise any of its borrowing powers. By the expression "minimum subscription" is meant that there shall be actually allotted the number of shares stated in the prospectus as being the lowest number applied for on which the Directors will make any allotment at all; and, if no such number is stated, then the whole issue must be taken up. This only applies to the first allotment of shares. This clause was passed to prevent a Company commencing business with inadequate capital, which is a frequent cause of loss and insolvency. A notice in the official form stating that shares equal to the minimum subscription have been allotted must be filed with the Registrar, who will then issue his certificate authorizing the Company to commence business, provided everything is in order. Whenever an allotment of shares is made a return thereof must be filed with the Registrar.

An important point to be decided before the issue of the prospectus—indeed before the Memorandum is completed—is the form and division of the capital of the Company. This may consist of one class of shares only, all ranking equally, or it may be divided into Ordinary and Preference shares, and occasionally Deferred or Founders' shares. The respective rights of the holders of these shares are set out in the Articles of Association (or Memorandum) and will vary in each case. The mere name given to a class of shares is practically no indication of the rights enjoyed by its holders.

The general lines followed are for the Preference Shareholders to have a certain fixed dividend out of the profits (before the ordinary shareholders are entitled to receive anything) and to receive no further share in the profits of the Company. For instance, if the former class are " Six per cent Preference shares," the holders of such shares will be entitled to receive six per cent on their holding (less income tax) out of the profits divided in each year, and the entire balance will go to the ordinary shareholders. Preference shares are usually " cumulative," i.e. if the profits of any one year are insufficient to pay the full dividend on such shares, then no dividend can be paid thereafter on the ordinary shares until all arrears of preference dividend have been paid, in addition to the six per cent for the current year. In the absence of express stipulation, all preference shares are cumulative. Under Section 46 of the 1929 Act Preference shares, if fully paid, may now be redeemed (i.e. repaid), if the Articles permit, either out of the proceeds of a fresh issue or by using profits for the purpose.

The rights of the holders of founders' shares (as, in fact, all other shares) are defined in the regulations of the Company, and usually take the form of, say, one-fourth of all profits after ten per cent has been paid to the ordinary shareholders. Founders' shares are not often created, as most ordinary shareholders prefer to retain all the profits, since they run the risk of losing all if the Company is not a success.

In the absence of agreement to the contrary in the regulations, all shares rank equally in the winding up of a Company and the sharing of the residue after payment of creditors.

The difference between Debenture holders and Preference Shareholders is that the former are loan creditors and receive their interest whether profits are made or not; whilst in a liquidation, if they hold a charge on the assets, they may exercise that charge, and so rank before all ordinary creditors, but, if not, they rank equally with other creditors (loan or trade) in their right to be paid out of the assets. Preference Shareholders, on the other hand, are entitled to their dividend only out of profits (if any), being shareholders only; and, in a liquidation, they are entitled to be repaid only out of assets remaining after the payment of all costs of liquidation, and after the claims of the Debenture holders and creditors are satisfied.

A Company is required by law to have the following—

(1) A Common Seal;
(2) Register of Members;
(3) Register of Charges;
(4) Register of Directors and Managers;
(5) Minute Book;
(6) An annual list of members and summary;
(7) Books of Account.

(1) The Common Seal must have the Company's name "legibly engraven" thereon, and since, in a trading Company, it is only on important or official documents that this Seal is required to be used, it should be kept in a box with two locks at least and with the keys, of course, in possession of different people, usually the Secretary and the Directors, and it should be used only under the authority of a special minute passed at a meeting of the Board or the Company. Many Companies have a Seal Register to record every document to which the Seal has been affixed, setting out the document, date and names of the witnesses to the act—also the destination of the document.

(2) The Register of Members must, by the Companies Act, 1929, be kept at the Registered Office of the Company and be open for at least two hours in each day to the inspection of members, free of charge, and to all other persons on payment of not more than one shilling, except for a period of not more than thirty days in each year, when the book may be closed to all. Any person is also entitled to a copy, at the rate of sixpence per hundred words. The penalty for default in either case is £5 per day. Under Section 95 of the Act, the book must contain the following information—

"The names, addresses and occupations (if any) of the members, and in the case of a Company having a share capital a statement of the shares held by each member, distinguishing each share by its number, and of the amount paid or agreed to be considered as paid on the shares of each member:

"The date at which each person was entered in the Register as a member:

"The date at which any person ceased to be a member."

All law stationers stock a ruling of this book, meeting all statutory requirements and, therefore, no form is given here.

(3) The Register of Charges is required to be kept by Section 88 of the Act of 1929, and must contain "a short description of the property charged, the amount of the charge and (except in the case of securities to bearer) the names of the persons entitled thereto." All members or creditors have a right to inspect or copy this book at any time free. The penalty in case of default is a fine not exceeding £50.

It must be remembered that, under Section 79 of the Companies Act, 1929, the following charges must be filed with the Registrar of Joint Stock Companies within twenty-one days of their creation—

(*a*) A charge for the purpose of securing any issue of debentures; or

(*b*) A charge on uncalled share capital of the Company; or

(*c*) A charge created or evidenced by an instrument, which, if executed by an individual, would require registration as a bill of sale; or

(*d*) A charge on land, wherever situate, or any interest therein; or

(*e*) A charge on book debts of the Company; or

(*f*) A floating charge on the undertaking or property of the Company.

(*g*) A charge on calls made but not paid; or

(*h*) A charge on a ship or any share in a ship; or

(*i*) A charge on goodwill, or a patent or a licence under a patent, on a trade mark or on a copyright or a licence under a copyright.

(4) A Register of Directors and Managers of the Company, setting out their names, addresses, nationality (and nationality of origin if not the same), and occupations, must be kept under Section 144 of the 1929 Act, and a copy must be sent to the Registrar annually. Notification of changes must be filed within 14 days.

In cases where a corporation is director of a company the corporate name and registered or principal office must be filed.

(5) The Minute Book contains a record of all proceedings of, and resolutions passed at, Shareholders' and Directors' meetings.

(6) The Annual List of Members and Summary requires to be in the official form and must be sent up to the Registrar every year. It is made up to the fourteenth day *after* the first Ordinary General Meeting in each year, and contains the names, addresses, and occupations of all who are at the time, or have been since the last return, shareholders and the following information as to capital—

The amount of capital; number of shares authorized to be issued; the nominal amount of each and amount called up; the number of shares issued respectively for payment wholly in cash, partly in cash and for consideration other than cash; total amount actually paid up in cash, amount considered as paid up and balance of calls in arrear; amount paid on shares forfeited (if any) and the amount of debts in respect of any mortgage or charge created by the Company requiring registration, or which would require registration, if created after the commencement of the Act. Every Company that is not a private Company must also include in its annual return a copy of the last audited Balance Sheet, including every document required by law to be annexed thereto. A private company avoids this requirement by signing a certificate, as part of the return, that it continues to be constituted as a private company.

The form of Return (Schedule VI of the Act) can be obtained from any law stationer, and must be sent to the Registrar with a copy of the Register of Directors and Managers, and the fee of five shillings, within 14 days of the date to which it is made up.

(7) Books of Account must be kept in which must be shown all sums received and expended by the company and the matters in respect of which the receipt and expenditure takes place; all sales and purchases of goods by the company; and the assets and liabilities of the company. The minimum particulars to be shown are mentioned in Sections 122 and 274. The books should be kept at the registered office or such other place as the directors think fit.

In addition to the above books, which are all necessary by law, a Company would require to have the following books—

Share Certificate Book, which is arranged with a Counterfoil like a Cheque Book, only larger, and the detached portion forms the actual Certificate issued to each holder of the Company's shares under the seal of the Company (if the articles so prescribe).

A Register of Transfers, which contains particulars in tabular form of all documents transferring shares in the Company.

APPLICATION AND ALLOTMENT SHEETS

SA[1]

ORDINARY SHARES

1	2		3	4	5	6	7	8	9	10		11	12	13	14	15	16	17	18	19	20	21
No. of Application.	Name.		Address.	Occupation.	No. of Shares Applied for	C. B. fo.	Deposit Paid.	Proposed Allotment.	No. of Shares Allotted.	Distinctive No. of Shares.		No. of Allotment Letter.	Amount Due on Allotment.	C. B. fo.	Amount Paid upon Allotment.	No. of Letter of Regret.	C. B. fo	Amount Returned.	Total Amount Paid up on.. 19..	No. of Share Certificate.	Fo. in Share Ledger.	Remarks.
										from	to											
							£ s. d.						£ s. d.		£ s. d.			£ s. d.	£ s. d.			
978	Saxon	John	—	—	10	29	10 0 0	—	—	—	—	--	—	—	—	47	32	10 0 0	—	—	—	
979	Strange	William	—	—	100	,,	100 0 0	80	60	59762	59821	941	80 0 0	37	80 0 0	—	—	—	180 0 0	941	941	

(*Form No. 53.*)

An Applications and Allotments Book, which is used in connection with the offer of shares to the public (the form and full working of this is described later).

A Fees Book for an account of all fees received for the transfer of shares, inspection or copy of Register of Members, copy of Memorandum, and Articles of Association, etc.

Other books are sometimes used to meet particular cases such as a Register of Share Warrants, Register of Debenture Holders, etc., but the above are the books required by practically every Company.

Having obtained the necessary books and issued the prospectus, the applications for shares will begin to come in through the bankers with an accompanying list. As soon as each list comes in from the Bank, it should be checked with the original form of application and then handed to the clerk in charge of the "Applications and Allotments Book." This book will consist at this stage (in the case of large Companies) of a number of loose sheets each headed alphabetically, and, if the number of applications justify, subdivided under the first vowel of the name of the applicant. The first sheet would, therefore, appear as Aa and would include such applicants as Adam, Aaronsberg, etc.; if one sheet were not sufficient for each subdivision, it would also be numbered, e.g. Ba^1, Ba^2, etc., for such names as Blair, Brain and Banbury. The sheet would be ruled according to the requirements of the Company, which would vary according to the calls payable after allotment.

At the time of the actual allotment each sheet should be signed by a Director and the Secretary for purposes of identification.

Form No. 53 supposes the case of a Company which is offering £10 shares, payable £1 on application and £2 on allotment. The first seven columns would be entered immediately the application was received, and column (7) would be agreed with the amount appearing to the credit of the Company in the Bank Pass Book. The 8th column would be filled in to assist the Directors in their allotment as soon as all the applications were received, in a flotation where shares were over-applied for and it was impossible to allot all applications in full. The 9th column would be filled in by the Directors on the actual allotment, and columns 10, 11, 12, 15, 16, and 17 would be filled in by the staff immediately after allotment. The actual Letters of Allotment and of Regret would then be filled up from the sheets, as already prepared, and posted to applicants.

Every Letter of Allotment must be stamped, before being signed and issued, with an impressed stamp value 6d., if the shares allotted are £5 or over in value, otherwise with a penny impressed stamp.

Where all the capital is intended to be called up shortly after allotment, columns are frequently added to show the amount payable on each call and the date of its payment. The sheets will have been added and summarized prior to the issue of the allotment letters, and it will be found that the total of column (9) will agree with the number of shares actually allotted; the total of the "Amount due on Allotment" (column 12) should be checked in total at the rate per share for the number of shares allotted. The Application and Allotment Sheets are then all signed by the Chairman and Secretary for identification. The Register of Members is then written up from these sheets, and they are finally bound together for safety and are known henceforward as the "Applications and Allotments Book." A "Loose-leaf" binding case will be found most useful for this purpose.

If various classes of Shares and Debentures are issued at the same time, each one should have the forms of application tinted a different colour, to avoid confusion, and there should be a separate set of Application Sheets for each. In the case of Companies of any size, a separate set of Registers will also be kept for each.

A Return of each allotment must be filed, in the official form, with the Registrar of Companies, accompanied by a five shilling fee, within one month of such allotment.

The Register of Members then becomes the official record of the shareholders of the Company, and, in the case of large Companies, will be put in the charge of a "Registrar"; or, in smaller concerns, in the hands of the Secretary, with or without the assistance of a Transfer staff. It will be the duty of this staff to receive all documents notifying an alteration of the names or standing of any shareholders by transfer, marriage (of a female shareholder), death, or otherwise, and to see that such documents are duly entered and recorded in the books, and that the fees (if any) to which the Company is entitled therefor are duly received and accounted for. The book in question might be ruled in form No. 54.

Prior to the passing of the Companies Act, 1929, shares could not be issued at a discount (although debentures could), but Sect. 47

REGISTER OF TRANSFERS

No. of Transfer or Description of Document	Date of Registration	Name of Transferor (Address and Description, if desired)	Old Certificate No.	Folio in Register	Name, Address, and Occupation of Transferee			New Certificate No.	Folio in Register	No. of Shares	Amount paid per Share	Distinctive Nos.	Fee
	19 .										£		
1	Jan. 29	Strange, William	59	174	Jones, John	—		72	206	60	10	17841-17900	2/6
Marriage Certificate	,, ,, etc.	Jenkins, Mary Ann	17	102	Smith, M. A.	—	Married Woman	73	102	50	10	8001-8050	2/6

(*Form No.* 54)

of the 1929 Act provides that shares of a class already issued may be issued at a discount, provided that—

(*a*) The issue is authorized by the company in general meeting and sanctioned by the Court;

(*b*) The resolution authorizing the issue states the maximum rate of discount;

(*c*) Not less than one year has elapsed since the company was entitled to commence business;

(*d*) The shares are issued within one month from the date of the Court's sanction, or such further time as the Court may allow.

Every prospectus relating to the issue, and every subsequent balance sheet must contain particulars of the discount allowed, or so much thereof as has not been subsequently written off (out of profits).

When a transfer is lodged with the company it should be compared with the certificate surrendered and the Register of Members, the signature of the transferor should be checked and the document should be submitted to the Directors at their next meeting for approval. To prevent fraud, it is usual to send a notice to the transferor, stating that a document purporting to be signed by him has been lodged and that, if he does not lodge an objection within 7 days, it will be submitted to the Directors for approval.

Many Articles, indeed practically all Articles of Private Companies, give the Directors absolute right to admit or reject a transfer, and many private Companies have clauses practically preventing transfers to persons other than present members of the Company, their wives and children. The Directors consider the transfer, and, if they decide to pass it, the old certificate should be cancelled in their presence, and they can then sign new certificates for the same number of shares as have just been cancelled. The Seal of the Company will then be attached to the new share certificates. When a member transfers his entire holding at once, no difficulty should arise, but it may happen that a holder of 100 shares desires to sell them and is obliged to do so in two lots of 50 shares each. If he has sold one lot before the other, he will probably direct the Company not to issue a new certificate for the second 50 shares, which, after the Directors' Meeting, will still stand in his name, but to retain the same until the sale of the second lot is completed. In these circumstances, a note must be given to the Registrar that 50 shares require a certificate from the old certificate No. — ; the old certificate will itself be endorsed to show this, and must be produced to the Board at the time the second lot of 50 shares is submitted for transfer. Immediately the second transfer is passed by the Board, the Registrar must enter it in the Register of Transfers and post the particulars to the accounts affected in the Register of Members, crediting the transferee and debiting the transferor in that book to show the present holdings of each.

The Register of Transfers, in a small Company, is usually bound in one book with the Register of Members, etc.

It will also be the duty of the Registrar to see that all calls are paid when due, and to submit the list of outstanding calls to the Directors, and take their instructions on the matter. The rights of the Company will depend upon their Articles, which usually reserve to the Company the right to forfeit the said shares after a formal notice to the shareholder in arrear, specifying a further date on or before which he must pay his calls overdue. The Articles of Association usually provide that shareholders whose shares have been forfeited lose all rights and interest in such shares, which lapse absolutely to the Company. Each shareholder nevertheless remains liable, even after forfeiture, for any calls made whilst he was a member. Forfeited shares may be re-issued to any other person for sufficient to pay 20s. in the pound in all; that is to say, if a £10 share had been forfeited after £3 had been paid on it, the Company could re-issue it for any figure they thought fit, not being less than £7. Of course, a formal resolution of the Board would be necessary, either to forfeit a share or to re-issue a forfeited share, the latter being in effect an ordinary allotment, subject to special terms of payment.

A trouble that is likely to arise in a Company which has been in existence a few years is the loss by a shareholder of his certificate, in which case he should apply to the Company for a new one. The usual course is to write him a formal note, asking him to make a thorough search for the document, and, if it is still missing, to issue him a new one on his making a statutory declaration that it has been lost, and that, in event of its recovery, he will hold the Company indemnified against any loss which may occur, and will, if it is subsequently found in his possession, forthwith return it to the Company. Many Companies charge a special fee for a certificate issued under this heading and, in important cases, require a guarantee for the performance of the indemnity.

Before leaving this section, it is well to remember that, when shares are issued for a consideration other than cash, the agreement embodying the terms of such issue or a statement in lieu thereof must be filed with the Registrar within one month from the time the shares are issued.

The first (or "Statutory") meeting of members must be held by public Companies not less than one month or more than three months from the date on which the Company is entitled to commence business. The notice calling this meeting must be accompanied by a special report which has been previously sent to the Registrar of Companies. Full particulars of this meeting are contained in the next chapter.

Another matter which is confined to Limited Companies is the issue of Debentures, the financial aspect of which has already been discussed. It must be remembered that, if these Debentures give any charge over the Company's assets, they must be registered with the Registrar of Companies, and also in the "Register of Charges" kept at the Registered Office. Where there are a large number of bonds issued, or where the Debentures take the form of stock held by a large number of different holders, it will be necessary to keep the same class of books for them as for shares, that is to say, an "Application and Allotment Book," "Register of Transfers," and "Register of Debenture-holders," and the particulars of the work will be the same as those described for dealing with shares, save that the Directors will not have the right to refuse to register the transfer, unless a clause limiting the right to transfer appears on the Bond or Stock Certificate itself, which is very unusual.

The only practical difference between Stock and Shares is that the former is always fully paid up, whilst the latter are not. Moreover, a share is a specific proportion of the capital of the Company, and can be transferred only in such portions, whilst stock can be subdivided to any extent desired, subject to the regulations of the Company. Thus, a person holding one £10 share could only sell it, as such, or keep it; whilst a man holding £10 stock could (in the absence of special restriction) sell, say, £5 6s. 8d. and retain £4 13s. 4d.

for himself. Stock Ledgers, therefore, require the usual money columns, instead of simple columns for the quantity (number) of shares or debenture bonds held or transferred. Often, however, the right to transfer even Stock is restricted to multiples of £1.

Another point peculiar to Company work is the method of distribution of the profits. Here again, reference to the Articles is necessary. For instance, some Articles of Association provide that the Directors have no right to distribute an interim dividend; whilst, in many Articles, it is provided that no higher rate of dividend shall be paid than is recommended by the Directors. But the point of immediate interest here is the procedure after the profits have been declared and the dividend sanctioned by a resolution of the Company. In large Companies, the Register of Members is closed before the Annual Meeting, and a list is prepared of all the members, with the number of shares held by each, and the amount of dividend to which each is entitled calculated out. The question of calculation even requires reference to the Articles, for it may be that the calculation must be worked on the nominal amount of the shares and not the amount paid up, so that two £10 shares, one fully paid up and one £5 paid up, would receive an equal dividend. In most cases, however, the Articles provide that the dividend shall be declared and be payable proportionately on the paid-up capital, and not on the nominal amount of capital issued.

The list is then prepared with the details shown in Form No. 55.

In the last column would appear any note as to calls being in arrear, or any other fact which would cause the dividend to be

DIVIDEND LIST

Folio in Share Register.	Name.	Address	No. of Shares held.	Amount paid up (where all shares are not equally called up.)			Amount of Dividend.			Income Tax deducted.			Amount payable.			Remarks.

(*Form No.* 55)

Form of Dividend Warrant.

No....... (*Date and Address.*)

The Earlham Manufacturing Co., Ltd.

SIR DIVIDEND NO. 56

In accordance with the resolution passed at the General Meeting of the above Company on 5th instant, I send you herewith dividend warrant as follows :—

	£	s.	d.
One year's **dividend at 5 % on** 10 shares of £10 each	5	–	–
Less Income Tax **at** 5s.	1	5	–
Amount receivable	£3	15	–

I hereby certify that tax on the above Dividend has been or will be accounted for to the proper authorities.

Yours faithfully.

HENRY BLANK.

Secretary.

Albert Rich, Esq.,
1015 Strand, W.C.2.

Shareholders seeking relief from Income Tax are informed that Inspectors of Taxes will accept the above statement.

Proprietors to retain this portion. Please note any change of Address.

- -

No.......

The Earlham Manufacturing Co., Ltd.

2d. Stamp impressed

Dividend Account 1. *Date* ....

To the Citadel Bank, Ltd.

Pay............ *Albert Rich, Esq*...*or order*

the sum of............ *Three pounds* 15/–...

£3 15s. –d.

For The Earlham Manufacturing Company, Ltd.,

....*Secretary* ....
.... } *Directors*

The Proprietor will sign here.

Name ....

This cheque must be presented within three months from date

(*Form No.* 56)

retained. The cheques, or rather "dividend warrants," would then be drawn on a special "Dividend Account" at the Bank. This account would be opened by the payment in of one cheque, drawn on the general account of the Company, in order to avoid a considerable number of cheques, frequently of small amount, passing through the general account, and also, in many cases, to save the Directors the trouble of signing all the cheques, since the Dividend Account has in it sufficient money to meet that dividend only, and the Secretary is very frequently authorized to draw on that account by his own signature only.

Under Section 33 of the Finance Act, 1924, "every warrant or cheque . . . in payment of any dividend or interest distributed by any company . . . shall have annexed thereto, or be accompanied by, a statement in writing, showing

(*a*) "The gross amount which, after deduction of the income tax appropriate thereto, corresponds to the net amount actually paid; and

(*b*) The rate and the amount of income-tax appropriate to such gross amount; and

(*c*) The net amount actually paid."

This means that, even in cases where a dividend is declared "free of tax," the net amount paid must be "grossed" by adding back such an amount of tax as represents the standard rate on the dividend so increased. A normal form is given in Form No. 56, but this must, of course, be suitably amended in (so called) "tax free" cases.

To show the care necessary in the case of a Limited Company, perhaps the best way is to close this chapter with a list of some offences, for which penalties (varying from £50 per day downwards) may be inflicted on the Company or its officials. Some of these penalties cannot, of course, apply to Private Companies—

Not keeping the books directed by the Acts (Register of Members, etc.), and not allowing inspection of the same to any applicant entitled, and not forwarding proper extracts from them to the Registrar:

Not having a registered office with the name legibly appearing outside:

Failure to file any document requiring filing with the Registrar, including—

Return of Allotments, contract to take shares other than for cash consideration, report for statutory meeting, mortgages or charges, any special resolution:

Neglect to return application money within 48 days after the first issue of the prospectus, if there has not been any allotment on account of the " minimum subscription " clause:

Inserting the name of a person who has not consented to act as Director as such in the application to register, or the acting as a Director of a person who is not qualified:

Omission to hold Statutory meeting:

Commencing business or exercising borrowing power without the Registrar's certificate:

Concurring in the issuing of any document (including share warrant, transfer, etc.) not duly stamped:

Neglect to send copy of Memorandum and Articles of Association to any member with copy of alterations made by any special resolution; and others.

CHAPTER XX

Company Work (*continued*)—Preparations for Committee, Board, and General Meetings—Agenda—Minutes—Reports—Methods of keeping papers pending production at Meetings—Procedure at Meetings

Too much care cannot be given to the preparation of information likely to be required at meetings of the Directors of a Company. The Secretary who wishes to stand well with his Directors will strive to develop a good system of collecting and preparing information regarding the business, which may be available at a moment's notice. The regular and methodical collection and analysis of current data should be arranged, so that it is not necessary to defer the consideration of a question until the necessary information is hurriedly and imperfectly looked up. It is the duty of a Secretary to keep in such close touch with the business that he is able to give his Board *precise* information on every point which may arise, whether its want was foreseen or not. A natural or acquired talent for method is an invaluable equipment, the result of which will be shown in the facility with which the business of the Board Meetings is carried through.

The exact nature of the records to be prepared will depend upon the nature of the business of the Company. A comparative financial statement is usually required by the Directors at each meeting of the Board. Such information is requisite for the proper conduct of the business, and the statement should show not only the cash actually in hand at the moment, but that which will be available shortly, together with the forthcoming liabilities, and the provisions made, or to be made, for meeting them. Not only should the financial position be known, but the Directors will naturally wish to have information as to the volume of business and the approximate profit which is being made, or the loss incurred. For this purpose, instead of the bare figures being given, it is becoming a common practice to present the information in graphic form. The general tendency is better and more easily shown by a good "graph" than by long columns of figures, and comparisons of certain periods are also facilitated by the use of differently coloured inks. Where the "graph" plan is not adopted, it may be found convenient for purposes of comparison to translate the figures into percentages.

The Directors have power to arrange for meetings to be held at such times and places as they may think fit, and (subject to the Articles) to determine what shall be the quorum necessary for the transaction of business. Every member of the Board should have due notice of the time and place of meeting, as it has been held that business done at a meeting of Directors, of which one Director had no notice, is invalid. Even if a majority of the Directors are present at a meeting, they cannot act unless due notice has been given to the whole body, nor must any Director be excluded from the meetings of the Board. It is not necessary that the notice should state the business to be transacted.

The Directors may elect a Chairman, and determine the period for which he is to hold office; but if, at any meeting, the Chairman thus elected is not present, the Directors may choose one of their number to be Chairman of that meeting. They may delegate their powers to Committees consisting of any members of their body they think fit, provided power so to do is contained in the Articles.

It is the duty of the Secretary to prepare the Agenda, or heads of business to be transacted at the meeting; and, in order that no items may be omitted, he should keep for his own use a rough Agenda Book, in which should be entered from time to time all matters requiring the attention of the Board. From this he can make up his Agenda for the Board Meetings. Perhaps the best form for the latter is that in which the various items are entered on one side of the page, with the other side left blank, in order that the Chairman may insert his own remarks as the matters are dealt with by the Board. The Secretary will, in addition, take minutes of all resolutions and proceedings, afterwards (in some Companies) submitting them to the Chairman before entering them in the Minute Book as a permanent record.

The following will be found a convenient form of Agenda for Board Meetings—

1. The verification of the Minutes of the previous meeting, certifying that they form a correct record of what took place:
2. Correspondence, or matters arising out of the Minutes. Reports as to the carrying out of resolutions or suggestions of the previous meeting:

3. Statistical information, financial statement, approximate trading accounts, analyses, etc. :
4. Reports of Sub-Committees, where such have been appointed :
5. Share transfers and issuing of new certificates :
6. Capital items, calls, loans, etc.

An Attendance Register should be kept, and signed by Directors present at each meeting.

The Minute Book, being the official record of the business done at each meeting, should receive careful attention. When signed by the Chairman of the meeting at which the proceedings were had, or by the Chairman of the next succeeding meeting, minutes are evidence receivable in Court proceedings. Under no consideration should a page be removed from the Minute Book, as such mutilation would give rise to suspicion in case of inquiry. Immediately after the meeting, and whilst the various matters which have been dealt with are fresh in his mind, the Secretary should proceed to draft the Minutes. The notes which he himself has taken will be supplemented by the Chairman's notes on the Agenda, and, as previously suggested, it is sometimes the practice to submit the draft Minutes to the Chairman before entering them in the Minute Book, so as to lessen the liability to alteration when the Minutes are submitted for verification. Should such alteration be deemed necessary, the correction should be made by the Secretary and initialed by the Chairman when the Minutes are signed. The Minutes should be indexed, in order to facilitate reference in case of need.

A great saving of time may often be effected by the Secretary sending to each Director, a few days before each meeting, a letter setting forth the subjects likely to come up for discussion, and giving such extracts from any important correspondence as will assist him to form a judgment upon them. It is also a good practice to send to each Director a copy of the Minutes of the previous meeting so that he may raise any point which occurs to him when these come up for verification. Each Director will thus be kept posted up in the current affairs of the Company, and a large amount of time which would otherwise be taken up by explanations will be saved.

The Secretary will find it useful to keep all the papers relating to each distinct subject in a separate portfolio, properly labelled on the outside. This will prevent papers and letters from being mislaid, and if the folders or portfolios are of different colours, and placed in a cabinet or drawer in alphabetical order, they are at all times easily accessible for reference. Such portfolios are not only cheap but in every way serviceable, and, by their use, documents and papers are kept together without the necessity of mutilating them by perforation, or spoiling their appearance by folding. Another plan is to file and docket all papers relating to the same subject, placing them in pigeon holes, or securing them by means of tape or rubber bands.

After each Board Meeting, the Secretary will turn his attention to his diary, recording therein on their proper dates the matters to be attended to. On no account should he rely upon his memory, however good that may have proved to be. It may happen that he may be prevented, either from illness or other cause, from carrying out his work, and he should be in a position to hand this over to the person who may temporarily take his place. Dates of future meetings should be entered sufficiently ahead of the actual dates as to allow for the sending out of the proper notices, and the preparation of the necessary Agenda. Where it is essential that replies should be received to important communications sent out, the date of the expected reply should be noted, so that in case it is not received a reminder may be sent if deemed advisable. A well-kept diary will ensure that important matters are not left to the last moment, and thus have to be dealt with hurriedly.

One of the most modern devices for keeping in touch with special business for fixed dates is that known as the "Office Tickler." This consists of a box or drawer in which cards are placed which have been specially prepared for the purpose. The first card is one indicating the month, say January; this is followed by other cards numbered from 1 to 31, after which follows a card marked February with 29 other cards behind it, indicating the days of the month, and so on for the whole year. Any matters which are to come up for consideration on any particular date are noted on loose cards or slips of paper. These are placed immediately behind the card indicating the day of the month required. From day to day, the front card is removed, and the matter requiring attention having been dealt with, the card is placed at the back of the set, that is, the card indicating 1st January is placed behind that representing 31st December, so that the whole of the cards are, like an endless revolving chain, gradually working round. In this way, it is possible to keep in constant touch with questions requiring attention, as, after a subject has been dealt with, e.g. after an important official letter has been sent, to which it is necessary that a reply should be received within a certain period—a note can be made which will bring the matter forward again in a few days' time, when, if the reply has not been received, a reminder may be sent or other necessary steps taken. The possibilities of this system are very great, as it can be applied not only to the business of the Company as connected with its administration, but also for the purpose of keeping in view the rendering of accounts, the due dates of Bills of Exchange, the dates on which certain returns must be made, insurance premiums renewed, and, in fact, it may take the place of a diary, to which in many respects it is superior.

Every Company must hold a General Meeting once at least in every year, and when the Directors have decided to convene a General Meeting, it is the duty of the Secretary to see that proper notice is given to every person entitled to receive such notice. The time at which the Annual General Meeting is to be held is usually fixed by the Articles, but the Act prescribes that it shall be held not more than fifteen months after the previous General Meeting. The place of meeting (unless fixed by the Articles) is determined upon by the Directors. The number of days' notice to be given is usually specified in the Articles, but, in the absence of express provision, at least seven clear days' notice must be given. The expression "clear days" means "exclusive of the day of giving notice and of the day of the meeting." Where it is provided by the Articles that notice is to be given by advertisement, the day of giving notice will be that on which the notice actually appears, and not that on which it was sent to the newspapers. The notice should specify the date, place and hour of meeting, and should state in general terms the nature of the business to be transacted, and in the case of special business it must state specifically what is in contemplation, so that the shareholders are in possession of full information as to what is intended to be brought forward. It may be pointed out that, in calling General Meetings, Directors are required to consider the interests of the Company, and they may be restrained, on the application of shareholders, from holding the meeting at a time which has been fixed for the express purpose of preventing a large number of shareholders from being present. If it is intended to proceed under any particular section of the Companies Act, the section should be clearly indicated in the notice. Just as in the case of a Meeting of Directors, a General Meeting would be held to be not duly convened unless every person entitled to attend had been given notice of the time and place and of the express purpose for which the meeting is proposed to be held, in order that he may exercise his own judgment as to whether he will attend or not. Omission to give notice (where such notice is possible) even to one member will invalidate the meeting. This is clearly laid down by Lord Campbell in *Smyth* v. *Darley* (1849), 2 H.L.C. 789.

Most Articles provide, however, that a member shall be deemed to have received notice, if such notice has been posted to him directed to his last registered address.

The Articles of most Companies, in making provision for general meetings, prescribe what business shall be considered " ordinary," and any other business which it is intended to transact at such meetings must be looked upon as " special," and due notice must be given of this.

" Extraordinary General Meetings " may be called by the Directors at any time they think proper, and, at such meetings, only the special business for which they are convened can be transacted.

The Directors are bound forthwith to convene an Extraordinary Meeting on the requisition of the holders of not less than one-tenth of the issued capital of the Company, upon which all calls, or other sums then due, have been paid. The requisition must be signed by the members concerned, and must state the objects of the meeting. If the Directors do not proceed to arrange for a meeting within 21 days from the deposit of the requisition, the requisitionists (or the majority of them in value) may themselves convene the meeting. It must, however, be held within three months from the deposit of the requisition.

The adjournment of a General Meeting may be brought about either (*a*) under the Articles by the absence of a quorum within the time fixed, or (*b*) by a motion for adjournment. Any member may move at any time, without notice, "that this meeting do now adjourn." Like other formal motions, this takes precedence of any other question or matter in hand. If the motion is carried, it should be followed by another, naming the time and place at which the adjourned meeting is to be held. As the adjourned meeting is a continuation of the original meeting, it generally requires no fresh notice to be given, except where no definite date had been fixed for the adjourned meeting. No business can be transacted at an adjourned meeting except that left unfinished at the first meeting, unless notice has been given in due form that such fresh business will be introduced.

The Annual General Meeting is the one occasion in the year (apart from extraordinary general meetings) when members of the company are able to exercise their right and duty to guide the affairs of the company and it is very important that proper arrangements should be made for the conduct of so important an occasion. The points in regard to the notice to be given to every member entitled to attend have already been indicated (page 267). With the notice (unless the company is technically "private") there should be sent out—

(1) A copy of the balance sheet, to which must be attached a copy of the auditors' report thereon, and

(2) A "report by the directors with respect to the state of the company's affairs, the amount, if any, which they recommend should be paid by way of dividend, and the amount, if any, which they propose to carry to the reserve fund, general reserve or reserve account shown specifically on the balance sheet, or to a reserve fund, general reserve or reserve account to be shown specifically on a subsequent balance sheet" (Section 123 (2)).

It is usual also to include with these documents a profit and loss account (albeit in very truncated form) although, strictly, under the statute (Section 123 (1)) it is sufficient merely to "lay before the company in general meeting" this document, i.e. to put it on the table.

The Articles usually provide that the Chairman of the Board shall preside but, otherwise, any member elected by the members present may take the chair.

The Secretary should arrange to check the credentials of persons attending either by taking their signatures and referring to the Register of Members or by inspecting their Share Warrants if these have been issued.

The first step in the meeting is customarily the reading, by the Secretary, of the notice convening the meeting. The purpose of this is presumably to enable persons to be sure that they are attending the right meeting. It is also obligatory under the Act (Section 129 (1)) that the Auditors' Report should be *read* before the company. The Chairman then usually asks the assent of the meeting that the previously circulated accounts and Directors' Report shall be "taken as read." The Chairman then delivers a speech (often, under a commendable modern custom, printed and circulated beforehand) in which he explains the position of affairs and enlarges on the matters dealt with in the Report, concluding by moving "that the Report and Accounts be now adopted." This motion is then seconded, usually by another Director, and the meeting is open for discussion.

Now is the opportunity for members to discuss and criticize the disclosures made to them, to state their views on the policy and activities of the Board and to ask for any further information they may desire. The Directors, however, are not obliged to give further information but must remember that their duty is to guard the interests of the company as a whole and it is obvious that to satisfy the curiosity of individual shareholders might conflict with this over-riding responsibility. Dissatisfied shareholders have four possible lines of remedy, viz. (*a*) To vote against the Chairman's motion. Rejection of the Report and Accounts is equivalent to a vote of censure on the Board; either another Balance Sheet must be prepared (to be accepted at an adjourned meeting) or the Board must be reconstituted. (*b*) To use whatever power is given by the Articles to appoint other directors. (*c*) To ask the Board of Trade to use its power (under Section 135) "to appoint one or more competent inspectors to investigate the affairs" of the company. (*d*) To pass a special resolution (see below) under Section 137 appointing inspectors to investigate the company's affairs.

The next step at the meeting is to elect or re-elect directors; the Articles will indicate which directors retire from office. It will also be necessary to vote the directors' fees unless the amount is fixed by the Articles. The relative resolutions on both these matters are usually moved and seconded by persons who are not directors.

It is also necessary for shareholders to move and second the appointment or re-appointment of auditors and to fix their remuneration, although the last named matter may be delegated to the Board.

The Minutes of the meeting must be taken by the Secretary; but there is no obligation upon the Directors to publish a report of the proceedings of general meetings, although it may be deemed advisable in the case of large Companies to have a report prepared and circulated amongst the shareholders. The Secretary will be responsible for the preparation of such a report.

Voting at general meetings is controlled by the terms of the Articles but usually it is, in the first instance, taken by show of hands, when each shareholder has a single vote, but cannot vote for any persons whose proxy he holds. But, if a sufficient number of shareholders are dissatisfied with the result of such a vote, they may demand a poll in order that the number of votes to which those present are entitled may be ascertained. Subject to the Articles proxies may be used on a poll. Unless special provision has been made in the Articles, three members, or those holding at least 15 per cent of the share capital, may demand a poll, which shall be taken in such manner as the Chairman directs, and the result of such poll shall be deemed to be a resolution of the Company in general meeting. It is at the discretion of the Chairman as to whether the poll shall be taken at the meeting then assembled or on a future day. In the latter case, it will be necessary, subject to the Articles, to give notice to all shareholders of the time and place.

An "ordinary" resolution is carried by a bare majority. An "extraordinary" resolution is one which is passed by a three-fourths majority of those voting at a meeting of which notice specifying the intention to propose the resolution as an extraordinary resolution has been duly given. A "special" resolution is similar, except that 21 clear days' notice must be given. Articles usually give the Chairman a second, or casting vote.

CHAPTER XXI

Legal Matters—Sale of Goods Act—Guarantees—Cancellation of Orders—Interest on Overdue Accounts—Carriers—Recovery of Debts—Deeds of Arrangement—Disputes with Employees—Truck Acts—Workmen's Compensation

THE business man who anticipates that he will be able to conduct his business without coming into contact with legal matters is very sanguine, and is likely to be disappointed. However anxious he may be to give the law a wide berth, he will find himself constantly in need of its aid, either to enable him to keep out of difficulties or, when once in, to get out again with a whole skin. It is an old and wise saying that " the man who acts as his own lawyer has a fool for a client," and, therefore, the best advice to a business man who requires the aid of the law is that he should consult a competent solicitor, and be guided by his advice.

There are, however, many cases in which it is necessary for the business man to act promptly, and, as ignorance of the law is no excuse, he should endeavour to make himself familiar with certain fundamental principles, and know where he is with regard to the law affecting matters of almost every-day occurrence. For this reason, it is proposed in this and the following chapter to draw the attention of the business man to certain matters of law and legal procedure with which it is desirable that he should be acquainted.

The great importance to commercial men of the law relating to the sale of goods has long been recognized, and the Sale of Goods Act, 1893 (which, by the way, has the enviable reputation of being the best drawn Act on the Statute Book), contains, in a codified form, all the law upon this important subject. It is well that a few of the leading features of this Act should be kept in mind, and one of the most important is Section 4, which provides that " A contract for the sale of any goods of the value of £10 or upwards shall not be enforceable by action unless the buyer shall accept part of the goods so sold and actually receive the same, or give something in earnest to bind the contract, or in part payment, or unless some note or memorandum in writing of the contract be made and signed by the party to be charged or his agent in that behalf." Acceptance does not mean an acceptance in performance of the contract. Any dealing with the goods which recognizes the fact that there has been a contract is sufficient. For example, if the goods are examined to see if they correspond with a sample, and even if rejected because they are not up to sample, there is an acceptance within the section. The section does not require the contract itself to be in writing but only a memorandum of its terms. The actual bargain may be made orally. In one case, the only memorandum was a letter containing the terms but repudiating liability, but it was held sufficient. Five things must appear in writing, viz., (1) the parties to the bargain, (2) the terms of the promise, (3) the consideration, or return given for the promise, (4) the promise itself, or an acknowledgment of it, (5) the signature of the party to be charged. Much litigation, valuable to the lawyer, but annoying and expensive to the litigant, would be saved if business men were more careful with their contracts for the sale and purchase of goods than they often are. An agreement, letter, or memorandum made for, or relating to, the sale of any goods, wares or merchandise does not need to be stamped. Doubt is often felt whether, on the neglect or refusal of a buyer to accept and pay for goods he has ordered, the seller is able to sue for the price of the goods or only for damages for breach of contract. As the latter is prima facie the difference between the contract price and the market price at the time of the neglect or refusal, it is often more to the interest of the seller to be able to deliver, and obtain payment for, the goods than to recover damages. This he can do only where the property in the goods has passed to the buyer, and the statute lays down certain rules which determine when the property in the goods has so passed. It is possible, however, for the contract to be so worded as to enable the seller to obtain the contract price for his goods in case of the buyer's neglect or refusal to accept delivery, and the wise business man will be careful to have an order form (to be signed by his customers) carefully drawn so that the latter may not wriggle out of an order with little or no loss to themselves.

The question as to whether or not the property in goods sold has passed to the buyer is also important in determining by whom the loss must be borne in case the goods are destroyed before actual delivery. If there is no agreement to the contrary, the goods remain at the seller's risk until the property in them is transferred to the buyer ; but, when once the property is transferred, the goods are at the buyer's risk, whether delivery has been made or not. An important proviso to this rule is that, where delivery has been delayed through the fault of either buyer or seller, the goods are at the risk of the party in fault as regards any loss which might not have occurred but for such fault. It may be useful to mention the principal rules for determining when, in the absence of special agreement, the property in goods passes to the buyer, and it must always be remembered that there is a great distinction between the *property* in the goods and their *possession.* Where there is an unconditional contract for the sale of specific goods (i.e. goods identified and agreed upon at the time a contract of sale is made) in a deliverable state, the property passes at the time the contract is made. If there is a contract to sell specific goods, and the seller is bound to do something to the goods before they can be delivered—as, for example, to polish furniture—the property does not pass until that something is done and the buyer is informed that the goods are ready for delivery. If there is a contract to sell specific goods and the goods are ready for delivery, but require to be weighed, tested, or otherwise dealt with for the purpose of ascertaining the price, the property does not pass until such act is done and notice given to the buyer. (The term "Specific" goods involves something more than description. A sale of "50 Southdown sheep" is not "specific," and can be satisfied by the delivery of any 50 Southdown sheep ; a sale of "the 50 Southdown sheep on my farm at Blackacre" is "specific" as the sheep are identified.) Where there is a contract for the sale of unascertained goods by description, and goods of that description and in a deliverable state are unconditionally appropriated to the contract, either by the seller with the assent of the buyer, or by the buyer with the assent of the seller, the property in the goods thereupon passes to the buyer. Such assent may be expressed or implied, and may be given either before or after the appropriation is made. It will be seen that the question of the passing of the property in goods is all important, and, as it may be determined by the contract, the document embodying the agreement should be carefully prepared, and the advice of a solicitor taken if the transaction is a large one.

It is also well for the seller of goods to bear in mind that if, while goods are in the course of transit, he hears of the buyer's insolvency, he may stop the goods and re-take possession of them while on their way, and retain them until payment. This step can only be taken while the goods are in course of transit, and provided the Bill of Lading, or other document of title, has not been assigned by the purchaser to a *bona fide* assignee for valuable consideration. If the buyer becomes insolvent before the goods, for which payment has not been made, leave the seller's possession, the seller may retain them until payment is made. A person is deemed to be insolvent who either has ceased to pay his debts in the ordinary course of business or cannot pay his debts as they become due, whether he has committed an act of bankruptcy or not.

A purchaser of goods should understand that by the common law the rule of *caveat emptor* (let the buyer beware) applies, and that he takes the risk of the goods not being suitable. The exceptions are given in the Act as follows : (1) Where the buyer, expressly or by implication, makes known to the seller the particular purpose for which the goods are required, so as to show that the buyer relies on the seller's skill and judgment and the goods are of a description which it is in the course of the seller's business to supply (whether he be the manufacturer or not), there is an implied condition that the goods shall be reasonably fit for such purpose, provided that, in the case of a contract for the sale of a specified article under its patent or other trade name, there is no implied condition as to its fitness for any particular purpose : (2) Where goods are bought by description from a seller who deals in goods of that description (whether he be the manufacturer or not), there is an implied condition that the goods shall be of merchantable quality ; but, if the buyer has examined the goods, there is no implied condition as regards defects which such examination ought to have revealed : (3) An implied condition as to quality or fitness for a particular purpose may be annexed by the usage of trade.

It often happens that a seller of goods who is doubtful of his customer's position, and anxious to avoid a bad debt, asks for a guarantee from some responsible person that payment will be forthcoming. There must be a written memorandum of an undertaking of this description signed by the party to be charged therewith if the customer is to remain primarily liable, but not if the liability to pay in any case rests upon the person giving the undertaking. For example, if A gives an order for goods, and B says to the seller, " If A does not pay you, I will," A remains primarily liable, and the promise of B, to be worth anything, must be put into writing. If, however, B says " Supply A with certain goods and I will pay," B takes the entire responsibility and his promise may be oral only.

An offer to purchase goods may be cancelled if cancellation is effected before the offer is accepted. If A writes to B offering a certain price for certain goods, he may withdraw his offer at any time before it is accepted by B. As many commercial contracts are made through the post, the following simple rules as to offer and acceptance through the post should be carefully noted. " The Post Office is the servant employed by the party making the offer to deliver the offer and receive the acceptance." Hence (1) an offer made by letter is made when the letter is *delivered* ; (2) such offer is accepted when the letter of acceptance is *posted*, even though it may never reach its destination ; (3) till the letter of acceptance is posted, but not afterwards, the offer may be withdrawn, e.g. by another letter or telegram. The moral of this is obvious : If an offer is worth accepting, accept at once.

Sellers of goods often make a mistake in thinking that they can recover interest on overdue accounts. Interest cannot be recovered unless there has been an express promise by the customer to pay interest, or unless such a promise can be implied from the usage of trade or other circumstances. The common practice of printing upon an invoice the words " Interest charged on overdue accounts," or words to the like effect, will not enable the seller to recover interest. The most effective way of making an extra charge where accounts are not promptly paid is to offer a rebate if payment is made within a stipulated time. When the time has elapsed, the rebate is forfeited.

The question of liability for goods lost or damaged in course of transit deserves attention. A common carrier is an insurer of the goods entrusted to him, except as to loss occasioned by the act of God, the King's enemies, or the inherent defect or vice of the thing carried. A carrier by land is, by virtue of the Carriers Act, 1830, exempt from liability for loss or injury to certain articles exceeding £10 in value, unless the value has been declared by the sender, and an increased rate paid. Among the articles are gold, jewellery, watches, pictures, china, and silk. The liability at common law and under the provisions of the Carriers' Act was often evaded by carriers putting notices, usually in very small type, upon the receipts given to persons delivering goods, to the effect that the carriers would not be liable for damage or loss except in certain circumstances. These notices were held to constitute special contracts, setting aside the carriers' common law liability, and, as they were often unreasonable and not properly brought to the notice of consignors, it was provided by the Railway and Canal Traffic Act, 1854, that, although special contracts may be made with railway companies, they shall not be binding unless they are just and reasonable, and signed by the consignor or his agent. It is very advisable, therefore, that a consignor, before signing the documents put before him by a Railway Company, should read and understand them. In the majority of cases, they provide that the Company shall not be responsible for loss of or damage to goods consigned to them unless negligence on the part of their servants is proved, and, in the case of certain goods, it is necessary to prove that the loss or damage is due to wilful misconduct on the part of the carriers or their servants. It is almost impossible for the unfortunate consignor to prove, in case of damage to his goods, that the damage has been wilfully done, and it is very often extremely difficult to prove that there has been negligence of any kind. The law will not assume negligence from the mere fact that goods have been lost or damaged, and the consignor wishing to recover compensation must be prepared to show how the accident happened, and place the responsibility on the right shoulders. Railway Companies are not philanthropists, and will not settle claims unless the blame is clearly brought home to them. Consignment notes which constitute special contracts are too often signed by business men or their servants as matters of course, but it is often advisable to pay an increased rate and insure the carriage of the goods at the carriers' risk. Care should be taken to see that goods are properly packed, as carriers may get rid of liability on the ground of insufficient packing. It is hardly necessary to point out that goods received should be carefully examined before a receipt is given to the carrier, and the attention of the carrier called to any loss or damage. It should also be borne in mind that, if damages arising from a carrier's negligence are recoverable, nothing in the nature of special damage can be obtained unless the special circumstances were made known to the carrier when the goods were consigned. If it is desired that, for some special reason, goods should reach their destination within a certain time, the matter should be carefully explained to the carrier, and he should understand that special loss will be occasioned if he fails to carry out his contract.

Next in importance to the selling of goods comes the question of obtaining payment from those who cannot or will not pay. Nothing that is satisfactory can be done with the former class. To sue them is often to throw good money after bad, and the best plan is to write off the debt at once as bad, and see that future orders are accompanied by cash. As to the latter class, they can be sued in the High Court or the County Court, but, in choosing the Court, regard must be had to the amount of the debt. County Courts have now jurisdiction to amounts not exceeding £100, but the procedure is sometimes slow and not always satisfactory. A writ can be issued in the High Court and judgment obtained in cases where no *bona fide* defence is possible, in little over a fortnight; but, if the amount is within the County Court jurisdiction, it sometimes happens that the plaintiff loses his costs altogether, or obtains costs on the County Court scale only. The procedure in the County Court may be (1) by ordinary summons or (2) by what is known as default summons. Judgment on a default summons may be signed if, within 8 days from personal service, the defendant omits to enter an appearance by signing and sending to the Registrar of the Court a notice at the foot of his summons to the effect that he intends to defend the action. The defendant need not, as in the High Court, show to the satisfaction of the Registrar that he has a defence, and it is not possible to set aside his appearance. If appearance is entered, the action proceeds as in the case of an ordinary summons, except that it can be heard only by the Judge and not by the Registrar. As defendants are usually quick enough to put in an appearance, proceeding by default summons is not as a rule satisfactory, especially as personal service is necessary and a defendant may be an adept at keeping out of the way. To enter a case in the County Court, two detailed statements of the claim are necessary if the sum claimed exceed £2, and it is also necessary to fill up a form (to be obtained at the Court) giving the names, addresses and descriptions of the parties, the amount claimed and what the claim is for. County Court fees are heavy. On entering a plaint for the recovery of a sum of money not exceeding 10s. the fee is 1s. and for £1 it is 1s. 6d., with an additional 1s. 6d. for each £1 up to £6. Exceeding £6 an additional 1s. is payable for each £1 up to £30. The fee for a sum exceeding £30 and not exceeding £35 is 30s., between £35 and £40, 32s., and an additional 2s. for each £10 up to £70. After £70 the fixed fee is 40s. On the trial or hearing of an action an additional fee is payable, this being equal to the fee payable on entering the plaint, but where the defendant does not appear only one-half of the fee is payable. If the person to be sued does not reside or carry on business within the jurisdiction of the County Court for the district in which the creditor's place of business is situate, it may be necessary to issue the summons in the Court for the district where the defendant resides or carries on business. Leave will be granted by the Registrar to sue in the creditor's district if the cause of action arose there. That is to say, a creditor may sue in his Court if (*a*) the order for the goods has been received at his place of business; (*b*) the goods have been delivered to the customer within the creditor's district, as, for example, if they are sent by carrier and the carriage is paid by the buyer, or (*c*) if the place for payment is the creditor's place of business. As it is often very inconvenient and expensive to attend a Court at a considerable distance to prove his case, a seller of goods should, wherever possible, arrange that the cause of action shall arise within his, and not his customer's district. This may be done in one way by putting on the invoice a notice to the effect that the place for payment for the goods is the seller's place of business.

In attending the Court on the day fixed for the hearing of the case, the creditor must take care to be in a position by witnesses, or letters from the debtor, to prove the order and delivery of the goods or an admission of the debt or a promise to pay. After judgment is obtained, payment of the debt may be enforced by levying execution upon the goods of the debtor. Care must be exercised in adopting this course, for considerable expense may be incurred if the goods levied upon do not happen to be the debtor's property.

The Judge of the County Court has power to commit to prison a debtor who has the means but refuses to pay, but legislation passed in 1935 has enjoined the strictest enquiry as to whether the refusal to pay is really wilful and our humane law now definitely discourages the imprisonment of debtors, except against contumacious persons. To obtain a committal, application must be made to the Registrar for a Judgment Summons, calling upon the debtor to appear and show cause why he should not be committed to prison.

On the hearing, the creditor must be armed with satisfactory *proof* of the debtor's ability to pay. It is for him to show that the debtor can pay, and it is not the duty of the debtor to prove that he cannot. Very often, the issue of the summons will bring about the desired result if the debtor has the wherewithal to pay, but it is the last resource and failure at this step leads to a bad debt. If the debt is £50 or over and if judgment is obtained against the debtor, or he commits an act of bankruptcy, a Petition in Bankruptcy may be filed against him. This course may sometimes be advisable to prevent other creditors taking the debtor's property, but the result is not generally satisfactory to the creditor unless there is reason to suppose that the debtor has concealed or alienated property, and should not be resorted to as a means of coercion, as the petition may not be withdrawn without the leave of the Court, and the Court will not grant leave without giving other creditors the chance of going on with the bankruptcy proceedings. Two or more creditors, where individual debts are under £50 but equal or exceed that sum in the aggregate, may present a bankruptcy petition by joining together.

It is often advisable to enter into arrangements with debtors who, by reason of their liabilities, are unable to pay their debts in full. Private arrangements are often more satisfactory to both debtor and creditor than the realization of estates under Bankruptcy laws. The cost of realization and distribution is considerably less, and, unless the debtor has been guilty of some offence deserving of punishment, or it is suspected he is concealing some of his property, an arrangement outside the Bankruptcy Court is to be recommended. The law as to arrangements with creditors outside the Bankruptcy Court is now contained in the Deeds of Arrangement Act, 1914, and all private arrangements between a debtor and his creditors are void unless registered in accordance with that Act. Private arrangements are usually carried out either by a Deed of Composition, or an assignment of the debtor's property to a Trustee for the benefit of the general body of creditors. The first scheme is adopted where a debtor proposes to pay a certain composition by instalments. The instalments should invariably be guaranteed to the satisfaction of the creditors, and the debtor's property is sometimes assigned to a Trustee who holds it in trust for the creditors until the composition has been paid. If the guarantee is satisfactory, the assignment of the property may be—and often is—dispensed with, but in any case a deed is necessary. The second scheme consists in assigning the debtor's property (except such property as would be excepted in case of Bankruptcy, i.e. the debtor's tools of trade, and the necessary wearing apparel and bedding of himself and his family to the value of £20) to a Trustee, who realizes it to the best advantage and distributes the net proceeds amongst the creditors assenting to the Deed in proportion to their debts; first paying in full claims which have priority in Bankruptcy as rent, wages, rates, and taxes. Any deed carrying out a private arrangement must be registered in accordance with the Act within seven days after its first execution by the debtor or any creditor, and with it must be lodged an affidavit by the debtor setting out in full the names and addresses of all his creditors, and the amount of their claims, and also stating the value of the property comprised in the Deed. A Register is kept of all deeds registered under the Act, and any person is entitled to inspect the Register and to obtain copies of, or extracts from, any registered deed. Deeds of Arrangement or Composition bind only those creditors who sign or assent to them, and as soon as executed by a debtor, are "Acts of Bankruptcy" upon which Bankruptcy proceedings may be taken within three months after execution by any creditors of the debtor who are not parties to the Deed of Arrangement or Composition, and are in a position to present a Petition in Bankruptcy. A creditor not assenting may, notwithstanding the Deed, sue the debtor for the amount of his debt; but, as he cannot touch the property comprised in the Deed, it rarely happens that he gains any advantage by keeping outside the Deed. If, however, the debtor should afterwards acquire any property the rights of the non-assenting creditors remain good, and they may be able to recover their debts. The assenting creditors can claim under the Deed only.

In general, there can be little doubt as to the expediency of those who are comparatively small creditors in an insolvency following the lead of the largest creditors, who (as being those most interested) may reasonably be expected to give the most trouble and attention to the matter, and, therefore, to arrive at the wisest course to be pursued. It is important to bear in mind, however, that the larger creditors in such cases owe no duty to the others, and are probably playing only for their own hand. It is probable that what is their interest will also be the interest of the general body of creditors, but it by no means follows. In particular, a large creditor will often desire that a business should be continued when such a course is not likely to lead to any increased distribution, solely because by that means he may be enabled to sell goods to the estate (perhaps at an enhanced price) for which he is certain to be paid, and thus somewhat reduce his loss. It is only under quite exceptional circumstances that the general body of creditors will derive any advantage from an insolvent business being continued: in the nature of things, a profitable business does not as a rule find itself in an insolvent condition.

With regard to failures in which a business is interested as a large (or as the largest) creditor, the most prudent course is undoubtedly to place the matter in the hands of the professional Auditor, and be guided by his advice—assuming, of course, that the Auditor is one who undertakes bankruptcy and insolvency work. In certain circumstances, it may be desirable that a member of the firm should represent it on the Committee of Inspection; but, with a Trustee of one's own nomination, such a course is quite unnecessary as a rule, and it may be mentioned, for what it is worth, that in such circumstances the firm would be debarred from supplying goods to the Trustee without obtaining, at its own expense, the leave of the Court so to do.

Where the debtor is a Limited Company, whether at the time actually insolvent or not, if there are Debenture-holders who have a floating security, it is, as a rule, undesirable to incur any expense in legal proceedings, as the only effect may be to bring the Debenture-holders into possession, when it will be quite doubtful whether there will be anything available for distribution among unsecured creditors. The position of creditors, where there are Debenture-holders with a floating security who can get a Receiver appointed as soon as an ordinary creditor has issued a writ and signed judgment, has been expressed in the following terms: "The cases are numerous in which the undertaking of a Limited Company is so loaded with debentures that the profits are barely sufficient, or perhaps not sufficient, to keep down the debenture interest, and that, if the Company is wound up, there is nothing for anyone but the Debenture-holders. In short, the facts often are that the undertaking is substantially carried on only for the benefit of the Debenture-holders who have a floating security over it. In this state of facts money is lent or goods consigned to the Company in respect of which a debt accrues to a creditor, and so long as the security floats, as it is termed, and no Receiver is appointed, the creditor has a possibility or expectation of being paid by the Company, for, as between the Company and the Debenture holders, the former may pay in the ordinary course of business. But directly a Receiver is appointed, this expectation of the creditor is intercepted. He may have lent his money or consigned his goods to the Company last week; but, if he has the audacity to ask payment, and to enforce his legal remedies to obtain it, the Debenture-holder obtains a Receiver in a proceeding to which the execution creditor is not a party, and thus closes the door against him, taking his money or his goods as part of the security, and leaving the creditor who supplied the money and the goods to go unpaid. I regret to be driven to the conclusion that, as the law stands, those are the rights of a Debenture-holder entitled to a floating charge." If, however, it is thought that the Debentures can be upset, the matter naturally assumes another aspect, and in that event the professional Auditor and the Solicitor might be consulted with advantage.

Disputes with servants are of frequent occurrence, and, to prevent them, written contracts should, when possible, be entered into. An indefinite hiring is a hiring for a year and terminable only at the end of the year, but many shorter notices have become customary. Thus clerks and servants of a like kind engaged otherwise than by express contract are very usually entitled to three months' notice only, and, in the case of servants of a lower grade, the notice required is generally determined by the payment of wages. For example, if paid weekly, a week's notice is sufficient; if monthly, a month's notice, but where there is the least doubt about the customary notice, the length of notice should be settled by express agreement and recorded in writing. An employer may dismiss a servant without notice, if (*a*) he is seriously incompetent to perform his duties;

(*b*) he wilfully disobeys his master's reasonable and lawful orders; (*c*) he is guilty of gross moral misconduct, whether pecuniary or otherwise; or (*d*) he is so negligent in the performance of his duties as to expose his master's business to serious injury. A servant summarily dismissed on one of these grounds loses any wages accrued since the pay day preceding his dismissal. Magistrates have, by virtue of the powers given to them by the Employers and Workmen Act, 1875, jurisdiction to settle disputes between employers and workmen; but the term "workman" is restricted to a labourer, servant in husbandry, journeyman, artificer, handicraftsman, miner, or person otherwise engaged in manual labour, and the amount in dispute must not exceed £10. The County Court must be resorted to in cases not falling within this Act. Magistrates have also, by the same Act, power to settle disputes between apprentices and their masters.

A master is responsible for wrongs committed by his servants, provided the servant is at the time acting either under express orders or in the course of his regular employment, and provided that his wrongful acts are not wilful and malicious. It may be well to remind the business man that, although he is not obliged to give a character to a departing servant, he must, in giving one, be careful to state only what he knows to be true, or he may lay himself open to an action for libel or slander.

The "Truck Acts," 1831, 1887, and 1896 contain much that is important to every employer. The Acts apply to and include every workman as defined by the Employers and Workmen Act, 1875, to which reference has already been made above, and the term "employer" includes masters, bailiffs, foremen, managers, clerks, and other persons engaged in the hiring of the workmen. It is proposed now to call attention to the principal provisions of the Acts, and to point out some of the pitfalls into which an employer may unwittingly fall.

The main provision of the Act of 1831 was that wages must be paid in legal tender, payment in kind being strictly prohibited by the Act. The workman is in a position to recover from his employer any sum not paid in money, and the value of the articles supplied in lieu of money cannot be recovered by the employer.

The Act of 1887 dealt with the case of a workman who is entitled by agreement, custom, or otherwise to receive a payment on account of his wages before the regular period of payment. In such cases, it is not lawful for the employer to withhold such payment or to make any deduction on account of interest, poundage, or other similar charge.

It also provides that the employer cannot insist upon a workman spending his wages at any particular shop, and a workman is not to be dismissed on account of the place at which his wages are spent.

The Act of 1896 has a much wider scope. Important provisions are made with regard to deductions or payments in respect of fines, damaged goods, or bad workmanship. Contracts may be made with the workmen for deduction from their wages of fines, if (*a*) the terms of the contract are contained in a notice kept constantly affixed where it can be easily seen, read, and copied by any person whom it affects, or the contract is in writing and signed by the workman, and (*b*) the contract specifies the matters in respect of which fines are imposed and the amount of the fines, and (*c*) the fines are in respect of matters likely to cause loss to the employer or interruption to his business, and (*d*) the amount of the fine is fair and reasonable. In addition, when fines are imposed and deductions made in respect of them, care must be taken to furnish the workman at the time with full particulars in writing. This part of the Act applies to shop assistants as well as to workmen, as already defined. Deductions from wages may also be made in respect of bad or negligent work, or injury to materials or other property of the employer, if similar regulations are carried out, and the deduction does not exceed the actual or estimated damage or loss occasioned to the employer. Under similar conditions, an employer may charge for use of materials or tools, standing room, light, heat, etc., so long as the charge is not in excess of the cost price. Workmen are entitled, on making request, to a copy of every contract or notice as to fines and deductions, and the employer is bound to keep a register and to enter therein every deduction or payment for or in respect of fines.

It is impossible within the limits of these pages to deal at all adequately with the important question of an employer's liability in case of accidents to workmen employed by him and the serious responsibility placed upon the employer by the various statutes which have now been consolidated in the Workmen's Compensation

Act, 1925, as amended in 1926 and 1931. Every wise employer of labour will be careful to insure himself against risks of this nature, and to make himself thoroughly acquainted with the terms and conditions of his policy. The Act does not purport to include within its scope all classes of workmen and all classes of employment; but Insurance Companies will issue a special policy to cover all accidents, whether within or without the Act, and it is well for employers to protect themselves against claims for compensation by taking out such a policy. As Insurance Companies naturally protect themselves as much as possible, and generally take advantage of the provisions contained in the policies they issue, care should be taken to see that all their requirements are complied with, and especially that immediate notice of accidents is given. This subject is referred to at greater length in Chapter XXIII.

CHAPTER XXII

Miscellaneous Legal Points—Tenancies—Distress for Rent—The Factories Act—Wages Boards—The Shops Acts

DIFFERENCES between landlord and tenant often give rise to litigation, and it is, therefore, necessary that, in entering upon the occupation of business premises, care should be taken to see first that the tenancy is made secure, and secondly that the terms of the tenancy are clearly expressed. Leases for terms not exceeding three years may be made by word of mouth, but *agreements* for leases, however short the term, must always be in writing. This is often important. A tenant may take premises for a term of two years, and, by taking possession, will, if the oral lease can be proved by evidence, be safe for the term agreed upon. If, however, an intending tenant agrees to take premises for a term of two years to commence at a future date, and does not immediately take possession, and, before the tenancy is entered upon, the owner of the premises changes his mind, the agreement cannot be enforced as, by law, it should have been in writing. Agreements for leases, however long the term, although bound to be in writing, need not be by deed under seal ; but a lease for a longer term than three years must be by deed under seal. For obvious reasons, it is highly desirable that tenancy agreements should be in writing. It often happens that a tenant enters and pays rent without any written document, and, in these cases, several points should be borne in mind. A tenancy is prima facie a yearly tenancy, but it may be inferred from the way in which the rent is paid that a shorter tenancy is intended. For instance, rent paid by the week in general establishes a weekly tenancy. But there is no such inference if the rent is paid quarterly. In the first place, to determine a yearly tenancy, six months' notice must be given on either side, and the notice must expire on the Quarter Day on which the tenancy commenced. That is to say, if the tenancy commenced on the 24th June, the six months' notice must be given on the 25th December preceding the June Quarter Day when it is desired that the tenancy should end. The yearly tenancy is, therefore, nearly always equal to a tenancy for two years certain, as, unless notice is given to terminate the tenancy at the end of the first half year, the tenancy cannot be terminated until the end of the second year. If, as sometimes happens, possession of premises is taken between two Quarter Days, and rent is paid for the broken portion of the quarter, and subsequently from quarter to quarter, the tenancy is considered to have commenced not when the tenant first entered but at the Quarter Day to which he first paid up, and notice must be given accordingly; but, if rent is not paid for the broken portion, the tenancy will commence on the day when the tenant entered and notice to quit at that time will be good. If a tenant wishes to terminate his tenancy, he may do so by giving an oral notice, but a written notice should always be given and may take the following form—

To A. B. of, etc. (Landlord).

Take notice that I wish to quit and deliver up on the 24th June next (or other day, as the case may be) possession of the premises situate at (describe the premises shortly) which I now hold of you as yearly tenant.

Dated this day of , 19. .

(Signed) C. D.
Address:

This notice should be served personally on the landlord, but may be served by sending it by registered post. If a yearly tenant gives notice of his intention to quit and does not leave at the expiration of his notice, he is liable to pay double the yearly rent of his premises for the time he remains in possession, and if notice to quit is given by a landlord and the tenant continues in possession, the landlord may recover double the yearly *value* of the premises. The rent cannot be increased during a tenancy, unless the tenancy is first determined by notice to quit; but, if the landlord gives a valid notice to his tenant to quit, or pay an increased rent, and the tenant does not quit, an agreement to pay the increased rent will be implied.

Various Acts of Parliament have been passed in recent years, the object of which is to restrict the landlord's right to raise the rent of his property. The Acts do not, however, apply to business premises.

As is well known, the premises comprised in a lease and all buildings and fixtures thereon revert to the landlord when the lease expires, but the Landlord and Tenant Act, 1927, provides for payment, in certain circumstances, of compensation for improvements and goodwill to tenants of business premises, or the grant of a new lease in lieu thereof.

A tenant from year to year, in the absence of an agreement, is bound to keep the premises wind and water tight, but is not responsible for general repairs. He will, however, be liable to make good all damage caused by his negligence, as, for example, if he breaks windows, or makes holes in the floors or walls. There is no obligation on the part of the landlord, in the absence of agreement, to do any repairs, and the tenant's only remedy, if the premises become unfit for occupation, is to give notice to quit, and to leave if the necessary repairs are not carried out. Where, however, the failure to repair constitutes a nuisance and a threat to health, the local Sanitary Authority may order the fault to be rectified and may charge the cost to either party at option. If there is no agreement to the contrary, the tenant is liable to pay all rates and taxes except Property Tax which, by law, falls upon the landlord and, if paid by the tenant, may be deducted from his rent up to the standard rate of tax on a year's rent.

When the agreement of tenancy or lease is in writing, all the terms of the tenancy must be included, as no agreement outside the written document will have any effect. The term for which the premises are to be let, the amount of the rent and when it is to be paid, and the notice required before the tenancy can be terminated, must all be included, and the obligations on the part of the tenant and landlord respectively should be carefully considered and expressed in plain language. The tenant usually agrees to pay rates and taxes, except Property Tax, and the tenant must see that the clause as to payment of rates does not include the words "duties," "charges," "impositions," or "outgoings." If any one of these words is inserted, the tenant may find himself called upon to pay charges under the Public Health Acts for the paving of streets, making of sewers, abating of nuisances, etc., which, in the absence of express agreement, are payable by the landlord. To avoid the possibility of having to pay these charges, which are often heavy, a clause should be inserted in the lease to the effect that they shall not be paid by the tenants. The tenant should also see that the lease clearly defines the duties of the parties as to repairs, and must bear in mind that, if the landlord is bound to repair any part of the premises and repairs are necessary, notice of the want of repair must be given to him, and an opportunity afforded him of doing the repairs. If the tenant executes such repairs without notice to the landlord that they are required, he cannot afterwards compel the landlord to pay for the work. The lease should contain provisions as to the insurance of the premises. In the absence of special agreement, the tenant is not bound to rebuild premises accidentally burnt down; but, if he has entered into a general covenant to repair without exception, he is liable to restore the premises which may be destroyed by fire, tempest, lightning, or any other accident. If the lease is silent as to insurance, the tenant remains liable for the rent although the premises have been burnt down, and it has been held that he cannot compel the landlord to expend insurance he may have received in rebuilding; but, under an Act of Parliament passed in the reign of George III, any person interested in premises destroyed by fire may require Insurance Companies to expend the insurance money in rebuilding. If, as is generally the case, the landlord undertakes to keep the premises insured against fire, the tenant must see that his lease contains a clause that, in the event of the premises becoming unfit for use or occupation by reason of fire, his rent shall cease or abate.

It is almost unnecessary to point out that, if the tenant is bound to keep the premises in repair, he should take care to see that they are in a proper state before he enters into possession.

The tenant has the power to sub-let the premises held by him, but it is usual for the landlord to provide that his consent must be obtained to any sub-letting. This clause should be drawn so as to give the tenant power to sub-let without consent if the proposed sub-tenant is a responsible person and the landlord unreasonably refuses to give the required permission. In the case of sub-letting, the tenant remains liable to the landlord for the rent, and he is also liable for repairs and other matters which he may have agreed to do. In fact, the sub-tenant is, for all purposes, a tenant of the tenant and not of the landlord.

Before entering into any agreement or lease, it is important that the tenant should ascertain that his proposed landlord has power to let the premises. It occasionally happens that the premises are in mortgage and the consent of the mortgagee is required to any lease. If, in these cases, a lease is granted without consent, the mortgagee may, if he takes possession of the premises, put an end immediately to the tenancy, and the unfortunate tenant is often left without remedy. If the landlord is also the owner of the adjoining premises, it may be well to insist upon a covenant by him that the adjoining premises shall not be let for a similar business to that carried on by the tenant.

A lease must be properly stamped. If the term does not exceed 35 years, the stamp duties are as follows—

				£	s.	d.
Rent not exceeding £5 per annum					1	0
Exceeding £5 and not exceeding £10					2	0
Exceeding	£10	and not exceeding	£15		3	0
,,	£15	,, ,,	£20		4	0
,,	£20	,, ,,	£25		5	0
,,	£25	,, ,,	£50		10	0
,,	£50	,, ,,	£75		15	0
,,	£75	,, ,,	£100	1	0	0

and 10s. in addition for every fractional part of £50.

For leases between 35 and 100 years these rates must be multiplied by 6 and for those over 100 years they must be multiplied by 12.

The costs of the lease, including stamp duty, fall on the tenant. The lease is usually prepared in duplicate so that one part may be retained by each party, and the landlord is liable for the costs of the duplicate. The tenant should, therefore, see that, in paying for the lease, he is not also charged for the duplicate.

Another important question which often arises is the right of a tenant to remove fixtures put up by him during the tenancy. By the common law, all things fixed to the freehold become part of it, and should not be removed without consent, but as this rule often works hardly upon the tenant it has been considerably mitigated in his favour. As a general rule, and in the absence of any agreement to the contrary, a tenant may now remove all fixtures erected by him for the purposes of trade, provided—and this is important—he takes them away before the end of his tenancy. If his tenancy expires and the fixtures remain, they become the property of the landlord, unless the tenant has obtained permission to leave them until they can conveniently be removed. Of course, any damage done to the property by the taking away of the fixtures must be made good by the tenant. Very often, a tenant giving up possession agrees to sell fixtures belonging to him to an incoming tenant. It is important that this agreement should be in writing and that the landlord should be a party to it, otherwise he might say that the outgoing tenant had forfeited all fixtures to him by not removing them, and so the incoming tenant might not be able to remove them at the end of his tenancy.

By the Factories Act, 1937, more particularly referred to later in this chapter, the owner of premises coming within the provisions of the Act is liable to maintain sufficient means of escape in case of fire, and the Act provides that, if the owner alleges that the tenant should bear, or contribute to, the expenses of complying with the requirements of the Act, he may apply to the County Court and that Court will have power to order by whom the expenses must be borne. If the tenant has agreed to pay all outgoings in respect of the premises, he may be liable to repay to the landlord the expenses of erecting and maintaining fire escapes. This point should be remembered when a lease of premises is being prepared, and the proposed tenant should see that a liability of this description, which may be heavy, is not thrown upon him.

One of the strongest weapons in the hands of a landlord is power to enforce payment of the rent by levying a distress upon all property on the premises, whether such property belongs to the tenant or to a stranger. There are some exceptions to this rule, and the following is a list of the principal things which are exempt from distress—

1. Things in personal use;
2. Fixtures fixed to the freehold;
3. Goods belonging to a stranger, and delivered to the tenant to be wrought on in the way of his ordinary trade;
4. Perishable articles;
5. Tools of trade, although not in actual use, provided other sufficient distress can be found; and
6. Loose money.

It is well to remember that machinery and other articles frequently obtained nowadays on what is known as " the hire system " may be taken by a landlord under distress for rent.

In levying a distress, a landlord or his agent cannot obtain an entrance by breaking open any outer door or window, but, if access is once obtained through an open door or window, inner doors may be forced open.

A distress must be levied upon premises held under the lease, but, if the tenant fraudulently or clandestinely removes his property after rent has become due in order to prevent it being seized by the landlord, the landlord may, if there is not sufficient property left to satisfy his claim, follow and distrain upon goods within 30 days of their being removed, provided they have not, in the meantime, been *bona fide* sold for value and to a purchaser who has no notice of the wrongful act.

The Law of Distress Amendment Act, 1888, as amended in 1895 and 1908, provides that no person shall act as bailiff to levy any distress for rent, unless authorized to act as a bailiff by a certificate of a County Court Judge, and any person not holding such a certificate who levies a distress is deemed to be a trespasser. The landlord may himself in person levy a distress without this certificate. The goods distrained cannot be sold until the expiration of 15 days from the time of their seizure, provided the tenant so require in writing and give security for any additional costs which may be incurred thereby.

The Factories Act, 1937, consolidates and considerably extends the law with regard to employment in factories. Under this legislation the word "factory" has a connotation much wider than in ordinary usage and includes "any premises in which . . . persons are employed in manual labour" as defined. Thus a shipyard or even a dry dock or a gasometer may be a "factory"; and activities so diverse as bottle-washing, net-mending, or the preparing of articles incidentally to the carrying on of building operations may technically be "factory" employment. The Act contains 160 sections directed principally to assuring the health, safety, and welfare of factory workers.

Some of the provisions of the Act are to be enforced by the local authority but for the most part administration and enforcement are in the hands of the Home Office, acting through its Inspectors in local districts. Penalties for non-compliance are heavy and it behoves every employer of factory workers to be familiar with all those sections (including Regulations made to cover special trades) which affect his case.

In the first part of the Act, containing 11 sections, general rules are laid down as to keeping the premises in a cleanly and well-ventilated state, and particular attention must be paid to the requirements of the law with regard to limewashing and cleansing of floors, walls, and ceilings. Overcrowding of factories and workshops must be avoided, and they are deemed to be so overcrowded as to be dangerous or injurious to the health of the persons employed therein if the number of cubic feet of space in any room is less than 400 per person employed therein, and for this purpose no space more than 14 feet from the floor is to be taken into account. It is important to remember that there must be affixed in every room a notice specifying the number of persons who may be employed therein. There are certain exceptions in favour of rooms in use before the passing of the Act but these will terminate after the lapse of specified times.

A "reasonable" temperature must be maintained in every room. Where work is performed sitting and does not involve serious physical effort, "reasonable," after the first hour, is defined as not less than 60 degrees. A thermometer must be provided in every workroom. Effective ventilation must be maintained and arrangements must be made for carrying off all noxious fumes, dust, etc. The Home Secretary may prescribe adequate standards of ventilation. "Sufficient and suitable" lighting is to be provided, and, in the case of wet processes, effective means of draining the floor must be provided. Proper separate sanitary accommodation is to be provided for persons of each sex.

It is now within the power of the Home Secretary, in cases where there have been outbreaks of disease in a factory, or where a dangerous process is being introduced, to order medical supervision of the persons employed.

Part II of the Act (29 sections) contains comprehensive general provisions directed to securing the safety of workers. All moving machinery, transmission gear, stairways, water-mill races, etc., must be securely fenced. Vessels containing dangerous liquids must have their edges at least 3 feet above the floor. So stringent is the law concerning dangerous moving machinery that even persons who sell, or let on hire, certain classes of machines now incur a penalty of £100 if specified precautions are not incorporated. Women or young persons must not clean any moving machinery; further, no young person must even work at certain prescribed machines "unless he has been fully instructed as to the dangers arising in connection with the machine and the precautions to be observed." Very detailed provisions are laid down in regard to lifts and hoisting tackle, work to be done in confined spaces, explosive dust, steam boilers, air compressors, gas holders, and other special matters.

All factories employing more than twenty persons (or more than ten on an upper floor) must be certified by the district council as being provided with reasonable means of escaping from fire, and effective steps must be taken by the employer to make the workers familiar with the means of escape and the routine in case of fire.

Part III of the Act contains six very important sections directed generally to providing for the welfare of persons employed in factories. For example, there must be "an adequate supply of wholesome drinking water" together with "adequate and suitable facilities for washing which shall include soap and clean towels." There must be accommodation for clothing not worn during working hours and, if reasonably practicable, arrangements for drying such clothing. For female workers whose work is done standing, there must be suitable facilities for sitting sufficient to enable them to take advantage of any opportunities for resting which may occur. Every factory must keep a first-aid box for every 150 persons employed. This box must be under the charge of a responsible person who must, if more than 50 persons are employed, be trained in first-aid treatment. The name of the person in charge of the first-aid box must be posted up in every workroom. The Home Secretary may make special regulations covering the welfare of workers in particular trades and he has in fact issued 32 such Orders.

Part IV of the Act provides for certain additional, and very detailed, precautions to be observed in regard to specified dangerous trades. Where an accident occurs in a factory, and disables any person for more than three days, notice must be given to the local factory inspector, and if a medical practitioner comes across a case of certain industrial diseases he is to notify the Home Office forthwith. Where a coroner holds an inquest on the body of a person whose death may have been caused by industrial accident or disease, the inquest is to be adjourned unless the Home Secretary is represented. The Home Secretary may also direct a formal investigation of any cases of industrial accident or disease.

The Act limits very closely the permissible hours of employment of women and young persons. Briefly, work must not begin before seven in the morning nor end later than eight in the evening (one o'clock on Saturday afternoons). The period of employment must not exceed 11 hours in any day nor must there be any continuous spell longer than 4½ hours without an interval of at least half an hour for a meal or rest. In any event the total hours worked, exclusive of intervals allowed for meals and rest, must neither exceed 9 in any day nor 48 in any week. After 1st July, 1939, the weekly hours of persons under the age of 16 will be limited to 44. Notice of the hours of employment must be posted up in every factory. In certain circumstances overtime is permitted but must not exceed either 100 hours in any year or 6 hours in any week and it must not take place in more than 25 weeks in any year. During the intervals allowed to a woman or young person for meals or rest, that person must not remain in a room in which a process is being carried on. Women and young persons must be granted as holidays every bank holiday (or a substituted day) or, in Scotland, six weekdays in the year. At least half of the holidays must be allowed between 15th March and 1st October.

No person under the age of 16 may be employed unless an examining surgeon has certified that he is fit for the particular employment. Further, where a factory inspector is of the opinion that the employment of a person under 18 years of age is prejudicial to his health, he may require that the employment shall be terminated unless an examining surgeon certifies that the young person is fit for employment in the particular kind of work.

The Act extends to outworkers in certain specified trades and lists of the names of these persons, showing the places at which their work is actually done, must be sent both to the factory inspector and to the local district council. The district council has power to require the occupiers of such home premises to abate conditions which are injurious or dangerous to the health of the persons employed.

Where piece-work is the rule in textile factories and in certain other specified trades, the employer must cause particulars of the rate of wages to be posted up and to be given in writing individually to every piece-worker. For this purpose mere symbols are not to be used.

Finally, a prescribed abstract of the Act must be kept posted at the principal entrance of every factory and there must be added the address of the factory inspector and of the examining surgeon. There must also be exhibited a notice specifying the clock by which the periods of employment are regulated. The employer must also keep a register, in a prescribed form, specifying particulars as to the young persons employed, the date when the premises were colour-washed or painted, particulars of every accident and of every special exception of which the occupier avails himself. No deduction is to be made from wages, nor is any payment to be exacted in respect of anything done or provided by the employer in pursuance of the terms of the Act.

WAGES BOARDS. Wages in certain trades are fixed by Trade Boards appointed under the Trade Boards Act, 1918. These Boards consist of representatives of employers and workers in equal numbers, together with members appointed by the Ministry of Labour, and, in addition to fixing a general trade rate of wages for time-work, they may also fix (*a*) a general minimum piece rate of wages for piece-work; (*b*) a minimum time rate to apply in the case of workers employed on piece-work; (*c*) a guaranteed time rate (whether a time rate or a piece rate) to apply in substitution for a minimum rate which would otherwise be applicable; and (*d*) an overtime rate. By a Provisional Order of the Ministry of Labour this Act may be applied to any specified trade.

SHOPS ACTS. The Shops Act, 1912, which is still in force, was a consolidating and amending statute embracing the whole of the Acts previously in force as to the hours and certain of the conditions of employment of shop assistants and extending the provisions thereof in various particulars. The Act has subsequently been amended by the Shops Act, 1913; the Shops (Hours of Closing) Act, 1928; and the (very important) Shops Act, 1934. The Acts refer to "shops" and "shop assistants" only. By the interpretation clause of the 1912 Act, it is provided: (1) "Shop" includes any premises where any retail trade or business is carried on; (2) "Retail trade or business" includes the business of a barber or hairdresser, the sale of refreshments or intoxicating liquors, and retail sales by auction, but does not include sale of programmes and catalogues and other similar sales at theatres and places of amusement; (3) "Shop assistant" means any person wholly or mainly employed in a shop in connection with the serving of customers or the receipt of orders or the dispatch of goods; (4) "Bank-holiday" includes any public holiday or day of public rejoicing or mourning; and (5) "Week" means the period between midnight on Saturday night and midnight on the succeeding Saturday night. Duties formerly laid on the "employer" of a young person are now imposed on the "occupier" of the shop. A person is "employed" even if he receives no remuneration.

With respect to the time of employment, no shop assistant, under 18 years of age, is to be employed for a longer period than 48 hours a week, including meal times, and a notice must be kept posted up in the shop in a conspicuous position, stating the exact number of hours during which such persons are employed. In times of seasonal or exceptional pressure, persons aged between 16 and 18 may work overtime provided such overtime (*a*) does not extend into more than six weeks, not necessarily consecutive, in any year and (*b*) does not amount to more than 50 hours in a year; and (*c*) does not exceed 12 hours in any week. Special exceptions provide for such cases as theatres, the catering trades, and the sale of motor and aircraft accessories.

In every period of 24 hours, ending midday, an interval of at least 11 consecutive hours must be allowed, including the hours 10 p.m. to 6 a.m. (or 10 p.m. to 5 a.m. in such cases as milk and bread rounds, and the delivery of newspapers). The occupier must keep a record of the hours worked and the intervals allowed for rest and meals in respect of every young person employed, particulars of overtime being separately entered therein. This record may be dispensed with (except as to overtime) if there is displayed in the shop a notice specifying the normal daily hours.

Intervals for meals must be allowed in accordance with the First Schedule of the 1912 Act (as amended), but this provision does not apply to a shop in which the only persons employed as shop assistants are members of the family of the occupier of the shop, maintained by him and dwelling in his house. The First Schedule, as amended, is as follows—

Intervals for meals shall be arranged so as to secure that no person shall be employed for more than five hours (or, on any day of the week in which he is not to be employed after half-past one o'clock, five and a half hours) without an interval of at least twenty minutes being allowed during the course thereof.

Without prejudice to the foregoing provision—

(1) where the hours of employment include the hours from 11.30 a.m. to 2.30 p.m., an interval of not less than threequarters of an hour shall be allowed between those hours for dinner; and

(2) where the hours of employment include the hours from 4 p.m. to 7 p.m., an interval of not less than half-an-hour shall be allowed between those hours for tea;

and the interval for dinner shall be increased to one hour in cases where that meal is not taken in the shop, or in a building of which the shop forms part or to which the shop is attached:

Provided that an assistant employed in the sale of refreshments or in the sale by retail of intoxicating liquors need not be allowed the interval for dinner between 11.30 a.m. and 2.30 p.m., if he is allowed the same interval so arranged as either to end not earlier than 11.30 a.m. or to commence not later than 2.30 p.m., and the same exemption shall apply to assistants employed in any shop on the market day in any town in which a market is held not oftener than once a week, or on a day on which an annual fair is held.

Certain alternatives are granted to this provision as to the meals of shop assistants employed in any premises for the sale of refreshments, by the amending Act of 1913, but as these are not obligatory, the later Act must be consulted for fuller information.

In every shop a suitable state of ventilation and temperature must be maintained and the lighting must be adequate. Proper sanitary and washing accommodation must be provided; any cost entailed in the working of this provision may be apportioned by the County Court between the owner and the occupier of the premises. Where females are employed, one chair for the use of every three assistants must be provided.

The Act directs that every shop to which the Act applies shall, subject to the exceptions set out, close at 1 p.m. on one day in every week, and the local authority has power to fix the particular closing day, though it is not essential that the closing day should be the same for all classes of shops, or for all parts of a district, or for all parts of a year. Again, if the local authority is of opinion that the majority of the shopkeepers of a particular district are opposed to the half day weekly closing, an exemption may be made. In any case the following trades and businesses are exempt by the Act itself—

(*a*) The sale by retail of intoxicating liquors.

(*b*) The sale of refreshments, including the business carried on at a railway refreshment room.

(*c*) The sale of motor, cycle, and aircraft supplies and accessories to travellers.

(*d*) The sale of newspapers and periodicals.

(*e*) The sale of meat, fish, milk, cream, bread, confectionery, fruit, vegetables, flowers, and other articles of a perishable nature.

(*f*) The sale of tobacco and smokers' requisites.

(*g*) The business carried on at a railway bookstall on or adjoining a railway platform.

(*h*) The sale of medicines and medical and surgical appliances.

(*i*) Retail trade carried on at an exhibition or show, if the local authority certify that such retail trade is subsidiary or ancillary only to the main purpose of the exhibition or show.

Where there exists an order as to the closing of the shop, the rule is relaxed where a shop is closed during the whole day on the occasion of a bank-holiday, and that day is not the day fixed for the weekly half-holiday, and it is then lawful for the occupier of the shop to keep his place of business open for the serving of customers either on the half-holiday immediately preceding or on the half-holiday immediately succeeding the bank-holiday.

Where a closing order is not in force, every assistant must in each week have a half-holiday commencing at 1.30 p.m. This rule will not apply to the week before a bank-holiday if, on one day in the following week the shop assistant is granted a half-holiday in addition to the bank-holiday. A notice must be conspicuously posted in the shop setting forth the names of the assistants and the days on which their holidays are granted.

It is almost unnecessary to add that there are many other points of interest to be found in the Acts, but those mentioned in this chapter are of primary importance for the consideration of the employer.

Sunday trading is now regulated by the Shops (Sunday Trading Restriction) Act, 1936, and Retail Meat Dealers' Shops (Sunday Closing) Act, 1936. Both Acts restrict the opening of shops and trading on Sunday, but make special provisions in the case of Jewish traders.

CHAPTER XXIII

Insurance—Provision against loss arising through Fire or Accident—Methods of preparing Proposals and Claims—Profits Assurance—Employers' Liability Insurance—Workmen's Compensation, Third Party Risks, etc.—Marine Insurance—Advantages of Insurance—Losses not covered by usual forms of Insurance—National Insurance

A GOOD knowledge of Insurance methods and practice is most useful to anyone holding, or aspiring to hold, a responsible position in the world of business. The principle is one the scope and operations of which are ever widening, and the idea having become firmly rooted in the public mind, numberless possibilities of adaptability and extension are continually being evolved.

The principle of insurance was first applied to marine risks, and the origin of marine insurance is lost in obscurity. The history of other forms of insurance, compared with that of marine insurance, is comparatively modern. Realizing the undoubted advantages offered by insurance, the principle was applied to life assurance, losses arising from fire, and, in more recent times, to losses arising from excess of bad debts, burglary, sickness, embezzlement by employees or agents, accidents to the person, to growing crops, to cattle, to plate glass windows, to machinery, lifts, boilers, the loss or destruction of documents by fire, mischance, theft, burglary, or in transit, the claims under the Employers' Liability Acts, and many other contingencies. Insurance does not, of course, prevent these accidents, but indemnifies the insured against any monetary loss which may result therefrom, and the prudent merchant and trader is always ready to take advantage of the opportunity presented for providing against loss, and, incidentally, of securing the peace of mind which naturally follows.

FIRE INSURANCE. The business of fire insurance in this country is almost exclusively in the hands of Joint Stock Companies. These are divided into two principal classes—

(1) "Tariff" Offices,
(2) "Non-Tariff" Offices,

and it is important that the essential differences between these two classes should be understood. The Tariff Companies have a working arrangement by which risks are carefully classified and a uniform scale of premiums agreed upon. These rates have been fixed as the result of the accumulated experience of the various offices. Risks and losses have been analysed and tabulated, and the premiums fixed on the basis of the data thus secured. The Tariff Companies are represented by the "Fire Offices Committee," which exerts a moral control over the transactions of the various Companies associated with it. The Non-Tariff Companies are those which are not represented on the Fire Offices Committee, and do not recognize its rules. They are free to charge whatever rates of premium they may deem proper, and profess to be in a position to consider each case upon its merits. It will be found, in practice, that they generally quote the same rates as the Tariff Offices, but are prepared to allow a certain amount of discount; they not infrequently allow their agents a larger commission than the customary 15 per cent.

It was formerly a custom for the person desirous of insuring against loss by fire to be requested to fill up a form known as a *Proposal*, giving full information as to the building or property to be insured. In the case of buildings, a full description of its construction with particulars of the trades carried on, not only in the building itself but in adjoining buildings, was insisted upon. As any mistake in this document might afterwards lead to the policy being considered void, it came to be recognized that, in order to prevent mistakes and misunderstandings, it was better for the Company itself to be responsible for the accuracy of this document. It is now the general practice for the building to be examined by an expert Surveyor, representing the Company, to whom the person seeking insurance gives as much information concerning the risk as lies in his power. When this inspection has taken place, the Company are in a position to give a quotation. The Companies in many cases send the proposal form to the insured for signature and, on receipt of the proposal thus signed, the Company will issue a "cover note," which covers the risk up to the time the actual policy is issued. The policy is handed to the insured on payment by him of the amount of the premium. Fire insurance policies generally run from year to year, from the date specified in the policy, but generally expiring on one of the regular Quarter Days. Fifteen days' grace is usually allowed for the payment of the premiums. It is important that the property insured should be correctly described in the policy, and, if any material alteration is made in the property, immediate notice should be given to the insurers, otherwise the policy may be rendered void.

It is necessary, in order to establish a claim under a policy of fire insurance, that the insured should be able to prove that he had an interest in the property at the time of effecting the insurance, and when the fire happens. A purchaser of the property will not benefit in case of fire, unless he has made an arrangement with the vendor, by which, with the consent of the Company, the policy has been transferred to him. The policy is not, however, assignable without the Company's consent. An ordinary fire policy covers all losses incurred by damage resulting from fire, such as may be caused by smoke or water, or by the removal of the goods to a place of safety. The insured should read carefully through his policy, noting the various clauses, as these differ according to the class of risk and the Company issuing them. The policy usually provides that notice of the damage shall be given to the Company within 15 days of the occurrence of a fire. The safest course is for the insured to give immediate notice; and if, as is frequently the case, it is not possible for him to furnish a detailed statement of claim within the period named, the Company will allow a reasonable time in which he may prepare the necessary particulars. Formal notice is given in order that the Company's assessors may have an opportunity of inspecting the premises, and instituting inquiries into the cause of the fire, etc. Claims are paid on satisfactory proof of loss or damage by fire. Assessors may require the production of books of account, invoices and vouchers, etc., in order to check the particulars given in the statement of claim which has been drawn up by the insurer. The production of an inventory of furniture and fixtures, together with carefully kept stock books, would be calculated to save a great amount of trouble in case of dispute. Anticipated profits are not recoverable, but only actual loss sustained by the insured. In case an "*Average*" clause has been inserted in the policy, the Company will be liable to pay to the insured only *pro rata* damages. Full damages will be paid only when the property or stock has, in the first instance, been insured *up to its full value*. If a business man has stock up to the value of £10,000, which he insures for only £5,000, he is deemed to be willing to run the risk so far as half the value is concerned, and he must be satisfied, in case a fire occurs, to receive from the Company the *pro rata* damages represented by the £5,000 insured. It is obviously unfair to expect a Company to insure £10,000 worth of goods for the premium on a £5,000 risk only.

In preparing claims for losses incurred by fire, it is necessary that the fullest available details should be furnished. In most business concerns, an inventory of furniture and fixtures is kept, and, if this has been brought up to date, say half-yearly, very little difficulty need arise in case a fire occurs in regard to the preparation of the claim on the Insurance Company, assuming, of course, that the inventory and books have been lodged in a safe place, and have not been destroyed by the fire. The production of such an inventory would be accepted by the Insurance Company as evidence that the claim was a *bona fide* one. In the case of stock-in-trade, the difficulty would probably be greater. Recourse would be had to Stock Books, Invoices, Sales Books, etc., and, in some cases, only approximate figures could be given. The Insurance Companies recognize this, and, provided there are no suspicious circumstances attending the fire, rely to a large extent on the good faith of the insured. As already stated, only actual losses can be claimed, and consequently the cost price only will be allowed in the claim in cases where the goods insured are rendered of no value; where the goods are not actually destroyed, the amount by which they are depreciated will be allowed. Should any dispute arise, it must be referred to Arbitration, this being invariably provided for in the policy.

In order to cover against loss, arising, as a result of fire, from the necessary acquisition of temporary premises, it is very general for business houses to insure against loss of rent to an extent equal to the annual value of the premises ordinarily occupied. In the event of the premises being rendered uninhabitable through fire, the insurance company will then pay a sum commensurate to the period during which they remain uninhabitable; or, if part only of the premises be damaged, a corresponding allowance will be made, which may be roughly regarded as sufficient to compensate for the double rent incurred while temporary premises are in use. It is not possible to insure against consequential loss (loss of future profits) arising from a fire with any of the ordinary insurance companies; but some companies make a speciality of such risks, and, for a quite reasonable annual payment, are prepared to pay compensation equivalent to the loss of profit during a limited period after a fire, such compensation being based upon the average profits of the past few years.

ACCIDENT INSURANCE. The usual form of policy covering accident insurance entitles the insured, or his representatives, to certain fixed payments in case he sustains bodily injury, caused by accident, which may result in death or disablement within three months of the accident. In this, as in every other form of insurance, the utmost good faith is presumed between the parties, and any misrepresentation, or false statement, or the suppression of any material facts, may afford a complete defence to an action under the policy. It is important, therefore, that great care be exercised in filling up the proposal form. The policy carefully defines the various degrees of disablement, as to what is to be considered as partial, total, temporary or permanent. Compensation is generally limited to the period of disablement, a maximum being fixed in respect of any single accident. The policy may cover any period agreed upon, or may be limited to a special journey, or particularized so as to cover a special set of circumstances. It is usual, however, for the policy to be a yearly one, renewable at the Company's option. The various classes of accident covered by the policy are clearly defined, and a proviso is generally inserted which excludes disablement resulting from natural disease or weakness. Death or disablement, in order to come within the scope of the policy, must be directly traceable to the accident.

CONTRACT GUARANTEES. When important contracts are advertised, a clause is frequently inserted to the effect that the contractor will be required to find sureties to be jointly and severally bound with him in a certain sum, the actual amount depending upon the magnitude of the contract. It is possible for the successful contractor to call upon his friends to act in the capacity of guarantors, or he may induce the firms from whom he proposes to purchase the materials required in the fulfilment of the contract to allow themselves to be bound as sureties. Or he may deposit a sum of money against the due fulfilment of the contract. In the latter case, however, he would be deprived of the use of his money at a time when, in all probability, he would have found it extremely useful. An Insurance Company will, for a fixed premium, take the position of guarantor, and either itself become a party to the contract, or be responsible for the payment of the stipulated penalty in case the terms of the contract are not fulfilled. The premium charged will be based, not only on the amount of the bond, but upon the nature of the work, and the character, experience and financial standing of the contractor.

BAD DEBTS. The covering of risks of loss connected with the giving of credit is not an easy matter for Insurance Companies to deal with, but the field of operations is undoubtedly large and a considerable and increasing volume of business is being transacted in this department. It is recognized that, seeing the form of policy, some proportion of the loss incurred must fall upon the insured himself. A policy may be issued which insures the solvency of certain specified debtors for a limited period. An agreed limit of liability is scheduled against each debtor, the Company taking a risk equal to one half the total loss in case of insolvency. Another form of policy may be had which covers any loss which may be sustained beyond the *average* annual loss as shown in previous years. By taking out such a policy, a trader may provide against losing more than he can well afford, and in this way save himself from disaster. The fact that he himself bears a certain portion of the loss safeguards the interests of the Insurance Company.

EMPLOYERS' LIABILITY AND WORKMEN'S COMPENSATION. The Employers' Liability Act was passed in the year 1880. Prior to that date, a workman, injured in the course of his employment, and through no fault of his own, could not obtain compensation, even though the injury was due to the negligence of some other person in the same employment. Proceedings could be taken at common law in case of injury due to the personal neglect of the employer. The Act of 1880 introduced a restricted liability, as, under it, the liability of an employer was, generally speaking restricted to cases where negligence had been shown by the employer or his subordinates. The injured workman had still no redress in case his injury had been brought about by the negligence of any of his fellow workmen. In 1898, the Workmen's Compensation Act of 1897 came into operation. The basis of this Act is the principle that the workman is entitled to compensation, whatever may be the cause of his disablement. Other Acts were subsequently passed and the whole statute law has now been consolidated in the

Workmen's Compensation Act, 1925. The main test of liability is whether the workman was injured by an accident arising out of and in the course of his employment. By degrees, the Courts have given a most liberal interpretation to the provisions of the Acts, and it is now very difficult for an employer to escape liability for injuries to his servant in the absence of fraud.

By Section 5 of the Act it is provided—

In this Act, unless the context otherwise requires—" Employer " includes any body of persons corporate or unincorporate and the legal personal representative of a deceased employer ; and, where the services of a workman are temporarily lent or let on hire to another person by the person with whom the workman has entered into a contract of service or apprenticeship, the latter shall, for the purposes of this Act, be deemed to continue to be the employer of the workman whilst he is working for that other person.

Under Section 3, " Workman " does not include any person employed otherwise than by way of manual labour whose remuneration exceeds three hundred and fifty pounds a year, or a person whose employment is of a casual nature and who is employed otherwise than for the purposes of the employer's trade or business, not being a person employed for the purposes of any game or recreation and engaged or paid through a club, or a member of a police force, or an outworker, or a member of the employer's family dwelling in his house, but, save as aforesaid, means any person who has entered into or works under a contract of service or apprenticeship with an employer, whether by way of manual labour, clerical work, or otherwise, and whether the contract is expressed or implied, is oral or in writing.

Under the Act an employer is liable if in any employment personal injury by accident arising out of and in the course of the employment is caused to a workman ; provided that the employer is not liable for an injury which does not disable the workman for a period of at least three days from earning full wages at the work at which he was employed. The compensation is disallowed (except in case of death or serious and permanent disablement) if the injury is attributable to the serious and wilful misconduct of the workman. No contract between employer and workman purporting to vary the provisions of the statute has any validity except where a special scheme may have been sanctioned by the Registrar of Friendly

Societies. A principal contractor is still liable even though the work may be in course of performance by a sub-contractor, the workman being directly employed by the latter.

The provisions made for compensation under the Act are complicated, but may result in awarding as much as £600 to the relatives of a workman whose life is lost.

It will be seen that the principle is now well established that some specific provision should be made for workmen who have been injured in the course of their employment, and that a workman disabled through an accident, and without means of support, should not become dependent upon private charity. The injured man's employer must be prepared to bear this cost, the obligation being laid upon him by law. Recognizing this, the employer will take the precaution of transferring his liability to an Insurance Company. The premiums payable on policies covering risks under the Employers' Liability and Workmen's Compensation Acts vary from ½% to 5% of the annual wages paid, and the average premium has been roughly estimated at 1¼%.

THIRD PARTY RISK. Another form of insurance is that in connection with Third Party Risks, or claims arising from injury to the person, or damage to property, of third parties (i.e. not the employers or employees). This is generally insured against by firms owning vehicles, such as carts, delivery vans, etc., and by omnibus and tramway proprietors, Companies, and Corporations. The premiums vary according to the class of risk, being sometimes based upon the number of vehicles run, or the mileage or—in the case of passenger-carrying vehicles—upon the gross receipts, the rate in the latter case ranging from 2 to 5%.

It is now part of the law of the land (Road Traffic Act, 1930) that no person may use, or permit to be used, a motor vehicle unless covered by a policy of insurance in respect of third party risks.

FIDELITY GUARANTEE. It has become a recognized practice for Government Departments, Corporations, and business houses generally to require some form of guarantee to be given by persons in their employ who hold responsible positions, such as Cashiers, Managers, Secretaries and others. Formerly it was necessary in such cases for private persons, generally friends or relatives, to act as sureties ; but this system has practically died out, having been superseded by a form of fidelity guarantee insurance. The advantages of the new method over the old are obvious. A private surety, willing to act as such, might himself be in a hopeless state of insolvency, or might become so by the lapse of years, and this would be discovered only in case it became necessary to make a claim upon him. Such a surety might even be lost sight of, having possibly left the country. On the other hand, where a policy is taken out with an Insurance Company, of recognized financial standing, absolute security against loss is offered in case of the default of the person concerned. The policy would be renewed year by year, and thus would be kept regularly under supervision, and, in case of default, the amount of the loss would be much more easily recovered from a Company than from private persons. Before issuing such a policy, the Company would inquire carefully into the character and history of the employee, and this fact in itself is a safeguard to the employer, being in the nature of an assurance of previous good conduct. Insurance Companies are willing to issue policies covering the risks of single individuals, or where, for example, a firm have a number of branches or retail shops, each having its own responsible Manager or official, the whole of the risks involved might be recovered by a single policy. In many cases, the employer pays the whole of the premiums, whilst others pay only a certain proportion, and require the employee to provide the remainder. The general principles of law applicable to other forms of insurance apply to guarantee insurance. Perfect good faith is essential on the part of the employee and his referees, as the Company, in estimating the risk, are compelled to rely largely upon the information thus given, supplemented by any inquiries which it may make on independent lines. A condition generally found in policies of this character is that the employer shall, if and when required by the Company, use all diligence in prosecuting the employee to conviction for any fraud or dishonesty in consequence of which the claim shall have been made under the policy. Other conditions relate to the giving of due notice of the claim, and the furnishing of proofs of fraudulent actions of the person whose conduct is insured against. The premiums vary very considerably according to circumstances, and the Companies will quote on being furnished with particulars.

Burglary Insurance. It is possible to recover loss incurred through burglary and housebreaking, and this class of insurance has made rapid progress during recent years. The principle is the same as that in case of fire, namely, an indemnity against loss, the loss in this case being sustained by burglary. A proviso is often inserted in a burglary insurance policy providing that the risk shall not apply where it is proved that any member of the assured's household, or of his business staff, or any other inmate of the premises is concerned as principal or accessory. A clear distinction is also drawn between burglary and mere theft, the latter risk not being covered by the ordinary burglary policy, although many policies are issued that cover the larceny risk as well.

Partnership Insurance. The death of a partner in a business firm frequently means the withdrawal of a certain amount of capital. Such a contingency may be guarded against by the firm taking out a joint policy on the lives of its partners, the amount of which becomes payable on the death of either. The premium may be paid by the firm or otherwise, as may be arranged. Such joint insurance, however, is being superseded by separate policies on the lives of the various partners. Not only are the premiums considerably lower in the case of single policies, but, should the partnership be dissolved for any reason, it is found that the single policies can be much more conveniently dealt with. It is only necessary for each partner to continue his own policy, paying his own premium.

No precise rules can be laid down as to how the premiums in respect of partnership insurance should be borne as between the partners, but as the object of effecting such insurances at all is to save the survivor from the inconvenience of being suddenly called upon to make a heavy payment, each partner is, in effect, insuring the life of the other, and the cost of the insurance should be apportioned between the partners upon this basis, having regard to their respective ages—and this whether a survivorship policy be undertaken, or the lives of the two partners separately insured. In the former event, on a dissolution of the partnership, the policy may be either surrendered or sold, as may seem advantageous, and the proceeds should be divided between the partners in proportion to their respective contributions by way of premiums, and not treated as a partnership asset. The same process should be followed in connection with separate policies, although these will, as a rule, be disposed of to the partners themselves, rather than sold to third parties or surrendered.

Marine Insurance. This is undoubtedly the oldest form of insurance. In a Statute of 43 Elizabeth c. 12, it is stated that it had been the *immemorial usage* among merchants, both English and foreign, when they made any great adventure to procure insurance to be made on the ships or goods adventured. From this, it may be inferred that insurance had been in use in England at least a century previously. A contract of marine insurance, although based upon the principle of indemnity, is not, in practice, a perfect form of indemnity, by which, in consideration of the payment of a certain premium by the insured, the insurer agrees to make good marine losses incurred in connection with the object insured. The insurer is frequently referred to as "the underwriter," and the contingency insured against is called "the risk." It is assumed that the transaction is entered into in good faith, and that the insured has an interest in the subject-matter of the insurance: without this condition being complied with, the insurance might be rendered void. A contract of marine insurance by way of gaming or wagering is void. Most policies are based upon "Lloyd's" form, but each Insurance Company issues its own special form, and different clauses are inserted to cover varying risks. When a firm is making regular shipments to certain ports, it is found most economical to take out an "open" or "floating" policy. This is one in which the value is not declared, but, as each separate shipment is made, notice is given to the Insurance Company, and the amount is endorsed on the policy. A lump sum is fixed when the policy is issued, in consideration of which a lower premium is charged than would be the case if a separate policy were issued for each shipment. As the various shipments are "declared," the amount is gradually reduced, until the whole sum has been declared against, when a fresh policy is taken out.

A "valued" policy is one in which the value of the goods insured is stated, together with their description, rate of premium, etc. "Lloyd's" is universally known as the head of the Marine Insurance business, but it should be understood that "Lloyd's," as a Corporation, does not transact insurance business. This is done by individual members of "Lloyd's," who accept risks in their own name.

It is a common practice for Marine Insurance business to be done through the medium of an Insurance broker. If it is intended to insure with "Lloyd's," the broker's clerk will ask certain underwriters to initial a slip containing brief particulars of the risk. When this has been done, a "covering note" is sent to the insured, which is afterwards followed by a policy. When the insurance is placed with an Insurance Company, the merchant furnishes the necessary particulars on an advice note. A covering note is sent to him at once, and this is followed later by the policy itself. In order to meet the requirements of English law, the policy must specify the name of the insured or his agent; the undertaking to insure; the subject-matter insured; the voyage or period of time covered by the insurance; the sum insured and the name of the insurer.

In Marine Insurance, the term "General Average" represents a contribution made by all parties interested in the ship, freight, and goods, towards a loss sustained by one for the benefit of all. Such a loss would occur, where, for the general safety, certain parts of the cargo are jettisoned. It would be manifestly unfair for the owner of such goods to bear the whole of the loss, seeing that the act was an intentional one and done for the general good. The loss of the individual whose goods are sacrificed for the benefit of the rest must be compensated, so that he will be placed in the position he would have held if the sacrifice had been made by another instead of himself.

The term "Particular Average" represents a loss which is not a general loss, and which falls exclusively on the owner of the goods, who has no right of contribution against other persons. A policy of marine insurance may be effected which covers "particular average," or—as it is sometimes expressed—"all risks," or, at a lower premium, a policy will be issued which covers only "general average." When that is the case, the policy is said to be "free of particular average," meaning that the underwriters are not liable for any claims for particular average.

A policy of marine insurance is assignable, either by special or by blank endorsement, the latter being most common.

It is impossible, within the limits here available, to describe fully the procedure in case of loss. If intelligence is received that the vessel carrying the goods has been wrecked, immediate notice of the fact should be given to the underwriters through the broker, and a claim made upon them for the value of the goods lost or damaged. There is usually some delay in settling claims, as the adjustment of the losses is generally found to be a very intricate and tedious process. This work is undertaken by experts known as average adjusters.

The ship itself may be insured in the same way as the goods, the same form of policy being used in each case.

TRADE DEPRESSION. In the nature of things, there can be no regular insurance effected against loss arising through trade depression and kindred causes. It is, however, obvious that, for many businesses, it would be highly desirable if some such form of insurance could be effected, with a view to minimizing the losses arising from such contingencies. Indirectly, such insurances are sometimes effected at "Lloyd's," more especially when, in times of international complications, it is thought desirable to guard against contingencies by effecting an insurance against war: that is to say, by making payment of a sum down in consideration of an agreement upon the part of the underwriters to pay a larger sum, if war breaks out within a prescribed period. Another form of "hedging"—perhaps less generally employed and less speculative, but probably, upon the whole, more efficient—is that of "going a bear" upon Consols or other Government stock: that is to say, the business man, who, on account of his commitments, is very desirous that there shall be no abatement in the existing state of general all-round prosperity, sells Consols, of which he is not possessed to an extent equivalent to the result sought to be attained. If his precautions have proved to be unnecessary, the worst that can happen is that Consols have risen, and that, in order to cover his "bear," he must buy Consols at a subsequent date at an enhanced price and be content to lose the difference—which, however, would as a rule not amount to any very serious sum, regarded as an insurance premium. If, on the other hand, his precautions have proved well founded, and the contingencies that he was fearing have, in point of fact, been brought about, the general losses which he sustains in consequence will, in part at least, be counterbalanced by a corresponding fall in Consols, which will enable him to cover his "bear" by purchasing at a lower price, thus making a profit upon the deal. A transaction of this description, so far from being a speculation, is, in point of fact, undertaken with a view to *reducing* the speculative risk that is inseparable from ordinary and legitimate business transactions. No transaction which has the effect of modifying extremes of risk can be regarded as speculative.

NATIONAL HEALTH AND PENSIONS INSURANCE. A matter of extreme importance to employers is their liability to contribute under the Acts relating to this matter, the law being embodied in the National Health Insurance Act, 1936, and several subsequent Acts. Pensions for widows, orphans and old age are legislated for in the Widows', Orphans' and Old Age Contributory Pensions Act, 1936. There is no intention of giving here anything other than a bare note on the law, but it is necessary for every employer to have a clear idea of the obligations imposed on him by this legislation, especially as far as the collection of contributions is concerned, seeing that he is the person responsible for the carrying out of this portion of the insurance scheme.

The general idea of the Acts, so far as sickness is concerned, is to include amongst the compulsorily insured all persons between the ages of 14 and 65, except those for whom special exemptions are provided, who are employed in manual labour whatever their remuneration, or who are otherwise employed at a remuneration not exceeding £420 per annum.

Although the principle of the Acts is to embrace as many workers as possible, certain classes of persons are specially *excepted*, no contributions being payable either by them or their employers.

Certain other persons who would normally be liable to compulsory insurance may, *if they so desire*, make application to remain outside the Acts; and if their application is granted, they receive an official Certificate of Exemption. It is to be noted with great care that the employers of such persons must pay the employers' contribution, only the persons themselves being excused from contributing.

The employer of an insurable person is liable, under heavy penalties, to see that a card is stamped in respect of each week (commencing on Monday) or part of a week during which employment lasts. Normally, cards are obtained by insured persons from their approved societies (see below), but "emergency" cards may be obtained from post offices if, for any reason, an insurable person fails to produce a card to his employer. The weekly contribution is divided between the employer and the employed person.

The whole scheme of Health Insurance is administered under the supervision of the Ministry of Health through voluntary associations of insured persons called approved societies. The societies are so constituted as to secure democratic control under safeguards designed to preserve actuarial and financial solvency.

Persons who are unable for reasons of health, or who neglect, to become members of approved societies may become insured through a statutory Deposit Contributors' Fund; but, although the contributions are at the standard rate, the benefits are less favourable.

Persons who have been compulsorily insured for a specified period, and who have ceased to be insurably employed, may apply to continue to be insured as "voluntary contributors," but they must then pay the whole of the contributions themselves.

The rates of contributions vary according to the sex and age of the insured person and (to some extent) according to the rate of remuneration. The employer is primarily liable to purchase the necessary stamp from the post office and to affix it to the card, but he has the right to deduct a prescribed proportion of the contribution from the wages of every employed contributor according to the rates in force at the time. These rates have been altered fairly frequently, so it has been thought better to omit them from this book.

UNEMPLOYMENT INSURANCE ACTS. Numerous statutes, now consolidated in the Unemployment Insurance Act, 1935, extended to agricultural workers by the Act of 1936, provide for relief to persons suffering from unemployment. The scheme is compulsorily applied to all persons between 14 and 65 who are in employment at a rate of remuneration not exceeding £420 per annum, or who are in employment by way of manual labour, whatever the remuneration. The scheme is administered by the Ministry of Labour through the Employment Exchanges, without the intervention of approved societies. Contributions are payable by means of stamped cards as in the case of health insurance. Current rates are printed on the appropriate insurance cards.

Full particulars of the conditions governing benefits and contributions can be obtained at any Employment Exchange.

INDEX

PAGE